LANGUAGE AND SOCIETY IN THE GREEK AND ROMAN WORLDS

Texts written in Latin, Greek and other languages provide ancient historians with their primary evidence, but the role of language as a source for understanding the ancient world is often overlooked. Language played a key role in state-formation and the spread of Christianity, the construction of ethnicity, and negotiating positions of social status and group membership. Language could reinforce social norms and shed light on taboos. This book presents an accessible account of ways in which linguistic evidence can illuminate topics such as imperialism, ethnicity, social mobility, religion, gender and sexuality in the ancient world, without assuming the reader has any knowledge of Greek or Latin, or of linguistic jargon. It describes the rise of Greek and Latin at the expense of other languages spoken around the Mediterranean and details the social meanings of different styles, and the attitudes of ancient speakers towards linguistic differences.

JAMES CLACKSON is a recognized world authority on the Indo-European language family. His research has focused on tracking the history and relationships of the ancient languages of the Mediterranean basin and Europe, ranging from Armenian to Volscian. His previous books include *The Linguistic Relationship between Armenian and Greek* (1994), *Indo-European Linguistics* (2007), *The Blackwell History of the Latin Language* (with G. Horrocks, 2007) and *The Blackwell Companion to the Latin Language* (2011). He is also editor of the world's oldest journal in continuous publication devoted to languages and linguistics, the *Transactions of the Philological Society*.

T0372704

KEY THEMES IN ANCIENT HISTORY

EDITORS

P. A. Cartledge
Clare College, Cambridge

P. D. A. Garnsey
Jesus College, Cambridge

Key Themes in Ancient History aims to provide readable, informed and original studies of various basic topics, designed in the first instance for students and teachers of Classics and Ancient History, but also for those engaged in related disciplines. Each volume is devoted to a general theme in Greek, Roman or, where appropriate, Graeco-Roman history, or to some salient aspect or aspects of it. Besides indicating the state of current research in the relevant area, authors seek to show how the theme is significant for our own as well as ancient culture and society. By providing books for courses that are oriented around themes it is hoped to encourage and stimulate promising new developments in teaching and research in ancient history.

Other books in the series

Religions of the Ancient Greeks, by Simon Price 978 0 521 38201 4 (hardback) 978 0 521 38867 2 (paperback)

Christianity and Roman Society, by Gillian Clark 978 0 521 63310 9 (hardback) 978 0 521 63386 4 (paperback)

Trade in Classical Antiquity, by Neville Morley 978 0 521 63279 9 (hardback) 978 0 521 63416 8 (paperback)

Technology and Culture in Greek and Roman Antiquity, by Serafina Cuomo 978 0 521 81073 9 (hardback) 978 0 521 00903 4 (paperback)

Law and Crime in the Roman World, by Jill Harries 978 0 521 82820 8 (hardback) 978 0 521 53532 8 (paperback)

The Social History of Roman Art, by Peter Stewart 978 0 521 81632 8 (hardback) 978 0 521 01659 9 (paperback)

Ancient Greek Political Thought in Practice, by Paul Cartledge 978 0 521 45455 1 (hardback) 978 0 521 45595 4 (paperback)

Asceticism in the Graeco-Roman World, by Richard Finn OP 978 0 521 86281 3 (hardback) 978 0 521 68154 4 (paperback)

Domestic Space and Social Organisation in Classical Antiquity, by Lisa C. Nevett 978 0 521 78336 1 (hardback) 978 0 521 78945 5 (paperback)

Money in Classical Antiquity, by Sitta von Reden 978 0 521 45337 0 (hardback) 978 0 521 45952 5 (paperback)

Geography in Classical Antiquity, by Daniela Dueck and Kai Brodersen 978 0 521 19788 5 (hardback) 978 0 521 12025 8 (paperback)

Space and Society in the Greek and Roman Worlds, by Michael Scott 978 1 107 00915 8 (hardback) 978 1 107 40150 1 (paperback)

Studying Gender in Classical Antiquity, by Lin Foxhall 978 0 521 55318 6 (hardback) 978 0 521 55739 9 (paperback)

The Ancient Jews from Alexander to Muhammad, by Seth Schwartz 978 1 107 04127 1 (hardback) 978 1 107 66929 1 (paperback)

LANGUAGE AND SOCIETY IN THE GREEK AND ROMAN WORLDS

JAMES CLACKSON

CAMBRIDGE
UNIVERSITY PRESS

Shaftesbury Road, Cambridge CB2 8EA, United Kingdom

One Liberty Plaza, 20th Floor, New York, NY 10006, USA

477 Williamstown Road, Port Melbourne, VIC 3207, Australia

314–321, 3rd Floor, Plot 3, Splendor Forum, Jasola District Centre, New Delhi – 110025, India

103 Penang Road, #05–06/07, Visioncrest Commercial, Singapore 238467

Cambridge University Press is part of Cambridge University Press & Assessment,
a department of the University of Cambridge.

We share the University's mission to contribute to society through the pursuit of
education, learning and research at the highest international levels of excellence.

www.cambridge.org
Information on this title: www.cambridge.org/9780521140669

First published 2015

A catalogue record for this publication is available from the British Library

ISBN   978-0-521-19235-4   Hardback
ISBN   978-0-521-14066-9   Paperback

Contents

The colour plates are to be found between pages 82 and 83.

Maps

The maps can be found in the colour plate section.

ix

Figures

Every effort has been made to secure necessary permissions to reproduce copyright material in this work, though in some cases it has proved impossible to contact copyright holders. If any omissions are brought to our notice, we will be happy to include appropriate acknowledgements in any subsequent edition.

Tables

Acknowledgements

I have relied on the help, advice and support of a large number of people to write this short book. My first debt of thanks is owed to Paul Cartledge and Peter Garnsey for suggesting that language would make a good topic for the *Key Themes in Ancient History* series, and for their kind encouragement, helpful suggestions and careful scrutiny of my text. I am honoured that Jim Adams agreed to read through a first draft of the manuscript, and I am very grateful to him for countless suggestions for improvement and for the notification of a number of bibliographic references that I would otherwise have missed. I am also indebted to two scholars from whom I learnt a lot when they were my PhD students, and from whom I continue to learn, Coulter George and Alex Mullen, who both read through drafts and, among many other things, ensured that my Phoenician and my Gaulish were better than they had been. I must record my deepest gratitude to two other readers of the manuscript who tried valiantly to ensure that the text might be understood by an undergraduate classicist or even an educated layperson: Calum Walker, now working in the film industry, and Véronique Mottier, sociologist *extraordinaire*. All of my readers saved me from numerous howlers, but undoubtedly others remain – they are not to blame; I am.

A number of other people were kind enough to answer queries, read shorter sections, suggest bibliography or send unpublished work. I owe particular and personal thanks to each of the following: Robert Crellin, Geoffrey Horrocks, Patrick James, Amanda Kelly, John Lee, Katherine McDonald, Rachel Mairs, David Oosterhuis, George Owers, Stephanie Posner, Janet Soskice, Pippa Steele, Rupert Thompson, Olga Tribulato, Bert Vaux, Sheila Watts, Peter Williams, Martin Worthington, Nicholas Zair.

This book is dedicated with much love to Véronique Mottier.

Abbreviations

CEG	Peter Allan Hansen, *Carmina epigraphica graeca*. Berlin 1983–1989
CII/P	Hannah M. Cotton, Eran Lupu, Maria Heimbach and Naomi Schneider, *Corpus inscriptionum Iudaeae/Palaestinae. A Multi-lingual Corpus of the Inscriptions from Alexander to Muhammad. Vol. I. Jerusalem.* Berlin 2010–12
CIL	*Corpus Inscriptionum Latinarum.* 1881–
DB	Darius I's rock inscription at Bisitun
Epist.	*Epistula*
ET	Helmut Rix et al., *Etruskische Texte: editio minor.* Tübingen 1991
ICS	Olivier Masson, *Les inscriptions chypriotes syllabiques: recueil critique et commenté.* Paris 1961
IG	*Inscriptiones Graecae.* 1873–
ILS	Hermann Dessau, *Inscriptiones Latinae Selectae.* Berlin 1892–1916
KAI	H. Donner and W. Röllig, *Kanaanäische und aramäische Inschriften.* Wiesbaden 1962–2002
LfrgE	Bruno Snell, *Lexikon des frühgriechischen Epos.* Göttingen 1955–2010
LGPN	Peter Fraser and Elaine Matthews, *Lexicon of Greek Personal Names.* Oxford 1987–
LSAG	L. H. Jeffery, *The Local Scripts of Archaic Greece: A Study of the Origin of the Greek Alphabet and its Development from the Eighth to the Fifth Centuries B.C.* Revised edition by A. W. Johnston. Oxford 1990
LSJ	H. G. Liddell, R. Scott and H. S. Jones, *A Greek–English Lexicon.* New (9th) edition. Oxford 1940

Migne PG	J.-P. Migne (ed.), *Patrologiae cursus completus. Series Graeca*. Paris 1855–
Migne PL	J.-P. Migne (ed.), *Patrologiae cursus completus. Series Latina*. Paris 1844–64
P.Amh.	B. P. Grenfell and A. S. Hunt, *The Amherst Papyri. Being an Account of the Greek Papyri in the Collection of the Right Hon. Lord Amherst of Hackney, F.S.A. at Didlington Hall, Norfolk*. London 1900–1
PCG	R. Kassel and C. Austin, *Poetae comici Graeci*. Berlin 1983–
P.Mich. VIII	H. C. Youtie and J. G. Winter, *Papyri and Ostraca from Karanis, Second Series*. Ann Arbor 1951
P.Münch.	A. Heisenberg and L. Wenger, *Byzantinische Papyri der Bayerischen Staatsbibliothek München*. 2nd edition enlarged by D. Hagedorn. Stuttgart 1986
P.Oxy.	*The Oxyrhynchus Papyri*. London 1898–
Praef.	*Praefatio*
P.Yadin	N. Lewis et al., *The Documents from the Bar Kochba Period in the Cave of Letters*. Jerusalem 1989–2002
RIB	R. G. Collingwood, R. P. Wright, R. S. O. Tomlin and M. W. C. Hassall, *Roman Inscriptions of Britain*. Oxford 1965–2009
RIG	P.-M. Duval et al., *Recueil des inscriptions gauloises*. 4 vols. Paris 1985–2002
RIL	J. B. Chabot, *Recueil des inscriptions libyques*. Paris 1940
SB	F. Preisigke et al., *Sammelbuch griechischer Urkunden aus Ägypten*. Strassburg 1915–
SEG	*Supplementum Epigraphicum Graecum*. Leiden and Amsterdam 1923–
SIG[3]	Wilhelm Dittenberger, *Sylloge inscriptionum graecarum*. 3rd edition. Leipzig 1915–24

CHAPTER I

The linguistic ecology of the Mediterranean

Introduction

All modern human societies are reliant on language. Human languages, whether spoken or signed, are unlike any other communication system in the natural world. Language has the capacity to allow us to express new ideas or to interact with each other in new situations, and to structure the ways in which we understand events and institutions. *Homo sapiens* is the only creature on the planet endowed with a communication system of such utility and complexity, and the origin of language is intricately bound up with the evolution of our species. Humans have been speaking to each other for at least 100,000 years;[1] but for 95 per cent of that time there was no means of keeping a record of speech. The first writing systems that could fully represent human language arose in the Ancient Near East around 3000 BCE, and thereafter the practice of writing, in numerous different scripts, gradually spread westward across the Mediterranean and into surrounding lands. With the advent of writing, the historic record begins. Surviving written texts from the ancient world, when understood, can provide unmatched detail about everything from the price of fish to philosophical speculation on the origin of the universe.[2] Writing also reveals something about the linguistic variety of past societies, both through the range of languages and dialects spoken, and through the different ways in which individuals and societies chose how to express themselves.

This book explores how ancient languages and language use can function as a window onto the history of the ancient world. My principal focus is the Greek and Roman civilizations between around 800 BCE and 400 CE.

[1] See Tallerman and Gibson (2012: 26–31) for an overview of possible dates for the origin of fully-fledged language among *homo sapiens*.
[2] Parsons (2007) shows how the written record of one city in Roman Egypt can give a vivid picture of everyday life.

I

Most of the historical evidence for this period comes from texts written in two of the major languages of the Mediterranean in the period, Greek and Latin, and much of this book will be concerned with evidence for ancient societies gleaned from the use of the Greek and Latin languages. But, as will become apparent, these were not the only languages spoken in this area – indeed, before the conquests of Alexander (356–323 BCE), Greek was but one of many languages spoken along the shores of the eastern Mediterranean, and, until the last century of the Roman Republic, Latin was a minority language even in Italy. For the bulk of the period under consideration in this book, the majority of the inhabitants of the lands around the Mediterranean spoke neither Greek nor Latin as their first language. By the end of the Roman Empire, this earlier linguistic diversity had largely disappeared, and a now unquantifiable number of languages had given way to Greek or Latin (in the eastern half of the Empire, and along the coast of North Africa, Greek and Latin were themselves later to yield ground in the face of migrations and conquest by speakers of Slavic languages, Turkish and Arabic). The mass extinction of ancient languages is one of the enduring effects of the Greek and Roman ascendancies in the Mediterranean, and I shall consider in later chapters of the book, particularly in Chapter 6, the factors accounting for the linguistic dominance of Greek and Latin, and the processes by which earlier languages ceased to be spoken. But in this opening chapter I shall give space to the other languages of the ancient world, most of which are now irretrievably lost. What languages were spoken in the ancient world, and how do we know that they existed?

Mapping the languages of the ancient world

The change in the linguistic landscape during our period can be seen most clearly by comparing the two maps of languages of the ancient world in 500 BCE and 400 CE (Maps 1.1 and 1.2). The first map is mostly a patchwork, bearing names that range from the familiar to the obscure. Greek is spoken (in various dialects) throughout Greece, and by colonists on the coasts of Sicily, Italy and southern France, and Phoenician is scattered across the whole length of the Mediterranean, but other than these, no language spreads beyond a territory of roughly 600 km at its furthest extent, while very few cover an area of more than 100,000 km^2 (roughly the size of the US state of Virginia). The same spaces occupied today by the largely mono-lingual modern states of Turkey, Italy and France were inhabited by speakers of a number of languages, many of which were completely unrelated to their neighbours. Even ancient Greece was home to speakers of languages other than Greek. The lack of shading in parts of the map shows that modern scholarship has little knowledge of languages at this period outside the ancient Near East and the Mediterranean basin. If we compare the second map, the picture is dramatically changed. Some languages still survive 900 years later, particularly in remoter mountains and deserts, but most of the earlier diversity has been lost, and Latin and Greek have extended their scope massively, with each covering well over 1 million km^2.

Neither of these two maps can be understood to be as accurate as a modern linguistic atlas would be. Both reflect the epigraphic and literary sources as closely as possible, but even so, much of the detail is filled in through guesswork and conjecture. There is no secure way of knowing what people spoke before the advent of writing, and there may well have been other languages that have left no record at all. The knowledge and use of script spread relatively rapidly from the east to the west of the Mediterranean basin after 1000 BCE, particularly in coastal sites, where either Phoenicians or Greeks traded and founded permanent settlements. The earliest surviving Phoenician inscriptions from the west come from Sardinia and are dated to the ninth century BCE (Amadasi Guzzo 1990:48); the earliest example of alphabetic Greek writing was found in a woman's grave near Rome from around 770 BCE (*SEG* 42.899). However, the practice of writing in the vernacular (i.e. the local language) on an imperishable material such as stone or metal only ever took hold in a very limited number of communities before the Roman Empire. For many corners of the ancient world, the only texts available are those associated with colonists, merchants, invaders or other incomers. Even where there is a surviving corpus of inscriptions from a particular locality, difficulties of decipherment or interpretation may mean that the linguistic situation is uncertain. Furthermore, in some cases where a modern decipherment has established a region's written record, these findings are not completely in accord with ancient accounts of the languages spoken in that area.

We can illustrate these points through consideration of various localities around the Mediterranean. First, Map 1.1 shows the existence of a language spoken in north-western Italy and into south-eastern France, called Ligurian. Many ancient sources identify a people called the Ligurians (in Greek *Lígues*, in Latin *Ligures*) living in an area of the north of Italy, the Alps and the south of France.[3] We even have some Ligurian glosses in

---

[3] Early Greek sources use the term far more promiscuously, and populate an area from the South of Tuscany to Spain with Ligurians; see Arnaud (2001) for details and discussion, and Mees (2003) for changing views of the Ligurian language over the last century.

ancient Greek and Roman sources (the term *gloss* refers to the citation of individual words with translations).[4] For example, the fifth-century BCE Greek historian Herodotus, discussing the name of the people called Sigynnae (Greek *Sigúnnai*) who live 'beyond the Danube', notes that the word *sigynnae* is in use among the Ligurians who live 'up beyond Marseille' to refer to traders (Herodotus 5.9.3). But there is scarcely anything that is identifiable as a sentence or even a phrase in the Ligurian language. Around sixty inscriptions written in a version of the North Etruscan alphabet, dating from as early as the sixth century BCE, have been found in the area, nowadays in Italy and Switzerland, around Lake Como and Lake Maggiore. Although scholars once identified these by the label Ligurian (or Celto-Ligurian), it is now clear that they are in a variety of Celtic (an Indo-European language family that includes Welsh, Irish and ancient Gaulish), known today as Lepontic.[5] Scholars of the Iberian language, known from inscriptions in Spain and south-western France, have some-times seen Ligurian (or what is more tentatively labelled 'Paraligurian') in the Iberian texts, but this is highly uncertain.[6] From the Italian province of Liguria, only a handful of pre-Roman inscribed items has turned up. All are very short, and written in forms of the Etruscan script, and most can be identified as Etruscan in language through the use of words or formulae known from Etruscan texts.[7] A few of these inscriptions may, however, display non-Etruscan elements: for example, a late sixth-century BCE stone stele from Zignago near Spezia has a text of just two words: *mezu nemunius* (*ET* Li 1.3).[8] It seems certain from the anthropomorphic design of the stele and parallels from elsewhere in Italy that the text *mezu nemunius* records the name of a deceased man. Neither of these names is attested in Etruscan sources, so it could be a Ligurian formula, although it isn't matched by other onomastic (i.e. name-forming) elements from the area (Untermann 2006). If this text really does represent the indigenous language of Liguria (and is not in a local variety of either Etruscan or Celtic), it does not shed much light. There is no way of testing whether it has any connection with the linguistic variety from which Herodotus's gloss *sigynnae* originally came. The label 'Ligurian' merely serves to conceal our ignorance.

In the absence of other evidence, the study of place-names (a science known as toponomastics) may help give a better understanding of the

---

[4] Collected in Conway et al. (1933 II 159–60).
[5] See Marchesini (2009: 62–4) for brief introduction and bibliography of these inscriptions.
[6] See Simkin (2012: 82).   [7] The texts are gathered in Rix et al. (1991 II 330–1).
[8] It would also be possible to read the name as *mezune munius*.

language of the Ligurians.[9] Place-names in Liguria recorded in ancient and modern sources often end in -*co* (after a vowel), -*sco* and -*nco*, which chime with Celtic place-names ending -*āco(n)* (such as the ancient name of York, first attested in a Greek source, *Eborākon* (Watts 2004: 711)). Was Ligurian perhaps actually a Celtic language then?[10] Further evidence to support this hypothesis may come from the striking similarity between the names of Genoa (ancient *Genua*) and Geneva (ancient *Genaua*). In the Celtic branch of the Indo-European language family, words beginning *genu*- or a derivative can mean 'mouth'; Geneva is indeed situated at the mouth of the Rhône on Lac Léman, while Genoa lies between the mouths of the Bisagno and Polcevera rivers (Falileyev 2010: 129). But toponomastic evidence can also support a conclusion that Ligurian was a member of the larger Indo-European language family (of which the Celtic languages form a subgroup), but not actually Celtic. There is a widespread Indo-European root *genu*- meaning 'knee', and it is possible to imagine that both Genoa and Geneva were so named because they were situated on a bend in the shoreline. The name of the river *Polcevera* itself has been given an Indo-European etymology: its ancient spelling is *Porcobera* (or *Procobera* or *Porcifera*), which has been explained as a compound meaning 'salmon-bearing' (Olsen 1906; for the element *porc*- compare Latin *perca* 'perch', not Latin *porcus* 'pig'!). Celtic languages lose the initial *p* of this word, for example in the Irish word for 'salmon', *orc* (the Orkney islands may have been originally 'salmon islands'), so this etymology can be used to argue against a specifically Celtic origin for Ligurian. Furthermore, a recent survey showed that in the area of the modern Italian province of Liguria there are few place-names that are solidly identifiable as Celtic (although a much higher concentration is found in western Switzerland).[11] The best single conclusion to draw from this is probably that place-names are always fertile ground for unverifiable speculation, but do not provide a secure basis for assigning language identity. We do not know whether separate elements of place-names all come from the same language: note the notorious example of the place-name Breedon-on-the-Hill in the English Midlands (Leicestershire), where the elements *Bree, don* and *Hill* mean 'hill' in Celtic, Old English and Modern English respectively, so the whole means 'Hill-hill on the Hill'. Even if we were sure that the elements come from the same language, there is no way to verify what feature the

---

[9] The following examples have been taken from Delamarre (2001) (with the review of Falileyev (2003)), Sims-Williams (2006), Falileyev (2010) and Delamarre (2012).

[10] See Falileyev (2011) for a recent review of the literature connecting Ligurian with Celtic.

[11] Sims-Williams (2006).

name-element refers to in the absence of speakers. Thus the element *genu-* of Genoa and Geneva may mean 'mouth' or 'knee', but it may mean 'settlement-by-the-water' in some language to which we no longer have access. The connection between *Porcobera* (or *Procobera* or *Porcifera*) and words meaning 'a type of fish' and 'carry' in other Indo-European languages may simply be a fortuitous coincidence; most Ligurian place-names cannot be so neatly explained.

Crete and Cyprus have much richer and longer epigraphic traditions than Liguria, and the distinct advantage that both are islands bounded by the sea, so that we can be sure that when ancient sources refer to Cretans or Cypriots we know exactly who they are talking about. However, the linguistic history of these islands is still full of uncertainty. Crete has the longest tradition of writing anywhere in Europe, with the first appearance of evidence for a local script (in the form of short hieroglyphic inscriptions, mostly found on seals) at the end of the third or beginning of the second millennium BCE.[12] There is no doubt that the Cretan origin of writing is one of a series of copycat innovations of literacy from the eastern end of the Mediterranean at around the same period. Contacts with the palace bureaucracies of Mesopotamia and Egypt led other emerging urban communities to adopt the idea of writing, even though they did not take over the same script-system or signs in use elsewhere; similar examples of what grammatologists term 'stimulus diffusion' are attested elsewhere in the world.[13] Early Crete has a rich tradition of scripts. The hieroglyphic script was the earliest, and it seems to have been replaced after about 200 years by a script now known as Linear A, which survives on a number of clay tablets as well as metal and stone prestige items.[14] A second hieroglyphic script, found on Crete, is principally known from one enigmatic object, a clay roundel (known as the Phaistos disc) which has signs imprinted in a spiral on both sides and which has proved a magnet for would-be decipherers. The Linear B script is a later development of Linear A, probably first in use around the middle of the second millennium.[15] Many more tablets survive written with Linear B than the other Cretan scripts (with archives of tablets also found on the Greek mainland). This abundance of material, and the brilliant insight of the amateur scholar Michael Ventris, led to its decipherment in 1952.[16] Ventris demonstrated that the language of the Linear B

[12] Cretan hieroglyphic inscriptions are collected in Olivier and Godart (1996); see Younger (1999) for an overview.
[13] Trigger (2004).   [14] Linear A texts are published in Godart and Olivier (1976–1985).
[15] Driessen (2008).
[16] Chadwick (1967) is still the most readable account of the scripts and the decipherment.

tablets was an early form of Greek, and that the script was a syllabary (unlike an alphabet, in a syllabary each syllable has a separate sign, so that the Greek word for 'bath-tub' *asáminthos* is written in Linear B with just four signs: *a-sa-mi-to*). Linear A and hieroglyphic Cretan are also likely to be syllabic writing systems of the same type, but no one has convincingly shown what languages (or language) they convey; the only certainty is that neither script conceals any form of Greek. In the sixth century BCE, nearly a thousand years later than the last Linear A inscription, a non-Greek language again makes an appearance in the epigraphic record. Half a dozen stone inscriptions survive from the east of the island in a script that can be read (they are written in the Greek alphabet) but in a language which has proved so far unintelligible; nothing in vocabulary or grammar corresponds to any other known language (Duhoux 2007).

In addition to this rich Cretan epigraphical tradition, there is also literary evidence to take into account. Crete is not just the first place in Europe to record writing, it is the first place for which we have something approaching a linguistic description by the ancient Greeks. In book 19 of the *Odyssey*, Odysseus attempts to convince Penelope that he is a travelling Cretan, and gives a brief linguistic and demographic description of the island:

> There is a land called Crete, in the middle of the wine-dark sea, an island fair and fertile. In it there are many men – a countless number, and ninety towns. Different languages are mixed together: there are Achaeans; great-hearted Eteocretans, Cydonians, the threefold[17] Dorians and divine Pelasgians. (Homer *Odyssey* 19.172–7)

Odysseus' description cannot be taken as a genuine ethnographic account. The poet doubtless wanted to project the account back to the time of the legendary kings Minos and Idomeneus of Crete, and give an impression of what the social mix of the island might have been at that time. Of the people listed by Odysseus, the Achaeans and Dorians are Greek speakers, but the other three groups, Eteocretans, Cydonians and Pelasgians, are usually understood not to have spoken Greek, although it is not clear what languages they did speak. The Pelasgians are notoriously difficult to pin down, since they are associated with different areas by different authors, sometimes in Athens, sometimes in Thessaly or on the Tyrrhenian coast of Italy; the tradition becomes so muddled that it is now impossible to link

---

[17] The Greek word *trikháïkes* is here translated as 'threefold', which seems to be how Hesiod interpreted it (fragment 233); the word may originally have meant 'with flowing hair', see Russo, Fernández-Galiano and Heubeck (1992: 84–5), Hall (1997: 42) and *LfrgE* IV 634–5.

the name with any certainty to a single region, or a defined ancient people or language.[18] In contrast, the meaning of the name 'Eteocretan' has aroused interest, since it can be translated 'true' or 'genuine' Cretan, and seems to recognize them as the aboriginal inhabitants of the island. It is no coincidence that modern scholars have labelled the language of the texts written in Greek letters, but not in Greek, 'Eteocretan'. But if we are to map the languages of Crete, should we also include Cydonian and Pelasgian?

Similar problems face the scholar trying to sort out the languages spoken on ancient Cyprus. One of the first pieces of writing from the island is a three-line text from the middle of the second millennium BCE, written in a syllabary linked to those found on Crete and called Cypro-Minoan (or sometimes Linear C).[19] There are well over 200 documents written in one of four varieties of this script from the island and the neighbouring Syrian and Turkish coasts before 1000 BCE, when the first evidence of Greek appears on Cyprus (also written in a variant of the Cypro-Minoan script).[20] In the first millennium BCE, inhabitants of Cyprus continued to write both Greek and a non-Greek language in the syllabic script derived from the earlier Cypro-Minoan writing system. Modern scholars (e.g. Masson 2007) refer to the non-Greek language of the tenth to fourth centuries BCE as Eteocypriot (on the analogy of Eteocretan discussed above). Eteocypriot has been identified in around two dozen inscriptions documented in the area around the town of Amathus, and may be preserved in a couple of later Greek glosses which attribute words to the speech of the Amathusians.[21] Owing to the paucity of inscriptions, Eteocypriot is little understood and, like Eteocretan, it seems to bear no relation to any other known language. There is no clear connection between Eteocypriot and anything found in the Bronze Age Cypro-Minoan texts (these themselves may be written in several different languages, Duhoux 2013). But this does not mean that Eteocypriot cannot be the same as an earlier language spoken on the island. We may miss the relevant links for a number of different reasons: the corpus of texts written in the Cypro-Minoan scripts in Cyprus is very small; the texts themselves have diverse functions, from accounting and administrative documents in the early period to

---

[18] Gruen (2011: 239–43).
[19] This tablet is edited in Olivier (2007: 60–1); Duhoux (2009) thinks it might be an *aide-mémoire* list of the signs of the script.
[20] The Cypro-Minoan corpus is edited in Olivier (2007) and in Ferrara (2013). The first text to use Greek is given as O170 in Olivier (2007).
[21] A bilingual text with Eteocypriot and Greek will be discussed in some detail in Chapter 3.

grave-markers and honorary decrees later on; and the language may have changed considerably over a millennium. Although there is a long tradition of writing on Cyprus, it is consequently very difficult to draw any firm conclusions about either the number or the nature of the native languages spoken there, or their long-term survival.

The examples of Liguria, Crete and Cyprus show just some of the pitfalls of attempting to map languages using inscribed textual remains, toponomastics and the statements of ancient writers. The epigraphic evidence is simply often not full enough, either owing to the paucity of actual inscriptions, or because of the underlying uncertainties of interpretation, and place-names are particularly hazardous if they are the only source of our information. In the face of these difficulties, scholars are often forced to rely largely on evidence from literary sources. But the Greek and Roman historians and ethnographers were on the whole not very interested in foreign languages. Unlike travellers in later Mediterranean cultures, such as the seventeenth-century Ottoman Evliya Çelebi who made transcriptions of several of the exotic languages he encountered,[22] no ancient writer made a serious attempt to present an accurate linguistic description of barbarous peoples. Although some individual authors, notably Herodotus, Varro, Plutarch and Jerome, did take an interest in languages other than Greek (and, later, Latin), they did not have the means or the desire to create anything approaching a technical linguistic survey. It is true that some ancient dictionaries include material from other languages: Hesychius' lexicon, a fifth-century CE compilation of rare and unusual Greek vocabulary, also contains some non-Greek entries; and a recently edited papyrus text from Oxyrhynchus of the first century CE is a fragment of an earlier glossary of foreign and unusual words (Schironi 2009). However, from what we can judge, the level of accuracy of these is not high. Hesychius assigns the correct meaning to *capra*, which we know to be the Latin for 'goat', but he ascribes it to the Etruscans, not the Romans. The Oxyrhynchus glossary includes *milēkh*, meaning 'noble', in the language of the Caucasian Albanians, but it actually seems to be a Semitic word for 'king'.[23] It also lists Persian *menemani*, 'water',[24] although this word does not occur in any attested Iranian language, and cannot have been the

---

[22] Examples of Çelebi's transcriptions of African languages are given in Dankoff (2004: 178–9); of Ladino in Dankoff and Kim (2010: 93–4); of German in Dankoff and Kim (2010: 247–8) and of Romani in Dankoff and Kim (2010: 277–8).

[23] *P. Oxy.* 1802 + 1842: 3 iii 12, following Schironi's correction of the text from the papyrus reading γένειον, 'chin', to γενναῖον 'noble'.

[24] *P. Oxy.* 1802 + 1842: 3 ii 17.

normal term for water, which we know to be *āp-, apa-,* or a derivative in all ancient and modern Iranian languages.

For most ancient writers there was an obvious (and self-fulfilling) correlation between 'people' and 'language'.[25] The general view in the ancient world was consequently that, if you were a Ligurian, what you spoke would be classed as 'the Ligurian language'.[26] We plot a language called Ligurian on the map, because this is where the people known as the Ligurians are reckoned to have lived, and the few ancient authors who happen to mention anything to do with the people give no indication that they spoke anything other than what we now term Ligurian. However, it is clear that the ethnographic term 'Ligurian' in ancient historical and geographical writers is, like 'Pelasgian', a fluid one (Shipley 2011: 92); this much is obvious from the Greek geographer Strabo's account (probably written at the beginning of the first century CE) of the various different peoples who have been included under the label *Ligues* (*Geography* 4.6.1-4). Just as the category of the Ligurian people can sometimes appear to be open-ended, capable of being applied to anything in northern Italy and Europe, so also the Ligurian language. This is the import of a story in Plutarch's *Life of Marius* about events at the Battle of Aquae Sextiae (102 BCE). Soldiers from Liguria were in the vanguard of the Roman army when they encountered the barbarian Ambrones, who were camped by the river Rhône. The origin of the Ambrones is unknown, but here they were partners to the Cimbri and the Teutones who both originated from what is now northern Germany. Plutarch states at *Marius* 15.4 that 'their speech and cries were unlike those of other peoples'.[27] When roused from their dinner and bathing by the camp-followers of Marius, the Ambrones shouted out their tribal name to encourage one another; the Ligurians, 'when they had heard and understood what the Barbarians were shouting, they themselves shouted back the word, claiming it as their own ancestral appellation; for the Ligurians call themselves Ambrones by descent' (Plutarch *Marius* 19.4, translation B. Perrin, Loeb Classical Library).

Even if we were inclined to accept that all the peoples encompassed under the label 'Ligurian' once spoke the same language, it would be hard to believe that they continued to do so over a period of centuries. The

[25] See Diodorus Siculus 1.8.4 or Dionysius of Halicarnassus 1.29 for the equation of language and people, and Herodotus 1.57 for a case where a change of language is taken to indicate a change of people.

[26] Although note Arnaud (2001) for speculation that the Greek name of these people originally simply meant 'barbarians'.

[27] Translation B. Perrin, Loeb Classical Library.

territory inhabited by peoples identified as Ligurian is largely mountainous and difficult to traverse. In early modern times, before the spread of mass education and the imposition of standard French and Italian, a wide variety of different Romance dialects were spoken in this region (all derived from Latin), many of them not easily understood by outsiders or even by inhabitants of the next valley.[28] It seems *a priori* unlikely that all speakers across this wide area continued to be mutually comprehensible for hundreds of years, even allowing for widespread mobility *via* pastoralism and transhumance.

However, the passage of the *Odyssey* cited earlier shows that the relation between people and language could be more complex than this. Odysseus refers to the mixture of languages and peoples in Crete, and, as we have seen, included Achaeans and 'threefold' Dorians.[29] Later Greeks recognized both Dorians and Achaeans as Hellenes, i.e. Greeks, speaking the same language.[30] Indeed, Dorian was the label in ancient grammatical writings (as Doric is in modern textbooks) for one of the major dialect divisions of Ancient Greek. We shall look in more detail in Chapter 2 at the interplay between the Greek dialects and the 'Greek language' in ancient accounts of the language, but for the moment the question that interests us is the larger one of what constitutes a dialect, and what constitutes a language. Might we be able to clarify some of the problems we have encountered in trying to pin down what it meant to speak 'Ligurian' or the pre-Greek language or languages of Cyprus by reference to a conception of language and dialect? Ligurians might all share the same language, for example, but did the Ligurian tribes identified by Strabo speak different dialects? Or might the four identified versions of the Cypro-Minoan script have been used to write four separate dialects of the same language?

Languages, dialects and varieties

Unfortunately, and disappointingly for non-linguists, most books on linguistics will not give a clear definition of the difference between a language and a dialect. Most people without linguistic training who have ever pondered the difference between a language and a dialect assume that the answer is something to do with mutual comprehensibility. Speakers of the same language should understand each other, although they may

---

[28] See Lewis (ed.) (2009: 551–3) for France, Lewis (ed.) (2009: 558–60) for Italy and Lewis (ed.) (2009: 576–7, 845) for Switzerland.
[29] See n. 17 above on the adjective 'threefold'.
[30] Hall (1997) traces the Greek and modern conception of the Dorians.

pronounce words in different ways, or favour different lexical items to refer to a pair of sneakers/tennis shoes/trainers, or call a carbonated beverage 'pop', 'soda' or a 'fizzy drink'. Linguistic textbooks will tell you that all these assumptions are wrong. Mutual comprehensibility is not a simple binary feature. I may understand you, but you may not understand me. Or I may understand you when you tell me about the forthcoming elections, but not when you talk about your garden. Moreover, a dialect speaker of language X may understand a dialect speaker of language Y who lives just over the national border better than another dialect speaker of language X who lives 500 miles away at the other end of the same country. Looking across any linguistic landscape, it is usually possible to identify dialectal continuums, that is, chains of related dialects, each one of which is easily comprehended by speakers of neighbouring dialects, but perhaps not by those at the other end of the chain.

There is no purely linguistic test by which it is possible to take two speech varieties and say whether they are the same language or not. What makes something count as a 'language' is dependent on factors beyond the purely linguistic. In the modern western world, the label 'language' usually designates something which has a codified written form. Thus one learns French, since there is a dictionary and grammar of the language, whereas there may be no agreed written form for the dialect spoken by residents of a Parisian *banlieue*. Languages today are further generally associated with nation-states, the boundaries of which may cut across the boundaries of dialect continuums: for example, Danish, Swedish and Norwegian carve up the Scandinavian dialects into three recognized languages. The language of a nation-state is the variety used in various official functions, which may include some or all of the business of administration, legal proceedings, education, religion, cultural and literary creation. Some nation-states, such as Switzerland, Belgium or Canada, may recognize more than one official language, and some multilingual societies distribute the official functions across several national tongues, so that one language will be predominant in, for example, religious discourse, and another in administration.

Languages associated with states are generally termed 'standard languages' by linguists, showing that they have undergone a process of 'standardization' and codification in a standard written form (we shall revisit the formation of standard languages in Chapter 2). Educators and functionaries, and often speakers themselves, tend to internalize the state's privileging of one linguistic form (the standard language as taught in schools or codified in grammars) over another (the dialectal variety actually spoken at home or in everyday conversation), and judge one form correct and the other substandard or incorrect, or indicative of 'stupid' or 'lazy' speakers. Linguists usually reject this promotion of the standard language at the cost of the dialectal, and judge that all linguistic varieties are equal. The often-repeated slogan 'A language is a dialect with an army and a navy'[31] neatly sums up the view that languages, as commonly understood, are just dialects that are more equal than others owing to the military or political power of their speaker group. The catchphrase is effective in making the point, but it can be misleading, since standard languages often have developed a greater range of vocabulary and technical styles, beyond the reach of varieties that only exist in spoken form. (It is significant that the phrase originally was reported in Yiddish: 'a shprakh iz a dialekt mit an armey un flot', since Yiddish is an unusual case of a written language that has never had any official recognition in a nation-state.)

Most speakers and writers in ancient Greek and Latin did not have the vocabulary to make a distinction between classing something as a language or a dialect. The Greek word *diálektos* only gains the meaning 'dialect', as opposed to 'discourse' or 'speech', in technical writings after the Hellenistic period, and there it has a slightly different sense from the modern term, in that it is applied only to varieties of Greek which are found in literary works (such as the Aeolic of Sappho or the Ionic of Herodotus), but not to regional spoken forms. In the description of Crete in the *Odyssey* cited earlier, and indeed in all ancient Greek authors, the same word *glôssa* could refer to one Greek dialect as opposed to another, or to a different language, and the same usage is found applied to non-Greek tongues. Thus a fragment of the fifth-century BCE historian Xanthus of Lydia (as reported by Dion. Hal. 1.28.2) says that the language (*glôssa*) of the Lydians and Tyrrhenians differs little, and compares their shared vocabulary to the Doric and Ionic dialects of Greek. Latin authors similarly use both the term *sermo* and *lingua* interchangeably for what we would specify as either a language or a dialect. The modern opposition between a standardized written language and a range of spoken dialects is in any case of limited relevance for the ancient world. As the discussion in Chapter 2 will show, it is possible to apply the label 'standard language' to certain varieties of Greek and Latin, but the absence of mass media, universal education or widespread literacy means that for the majority of ancient speakers

---

[31] The phrase is first reported in Yiddish in Weinreich (1945), who later reported that the phrase was given to him by an audience member at one of his lectures.

the experience of a standardized language was very different from the modern one.

Yet despite these caveats, the naïve conception of a continuum of dialects subsumed under a larger abstract identity considered as a language can be helpful, indeed necessary, for describing the ancient world, and in some cases captures the ancient conception more closely than anything else. Take the case of the language called Oscan, and spoken in central and southern Italy (it is one of a closely related group of languages which are labelled 'Sabellian' on Map 1.1, in the plate section). This area of the linguistic map is relatively well charted in terms of epigraphy and ancient testimonia. We have several hundred, mostly short, inscriptions from before the Roman hegemony written in Oscan, which is generally well understood by modern scholars since the Sabellian languages are closely related to Latin.[32] The majority of Oscan inscriptions are inscribed in the Oscan alphabet, an offshoot of the Graeco-Etruscan alphabet with a few idiosyncratic letter-forms and some additional signs found in no neighbouring script; a smaller number of Oscan inscriptions from Lucania in the toe of Italy are written in the Greek alphabet. Many of the short Oscan inscriptions are formulaic records of dedications, buildings or funerary monuments, but they share a remarkable consistency of language and orthographic conventions (i.e. spelling rules and such like). The Paeligni, Marrucini and Vestini, situated in central Italy to the north of the Oscan speakers, are also included under the Sabellian label in Map 1.1. These peoples did not use the Oscan alphabet or Oscan spelling, but left inscriptions in the Latin alphabet, and their language often shows grammatical or lexical influence from Latin. Linguistically, however, their language looks little different from Oscan.[33] It is true that there is not a lot of material to support a sound linguistic judgement; there are only three short inscriptions in the native language from the territory of the Vestinians, for example (discounting texts which only give names). But it would give a skewed picture to set up a separate Vestinian language on the basis of texts which are in fact no more different from Oscan written in the Oscan alphabet than the Lucanian Oscan texts written in the Greek alphabet. In this case, it seems best to view Oscan as a language that stretched in a dialectal continuum from Sulmona (ancient Sulmo) in central Italy all the way to Lucania in the south. The references in Latin sources also generally

---

[32] See Wallace (2007) and Marchesini (2009: 72–80) for overviews of Oscan.

[33] Conway (1897: 233–4) was the first to use the term 'North Oscan' for the language of these peoples, followed by later scholars, most recently Rix (2002).

observe a distinction between language and peoples when describing this area.[34] The peoples are designated variously as Marrucini, Vestini, Samnites, Campani and Lucani, but the language is referred to as *Lingua Osca* or *Osce* 'in Oscan'. Where the term *Osci* 'the Oscans' is found, it is restricted to statements about language such as 'the *Osci* say … '[35] Moreover, Latin authors do not usually speak of the language of the Samnites, or the Campanians, or the other peoples of the region. Chapter 3 will revisit the question of how far the shared language of these peoples reflected any shared cultural or political unity, but for now the key point is that the Roman intuition that these peoples did not differ that much in language correlates well with the linguist's judgement of their epigraphic record.

The Romans did not expend a lot of energy conceptualizing or categorizing the speakers of Oscan (Dench 1995), but the dimly realized notion of an Oscan language spoken by various different peoples was intertwined with a view of the shared descent of the Samnites, Campanians and other peoples of Italy. Most ancient accounts of the spread of populations around the Mediterranean were based on the idea of a founder-hero after whom the people took their name.[36] The language of the people naturally followed that of their ancestors, and hence spread of language was associated with a shared family or clan.[37] This implies a model of language transmission and spread in which language is static: children always maintain the speech of their parents unchanged, and most speakers are monolingual. However, even in antiquity it was recognized that this was not the only means for the propagation of languages. Many ancient ethnographic accounts speak of hybrid populations and 'mixing' of peoples, and by extension, mixing of languages: Odysseus' account of Crete refers explicitly to the mixing of languages; the fourth-century BCE mathematician and geographer Eudoxus of Cnidus states that the early inhabitants of southern Italy 'mixed languages';[38] and mixed languages were understood to reflect a mixed origin of peoples by Xanthus of Lydia (when discussing the Anatolian people called the Mysians, as reported by Strabo *Geography*

[34] The earlier Greek sources seem less well informed, or at least are more difficult to match with the epigraphic evidence. See for example Pseudo-Scylax 15 on the five *glôssai* of the Daunitae (see Marcotte 2001, Shipley 2011).

[35] Dubuisson (1983: 535), Clackson (2012a: 135–6).

[36] Bickerman (1952), reprinted in Bickerman (1985: 399–417).

[37] Note that the famous remark of Herodotus on Greekness, *tò hellēnikón* (8.144.2 cited in Chapter 2), explicitly links shared descent and shared language.

[38] Preserved in the work of Stephanus of Byzantium, writing a thousand years later, frag. 321 in Lasserre (1966).

12.8.3). It will be useful in the next section to sketch out theories from modern linguistics about the spread and diversity of human languages, which also combine the metaphors of linguistic descent as a family (called the genetic or family-tree model) and as a mixture (the contact model).

Language origins and language change

First, all modern accounts of linguistic variation rely on an assumption that all spoken languages change over time. Change may occur as speakers themselves vary their grammar, vocabulary or pronunciation over their lifetime, or as a younger generation adopts or creates new forms and structures. Within any speech community there will therefore inevitably be variation, and often speakers themselves will employ different variants according to their audience or the context of utterance (this variation will be explored more in Chapter 4). As long as there is sufficient intercommunication between all parts of the community, speakers will share the bulk of new linguistic forms, and the language of the community evolves while still remaining undivided. However, if a community divides, and speakers lose regular contact with each other, then, over several lifetimes, one language may develop into two or more distinct variants. Indeed, the process may be hastened if a group of speakers choose, either deliberately or subconsciously, to distinguish themselves from the crowd. The genetic model of language change thus assumes a kinship between different historical stages of a language comparable to a parent–child relationship; the connection between two or more languages spoken at the same time is analogous to that of siblings. Hence it is possible to say, for example, that French is a daughter of Latin and sister to Spanish. This family-tree model is an immensely powerful way for explaining language diversity, particularly so since it allows researchers to identify genetically related languages even in the absence of the parent. Thus Latin and Oscan, for example, are undoubtedly sister languages, although there are no written or other records of the parent language from which they both descend. Their parent language, referred to as 'Proto-Italic', is itself reckoned to be part of a larger family, headed by a lost *paterfamilias* called Proto-Indo-European.

Similarities between languages may thus be explained through the genetic model, but they can also be explained by a model of language contact. In communities where some or all speakers have experience of more than one language, it is not unusual to find features transferred from one to another. Transfer (usually referred to as 'borrowing') of vocabulary is the most obvious and widespread effect of language contact, but it stands at the end of a scale of progressively more intense linguistic interaction. At the other end of the scale are what modern linguists refer to as 'mixed languages', where parts of the grammar are taken wholesale from two different languages. One of the best-documented examples of a true 'mixed language' is Michif, whose few remaining speakers in Saskatchewan, Manitoba and North Dakota combine verbs conjugated as in the Native American Cree language with nouns which follow French grammatical structures. Other languages combine elements of more than one language in different ways. The generic term 'creole' is used to describe a language that results from children creating a new language out of pidgins, i.e. trade languages of limited vocabulary and grammar, spoken by their parents. Tok Pisin, an official language of Papua New Guinea, has been classed as a creole; it is based on a reduced form of English with some vocabulary coming from other, local languages. True 'mixed languages' are extremely rare in the modern world, and usually result from very particular circumstances. The Métis, for example, speakers of Michif, are descended from the children of Native American women and French-speaking fur-trappers.[39] Some of the ancient testimonia for 'language mixture' refers explicitly to similar social situations, for example, the story of the non-Greek-speaking Lemnians who kidnapped Athenian women from Brauron and had children by them (Herodotus 4.145); Plutarch (*De mulierum virtutibus* 247a) calls these offspring 'mixed barbarian' (Greek *mixobárbaroi*). Unfortunately, there is no surviving epigraphic evidence or any representation of what these ancient 'mixed' peoples spoke, and no mixed language ever became established in the written record in the ancient world.[40]

Modern linguistic explanations for language diversity thus share with the ancients a conception of shared descent of language and language mixture. However, the modern view is also radically different: first, linguists now recognize change to be an inherent part of language, whereas the common ancient view was that change is necessarily degradation of language and best avoided if possible (a position still met with today);[41] second, today descent and mixture are not seen as binary opposites, but contact between languages is envisaged as one of the major factors in

---

[39] See Bakker (1997: 9–26) for a synopsis of theories about the origin of Michif, and its importance for studies of language contact.

[40] See Adams (2003a) for the fullest discussion of ancient 'mixed languages' and especially 2003: 93–103 for discussion of possible examples of ancient language mixture.

[41] Jerome is a notable and extraordinary exception to the ancient view, see discussion of his remarks at *Comm. in Gal.* 357a (cited in part in Chapter 3) at Adams (2007: 116 with n. 2).

language change. The modern account holds that a language such as Oscan may show the result of speakers' interaction with other languages, incorporating words and structures from other languages, but that this promiscuity does not alter its place within the Italic or Indo-European family. All languages, except the rare creoles and mixed languages, are the end-result both of a mutating inherited tradition and of features incorporated from other languages. A better metaphor for language change than the biological family-tree model is thus a manuscript stemma, such as might be seen at the beginning of an edition of a classical text, where divergent texts have arisen through a chain of copying and miscopying of an earlier original, but may also show the effects of cross-contamination from parallel traditions. Linguists usually believe that they can untangle, without too much difficulty, which features of a language are inherited and which arise from language contact. In general, vocabulary is more apt to be transferred from one language to another – the usual metaphor of vocabulary 'borrowing' and 'loan-words' perhaps reveals an underlying assumption that this is somehow a transitory linguistic change, although of course there is no question of words ever being handed back. Grammatical structure and in particular inflectional endings are most likely to reveal inheritance, and it is these features that linguists rely on in order to construct family-trees (which is why Michif, with grammatical structures half-Cree half-French, is fascinating for linguists).

The ability to separate out linguistic descent from the effects of linguistic contact furnishes the modern historian of languages with a tool of a power and sophistication that would have astounded ancient ethnographers. Take, for example, the case of the Phrygians. There is a wealth of ancient statements about the connections of the Phrygians and of the Phrygian language. Herodotus (2.2) relates the story of some of the earliest linguistic fieldwork, the Egyptian Pharaoh Psammetikhos I's attempt to find out the oldest people in the world through imprisoning new-born babies in a goat-shed and seeing which language they spoke. When the babies cried 'bekos!', which was found to be the Phrygian word for 'bread', the pharaoh was able to identify Phrygian as the first language spoken and hence the Phrygians themselves as the first people on earth. In Homer, Phrygians are closely allied to the Trojans, and in later poets the two words become synonymous, yet in the Homeric Hymn to Aphrodite (113–16), Aphrodite explains how she can speak Greek since a Trojan nurse taught her while she was growing up in the house of her Phrygian father. Socrates mentions that the Phrygians have many similar words to Greek in his discussion of word origins in Plato's *Cratylus* (410a). Ethnographers linked the Phrygians with the Lydians, the Thracians, the Armenians, the Mysians and other peoples of Anatolia. The epigraphical remains of the Phrygian language are attested over a very long time-scale, from the eighth century BCE to the third century CE (with a noticeable, and as yet unexplained 600-year gap from *c.* 400 BCE to 200 CE), but the texts themselves are not extensive, and the language and the meaning of the inscriptions are still imperfectly understood.[42] Even so, modern linguists can make a number of definitive statements about the Phrygian language: it is not the oldest language in the world, although the word *bekos*, which occurs in some of the later Phrygian inscriptions, does appear to mean 'bread'. Comparison of Phrygian vocabulary items, and Phrygian word-endings, makes it clear to modern scholars that it is a member of the Indo-European family. (Indo-European is the name for a large group of languages which includes Latin and Oscan, Greek, the languages of Iran and northern India among which is Sanskrit, as well as many of the other languages spoken in the ancient Mediterranean, including Lydian, Thracian and Armenian.)

Furthermore, modern linguistic research can clarify that Phrygian belongs to a different branch of the Indo-European family from Lydian and Lycian, both of which, together with other ancient languages such as Hittite and Luwian, form a sub-family known as the Anatolian branch. The Anatolian languages are an offshoot of the Indo-European family; all other Indo-European languages can be shown to have undergone developments made in common, developments that did not take place in the Anatolian sub-family. Hence Phrygian, together with Greek and Armenian, is a member of what may be called the 'nuclear' Indo-European family, which also contains the other Indo-European languages we have met so far in this chapter: the Celtic branch (including Irish, Welsh, Gaulish, and other extinct ancient varieties such as the Celtiberian language of Spain, and modern varieties such as Breton, Cornish and Manx); Latin, Oscan and the other Italic languages of Italy; the Iranian languages, including Old Persian and many modern varieties. The Germanic languages (of which English is one), the Baltic and Slavic language families (whose members include Lithuanian and Russian respectively), and the Indian languages, including Sanskrit, are also all subsumed within the nuclear Indo-European. Figure 1.1 aims to clarify the position of the Anatolian languages with regard to Phrygian, Greek and Armenian by plotting them on a family-tree. In order to avoid 'language-overload', the family-tree does not show the internal relationships of the Anatolian

---

[42] See Brixhe (2004) for a recent survey of Phrygian.

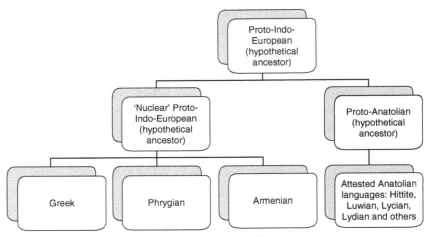

Fig. 1.1 A (partial) family-tree of Indo-European languages.

languages, nor does the tree include all the different branches of nuclear Indo-European. Note that only the languages listed on the bottom row of the family-tree are actually attested; the 'proto-languages' at higher levels are assumed to have been spoken languages, but we can only make hypotheses about what they were like.[43]

Modern linguistic analysis can thus elucidate something of the prehistory of the Phrygian language and its place in the Indo-European family. It can also give some information about other languages that earlier speakers of Phrygian encountered. The most interesting finding for the classical historian is that speakers of Phrygian used a word *lavagta-* to describe a military title, a word which almost certainly is borrowed from Greek, probably at around the time of the Mycenaean palace economies in the second half of the second millennium BCE, since the word is attested in Linear B tablets as the title of a particular office holder (written *ra-wa-ke-ta* but pronounced *lawagetās*), but in later Greek only in poetic texts with the generic meaning 'hero' (*lāgétās*, a contraction of *lawagetās*).[44] Phrygian speakers also adopted onomastic elements (i.e. names and naming practices) from other languages spoken in the region, and possibly other

---

[43] See Clackson (2007) and Fortson (2010) for introductions to and descriptions of the Indo-European language family. The term 'nuclear' Indo-European is taken from Garrett and Weiss (eds) (forthcoming).

[44] For the Greek word, see Trümpy (1986: 26–9); for the connection with Phrygian, see Neumann (1988: 16).

vocabulary, although most of the loans so far suggested have been queried.[45]

Linguistic evidence of the sort that has enabled linguists to position Phrygian on the family-tree of Indo-European is open to different kinds of interpretation. We have already mentioned the potential pitfalls of a simplistic equation of languages and peoples, but this was exactly the approach of most scholars who worked with the then fresh insights of the hypothesis of an Indo-European language family in the nineteenth century. The assumption of a tree model for the Indo-European language family presupposes that these different languages evolved from a single language. Many scholars have attempted to locate this language (Proto-Indo-European) and its speakers (often referred to as 'the Indo-Europeans', a term which I will avoid) in space and time.[46] In the nineteenth and early twentieth centuries, the most widely accepted theory held that the Indo-European homeland was in the steppe lands of southern Russia, and various waves of migration or invasions swept speakers of Indo-European languages west and south (Schrader 1883). In the 1980s the archaeologist Colin Renfrew, building on the new dating for prehistory obtained by the recalibration of carbon-14 dates, reopened the debate (especially in Renfrew 1987). Looking for an explanation beyond a simplistic equation of language and archaeological culture, he linked the spread of Indo-European languages to the spread of farming, and located the original speakers of Indo-European languages in central Anatolia *c.* 7000 BCE, much earlier than scholars had generally dated the existence of the proto-language. In support of Renfrew's thesis is the supposition that the Anatolian language branch of Indo-European is the first to have split off the family-tree (see Fig. 1.1); but the fact that the relationship between Greek, Latin, Celtic, and the languages of Iran and India (i.e. the 'nuclear' Indo-European family) seems to be more close-knit than the ties between any of these and the Anatolian varieties argues against the slow dispersal from the centre that Renfrew posits.[47] Moreover, evidence from vocabulary shows that Greek and Latin, as well as Armenian, all borrowed the same Mediterranean words for botanical and cultural items (from a

---

[45] On Phrygian and Anatolian onomastics, see Brixhe (2004: 787); Gorbachov (2008: 98–9 and 106–7) rejects earlier identifications of Phrygian loans from Hittite or Luwian, although in (2008: 103–4) he himself suggests that the Old Phrygian hapax (i.e. it only occurs once) *pupratoy* is a loan from a Hittite verb *paprezzi* 'he defiles'.

[46] See Anthony (2007) and Lewis and Pereltsvaig (2015) for recent surveys of the vexed relationship between linguistic evidence and archaeology. I have argued that too much confidence in the reality of lexical reconstructions for Indo-European is misplaced (Clackson 2007: 187–214, Clackson 2010).

[47] See the criticisms of Renfrew by Anthony (2007: 75–81) and Lewis and Pereltsvaig (2015).

language or languages now lost), probably including the terms for 'fig' and 'elm', which suggests that the earlier speakers of the Indo-European languages were not acquainted with these items, and therefore not indigenous to the area.[48] Indeed, it is difficult to find experts in Indo-European linguistics who agree wholeheartedly with Renfrew, although his entry into the fray has had the benefit of challenging linguists to justify many of their assumptions (such as the simple equation of speakers of Indo-European languages with nomads on horseback charging in from the steppes) and sharpening the reactions of linguists to contemporary archaeological debate. The temporal and spatial confines of this book (and the complexity of the issues) mean that we shall not concern ourselves further with the question of the homeland or date of the speakers of Proto-Indo-European. We shall, however, return to the question of migrations and invasions as opposed to other mechanisms of language dispersal in Chapter 2, when we examine different explanations for the diffusion of the Greek dialects.

Language families in the Mediterranean

Indo-European is not the only big language family attested in the Mediterranean: on the eastern and southern boundaries of the Mediterranean speakers of languages in the Afro-Asiatic macro-family were abundant in antiquity. Afro-Asiatic includes among its members Ancient Egyptian (and its later forms Demotic and Coptic) and the Berber languages, as well as the Semitic family, which embraces Akkadian, Ugaritic, Hebrew, Aramaic, Phoenician (and the later form of Phoenician spoken in North Africa, Punic) and Arabic.[49] The Semitic family is well understood, and it is possible to divide it into two basic branches: Akkadian is the most prominent member of East Semitic, and all the other languages mentioned here belong to West Semitic (Faber 1997, Rubin 2008).[50] The interrelationships within the ancestor of the Semitic languages, the macro-family Afro-Asiatic, are, however, not so well mapped out. This may be because the original unity of these languages existed much earlier than that posited for Indo-European. As languages diverge over time, the core of shared material gradually diminishes up to a point when it is difficult to pick it out against the surrounding noise; it is

---

[48] Beekes (2010: 1420) s.v. σῦκον 'fig' and (2010: 1247) s.v. πτελέα 'elm tree'.
[49] Woodard (ed.) (2004) has surveys of most of these languages.
[50] Note that on Map 1.1 I have used the designation West Semitic to denote an area in which several of these different varieties were spoken c. 500 BCE.

reasonable to assume that there is a temporal limit beyond which it would no longer be possible to group a language family with any certainty. The Afro-Asiatic language family may be near that limit. Although it has proved impossible to quantify rates of language change, or indeed make firm conclusions about whether all languages change at similar rates, one tentative conclusion from such attempts is that the Afro-Asiatic language family is older than the Indo-European (Frajzyngier and Shay 2012: 13–14 record suggestions that the origin of the language family may be in the eighth millennium BCE). The dispersal of languages on the southern and eastern shores of the Mediterranean thus seems to have taken place over a longer period prior to the rapid expansion of the Phoenicians in the first millennium BCE.

Comparative linguistics, and research on both the Indo-European and Semitic language families, have allowed many languages of the Mediterranean area known only through epigraphic means to be deciphered and understood. Although our knowledge of Phrygian and Phoenician, for example, is far from perfect, we have a much better chance of getting meaning out of an inscription written in either of these languages, for which we know something of their family background, than we do of one in Etruscan or Iberian, even though they are represented by far larger textual corpora.[51] Even the Lusitanian language, known from only half a dozen inscriptions, is better understood than its neighbours Iberian and Tartessian (with ninety-six inscriptions),[52] since it has a clear Indo-European verbal morphology and verbal roots, so that a word such as *doenti* is readily understood to mean 'they give' by someone who has studied only a rudimentary amount of comparative linguistics. Without the assistance afforded by etymology and parallel languages, it can be frustrating to work on epigraphical corpora in these 'non-affiliated' ancient languages (i.e. languages that cannot be related to any known language family, such as Etruscan, Iberian or Tartessian). Even if the script is close enough to recognize alphabets or syllabaries to enable it to be read with ease, in the absence of a body of parallel texts in a known language, progress in interpretation is painstaking and slow.

[51] There are around 9,000 inscriptions in Etruscan (published in Rix et al. 1991), and over 2,000 in Iberian (published in Untermann 1980 and 1990), but under 400 Phrygian inscriptions (mostly gathered in Haas 1966 and Brixhe and Lejeune 1984) and fewer than a hundred Phoenician (Donner and Röllig 1962–2002).
[52] Lusitanian and Tartessian inscriptions are published in Untermann (1997), with new finds (also of Iberian and Celtiberian inscriptions) published in the journal *Palaeohispanica*. The size of the Lusitanian corpus has doubled since 1997, when Untermann only knew of three inscriptions.

Consequently, several languages of the ancient world languish in a state of 'semi-decipherment'. Etruscan is perhaps the most famous example of an ancient 'unknown language', though in fact it is probably the best understood of any of these semi-deciphered languages. The majority of short Etruscan texts can be translated with confidence today. This is because most of these texts say similar things, recording gifts, dedications, and the name and family relations of individuals commemorated by grave-markers. The existence of more than a dozen Latin–Etruscan memorial stones, and parallels in the style of other short documents with other texts from ancient Italy, have allowed scholars to get a good idea of the basics of Etruscan verbal and nominal morphology.[53] This knowledge has been supplemented by discoveries in the past fifty years, including the famous Pyrgi tablets, dated to the fifth century BCE, which comprise three nearly parallel inscriptions on gold leaf, originally nailed to a wooden board in an Etruscan sanctuary, one of which is in Phoenician, and the other two in Etruscan. In the absence of further bilingual texts, progress in understanding Etruscan has only been reached by inspired linguistic detective work, not all of which is universally accepted. Many uncertainties remain, and Etruscan continues to attract speculation ranging from the useful and informed to the crackpot. In contrast, although most texts in the semi-deciphered Iberian language can now be transliterated into the Latin alphabet, their meaning, and even the basic nature of the structure of the language, largely elude researchers. Next down the scale come languages encoded in scripts such as Linear A, or Cypro-Minoan, where even the correct reading of the sound values of the individual signs is still unclear.

Although the non-affiliated languages are thus only imperfectly known, their resistance to elucidation through attempts to relate them to known languages or language families is in itself revealing, since it tells us something about the range of expansion of language families other than the well-attested Afro-Asiatic and Indo-European. Type 'Etruscan language origins' into an internet search engine and it is possible to find theories linking Etruscan to Basque, Turkish, or the Kartvelian language group (which comprises languages of the South Caucasus including Georgian), or almost any other family, but none of these theories has met with general acceptance. Etruscan can, however, be linked to two other languages known only from epigraphic remains: Rhaetic, found in 300 very short inscriptions mostly in the Italian and Swiss Alps (Schumacher 2004), and Lemnian, known principally from one long inscription from Lemnos

---

[53] Wallace (2008) is a reliable and accessible introduction to Etruscan.

(recall the stories about the barbarian Lemnians kidnapping Athenian women, and Xanthus of Lydia's statements about Tyrrhenians and Lydians both given above).[54] Iberian may be distantly related to the language isolate Basque (itself attested only in personal names in the ancient epigraphic record),[55] but it is clear that Basque is not the daughter of Iberian, and many doubt that there is any genetic connection between the languages at all.[56] The language usually known as Tartessian, attested in inscriptions from the south-west of Spain, is almost certainly unrelated to either Iberian or Basque, or any other known language.[57] Eteocypriot and Eteocretan appear to belong to separate language families, and neither can be confidently assigned to any other language group. The affiliations of Elymian on Sicily[58] and the Libyan language of North Africa are similarly obscure, although in the case of Elymian the textual material (other than the onomastic) is so scanty that we can barely speak of knowing the language at all.[59]

Linguistic ecology of the Mediterranean

This chapter opened with the discussion of a map of language-distribution around the Mediterranean that was constructed from a combination of epigraphic evidence and ancient testimonia. Problems inherent in these sources meant that we could not be sure that some languages were not missed off the map completely, or that others were allocated a larger area than was really inhabited by their speakers. Furthermore, the epigraphic record may conceal ancient peoples who regularly wrote in a different language from the one they usually spoke. There are also documented cases where the written record in one language was designed to enable readers to understand a different underlying spoken language, so that readers would be able to convert the written signs of one language into the spoken utterance of another.[60] Examples include the use of Sumerian by scribal schools throughout the Ancient Near East, or early texts written in Japanese which contain only Chinese characters, and which can also be

---

[54] de Simone (2011) reports the discovery of a new, shorter Lemnian inscription.
[55] Gorrochategui (1995).   [56] Simkin (2012: 90).
[57] Koch (2010) claims that Tartessian is Celtic, but this has not been generally accepted by scholars. See Clackson (2007: 4) for brief discussion of the difficulty of interpreting the Tartessian inscriptions.
[58] See Marchesini (2012).
[59] Libyan texts are gathered in *RIL*. On the difficulty of connecting Libyan with modern Berber languages, see Galand (1996); on the question of Latin loans in Libyan, see Adams (2003a: 245–7).
[60] A practice sometimes known by the term 'alloglottography' following Gershevitch (1979); see further Rubio (2006) for discussion.

read as Chinese. In this section I will ask whether it is possible to gain any rough estimates about the likely extent of language spread and the diversity of dialects in the Mediterranean before the Greeks and Romans from comparison with other pre-modern societies.

In recent years, linguists and others have become increasingly interested in searching for correlations between language diversity and variation and a range of other factors, including the geographical environment, population size, social organization and economic means of production. Nichols (1992) hypothesized that in prehistory older populations tend to get driven back into mountainous, inaccessible and remote areas (which she calls 'residual'), while more recent incomers occupy more easily accessible open plains or steppes (in her terms a 'spread zone'). In the residual zones, there is a greater concentration of different language families, but in the areas of recent population spread, there is less linguistic diversity and a greater number of speakers of each single language. As we have seen, Renfrew (1987) linked the spread of the Indo-European population with what he called a 'wave of advance' of the first farmers, who gradually pushed earlier populations into the geographical margins as they progressively put more land under cultivation.[61] Some have seen more complex connections between environmental and social factors and linguistic diversity. The archaeologist John Robb (1993) proposed a model accounting for fluctuations in the size and number of languages in prehistory according to the dominant means of social organization. In the Palaeolithic period, he reasoned that languages would have been spoken by small bands of hunter-gatherers who ranged over a wide area, but that there must have been a proliferation of languages, each with more speakers, in the Neolithic period, as farming and other social changes led to larger, more sedentary populations. Then, in the Bronze Age, from the end of the fourth millennium BCE onwards, military expansions and colonization led to the enslavement and destruction of a number of peoples and, with that, to the loss of linguistic variety. Nettle (1999) developed computer simulations of language change and spread to support some commonplace observations such as that languages supported by a literate culture and a greater number of speakers change at a slower rate than varieties spoken by only a small, illiterate population. Nettle further theorized that in areas of greater 'ecological risk', i.e. threats to the continuation of the food supply and the maintenance of livelihoods, extensive social networks would develop to

[61] Renfrew and Bellwood (2002) attempted to generalize the link between language dispersal and farming across other language families of the world.

minimize the effects of disasters, leading to less linguistic diversity in the area. The effect of different types of social organization on language has also been studied by Sandøy (2003), who contrasts the dialect diversity of modern Faroese (spoken on the Faroe Islands), where the traditional speech communities have been concentrated in villages of roughly 150 inhabitants apiece, with the lack of variation in modern Icelandic, spoken by a population dispersed over small family farmsteads, usually numbering no more than ten.

However, all of these models presented for understanding and explaining linguistic diversity have proved controversial (Campbell and Poser 2008). Some parts of the world, such as Central America, display environmental factors concomitant with a spread zone, but are home to speakers of many different language families. Some instances of language dispersal are linked to farming, but others are not, and there are many regions, again including Central America, where shared innovative agricultural practices have not led to linguistic change. The theories of Robb and Nettle suggest that we should encounter similarly sized languages across populations which share the same social and environmental features, but this is demonstrably not the case: in the Andes, Quechua, spoken by 8 million people, is surrounded by indigenous languages with far fewer speakers. Social factors, including the openness of communities to change, gender roles and marriage patterns, and community size and organization also play important roles in language change and diversity, probably much greater than environmental, economic or geographical differences. Furthermore, the historical effects of migrations or invasions may linger in the linguistic record for centuries, and each wave of population movements is imprinted upon a well-trodden linguistic terrain.

Applying any of these models of language diversity wholesale to the ancient world will consequently not answer the question of how many languages were spoken around the shores of the Mediterranean in antiquity. Population genetics is also largely unhelpful for tracking prehistoric languages, since it normally assumes a model whereby monolingual children speak the same language as their parents (or one parent), no more likely for ancient societies than for modern ones (Soares et al. 2010). It is also clear that linking languages to archaeological cultures is fraught with uncertainties (Lang 2001, Mullen 2013: 4–22). For example, there are no diagnostic features which allow archaeologists to separate out a 'Ligurian' settlement from a Gaulish one (Mullen 2013: 28), but this does not mean that we can confidently describe the unknown language of the Ligurians as a Gaulish language. However, other aspects of the theoretical study of ancient language diversity are relevant to the study of antiquity. There is a clear correlation, for example, between identifiable speech communities and distinctive dialects in Classical Greece, as we shall see further in Chapter 2. A large, partly mobile and partly literate population of speakers whose centre was a single all-consuming metropolis is theoretically unlikely to show a great deal of linguistic change in their dominant language, which helps explain the scanty evidence for dialectal variation in Latin (see further Chapter 4). But it is more difficult to apply similar considerations to the many poorly attested or ill-understood languages of the ancient world.

Perhaps the most helpful model for language dispersal around the Mediterranean basin is the insight into spread and residual zones. In the first millennium BCE, speakers of two of the largest and best-studied language families, Indo-European and Afro-Asiatic, occupied much of the coastal strip and inland area going clockwise from Spain to Libya. But there are also pockets of apparent linguistic orphans, particularly associated with islands (Crete, Cyprus, Lemnos, Sardinia and perhaps Sicily) or with mountainous and more peripheral regions (Basque in the Pyrenees, the Rhaeti in the Alps, the Tartessians between the Sierra Morena and Sierra Nevada). The distribution of language areas can thus be roughly divided up between a series of 'spread' zones, prone to incursions and rapid movements and changes of populations, and 'relict' areas, such as islands and mountains, where the last speakers of earlier widespread languages tend to hold out the longest.

The ancient Near East, where writing, and hence languages, are attested earlier than in the Mediterranean, gives an interesting point of comparison. The earliest Near Eastern scripts are termed cuneiform, and rely on wedge-shaped marks made in tablets of wet clay. Of the languages attested in cuneiform sources, some are Indo-European (such as Hittite and Luwian, members of the Anatolian branch), one is Afro-Asiatic (the East Semitic language Akkadian). But there is evidence for at least four other language families in the area: Sumerian, Elamite, Hurrian and the related Urartian, and Hattic.[62] It is also possible that there were languages spoken in the area which were never recorded: the Kartvelian language family of the southern Caucasus has every chance of having been spoken in the same area for the last four millennia (it is first attested in the early first millennium CE), but

[62] Again, Woodard (ed.) (2004) provides a useful introduction to Sumerian, Elamite, and Urartian; for Hattic see Goedegebuure (2013). Note also that the undeciphered script known as 'Proto-Elamite' may have been the writing of a different population than the later Elamites (Englund 2004: 141).

has not been related to any of the languages attested in cuneiform records. Proto-Elamite (a term for a still undeciphered writing system from Iran) disappears from the inscriptional record by the end of the fourth millennium BCE, Sumerian by the second millennium, while other languages lose out in the second and first millennia BCE in the face of the advance of imperial idioms including Greek and the Semitic language known as Aramaic. By the beginning of the Common Era, only Indo-European, Semitic (and we presume Kartvelian) languages were spoken in the same broad area. The most archaic branch of the Indo-European family, Anatolian, and representatives of the other language families have all vanished from the record.

The Near Eastern picture of early diversity and language loss already in the third and second millennia affords a suggestive backstory to the Mediterranean basin in the first millennium BCE. It is not known what happened to the speakers of Proto-Elamite in ancient Iran, but by the first millennium Persians and other speakers of languages of the Iranian branch (and, in the case of the Mitanni, the Indian branch) of Indo-European are firmly established in the area. Elamite survived for a while alongside Old Persian (as we shall see in Chapter 2) before going the way of Proto-Elamite. In Mesopotamia, Sumerian was replaced by Akkadian after a period of bilingualism (Woods 2007). In neither case is the cause of language change a wave of advance of farmers, and it is not clear that there is any dramatic population movement at all involved in the death of Sumerian. The situation in the first millennium in Europe bears some similarities to the Near East. Just as the Iranian languages are spread over a wide area, so the Indo-European Celtic languages occupy a band stretching from Spain to Italy (and are attested later in Britain as well). Speakers of Greek are dispersed across Greece and the Aegean, and the Italic languages cover most of central and southern Italy. If we were able to go further back in time, we might see these languages retreating on the map, and perhaps find a similar level of linguistic diversity in the Mediterranean world to match that of the Near East in the fourth millennium.

Cross-linguistic communication in the ancient world

They were all filled with the Holy Spirit, and began to speak with other languages, as the Spirit gave them the ability to speak. Now there were dwelling at Jerusalem Jews, devout men, from every nation under the sky. When this sound was heard, the multitude came together, and were bewildered, because everyone heard them speaking in his own language. They were all amazed and marveled, saying to one another, 'Behold, aren't all these who speak Galileans? How do we hear, everyone in our own native language? Parthians, Medes, Elamites, and people from Mesopotamia, Judea, Cappadocia, Pontus, Asia, Phrygia, Pamphylia, Egypt, the parts of Libya around Cyrene, visitors from Rome, both Jews and proselytes, Cretans and Arabians: we hear them speaking in our languages the mighty works of God!' (Bible New Testament, Acts 2: 4–12 (World English Bible))

The discussion of linguistic diversity raises the question of how people who spoke different languages understood each other, which we shall briefly consider in this final section of the chapter. The story of speaking in tongues from Acts gives a memorable picture of the diversity of languages spoken by all the Jews and others gathered in Jerusalem, and the miraculous event of sudden communication without an interpreter. No other surviving text from the ancient world captures so well the babble of languages and dialects that was undoubtedly a feature of many larger towns during festivals or markets. (Note that this version renders both Greek *diálektos* and *glôssa* as 'language', but each of the terms in this passage probably refers to languages and dialects collectively, since it is likely that all Cretans, for example, were speaking Greek at this date.)

Most Greek and Roman sources give little space to problems of communication across language barriers. Herodotus, usually sensitive to language use, recounts that the Persian Cyrus gets an interpreter to tell him what the Lydian Croesus shouts out on his funeral pyre (1.86.4), but thereafter the two men are presented as conversing directly in Greek throughout the history. Perhaps both rulers did have a knowledge of Greek: the Lydians made use of the Greek oracle at Delphi (Herodotus 1.85) and, despite the Persian ambassador Pseudartabas' comic broken Greek in Aristophanes' *Acharnians*, some high-ranking Persians seem to have known the language, if we may extrapolate from the presence of a Greek text among the Persepolis archive[63] and an inscriptional copy of a Greek letter from Darius I to the provincial satrap Gadatas in Magnesia (last discussed at *SEG* 56, 1230). But it is equally likely that Herodotus felt no hesitation in ignoring the role of the interpreter after the first mention. Interpreters must have been so common in the ancient world that their presence and availability could be taken for granted. Indeed, those individuals who did not need interpreters, and who were able to switch to languages other than Greek and Latin, are normally the exception,

[63] See the discussion in Chapter 2 of the languages in the royal archive of the Persian capital Persepolis.

and noted as such in the sources (Mairs 2011, Mairs and Muratov forthcoming). Hence Cleopatra and Mithridates, multilingual monarchs who can speak directly to their subjects, are cited with amazement by Plutarch (*Life of Antony* 27. 3) and Pliny (7.24.88; Mithridates' accomplishments are also mentioned by Valerius Maximus and Aulus Gellius). Caesar's protégé C. Valerius Procillus, a second-generation Roman citizen who can speak Gaulish (and thus converse with the Suebian chief Ariovistus), is explicitly referred to as a youth of good family and culture (*Gallic War* 1.46–7).

The Greek and Latin terms which are normally translated 'interpreter' (*hermēneús* and *interpres*) do not turn up often in documentary sources. Even in the abundance of papyri from multilingual Egypt only a handful of *hermēneîs* are mentioned, and these, like the Roman *interpretes* who are found in the military documents at Vindolanda and in funerary inscriptions from the Danube provinces, seem to have been people who acted as middlemen or brokers as well as translators (see Mairs 2012, Mairs and Muratov forthcoming). Only when outside the normal confines of the known world was it worth noting the availability of a Greek or Latin speaker (e.g. *Periplus of the Red Sea* 5, which includes the information of a man versed in Greek literature in the far south of the Red Sea). In the absence of interpreters, merchants may have made silent exchange of their goods (as recounted by Herodotus 4.196),[64] or travellers could make their needs understood through dumb show, as Xenophon's men did in Armenia (*Anabasis* 4.5.33), while their commanders employed a Persian interpreter to interact with the Armenians.

The reticence of many of the ancient sources about interpreters may also be partly due to a mistrust of those who straddled two languages and two cultures. Interpreters and translators have been objects of suspicion in many different cultures at different times. Indeed, until the peculiar bilingual phenomenon of the Roman Empire (which will be explored further in Chapter 3), bilingualism of any sort was treated as evidence of divided loyalties; thus the word *bilinguis* in Latin means not 'bilingual', but either 'having two tongues' (as of a snake or monster) or 'shifty'. But, as Mairs (2011) notes, the Graeco-Roman blind-spot towards multilingualism is a typical defect of largely monolingual and dominant cultures. In most of their interactions with 'barbarians', the Greeks and Romans were dependent on interpreters. But for many of the cultures with which they came

---

[64] But see Curtin (1984: 12–13), cited by Morley (2007: 58), for doubts about silent trade, noting the absence of good parallels from the early modern and modern periods.

into contact, much of the population may have been comfortable with speaking more than a single language. Indeed, this is clearly the case with the Suebian chief Ariovistus, whose native language was Germanic, but who was equally fluent in Gaulish. It was also true for the Armenians whom Xenophon's Ten Thousand encountered in their march from Babylonia, who spoke ancient Iranian varieties as well as Armenian. Most of the speakers of diverse languages listed in Acts who had gathered for the Pentecost in Jerusalem were doubtless able to speak Greek (if not also a Semitic variety as well) alongside their vernacular language. In non-western societies today multilingualism is extremely common, and it is estimated that a greater number of people are bi- or multilingual than monolingual.[65] There is no reason to believe the ancient world was any different. Moreover, as populations switched over time to Latin or Greek, bilingualism across at least a couple of generations is likely. Bilingualism will be explored in more depth in Chapter 3.

[65] Bhatia and Ritchie (2013: xxi).

CHAPTER 2

States of languages/languages of states

The case of Old Persian

'Darius the king proclaims: This is what I did after I became king.'[1] In around 520 BCE the Persian King Darius thus recorded his achievements in a massive *Res Gestae*, a rock inscription covering over 350 m^2, located over 100 m up a cliff face on Mount Bisitun in western Iran. The rock is engraved with Darius's own record of his achievements in three different language versions. The first version is in Elamite, a non-Indo-European language of ancient Iran which had been used as the administrative language even before the advent of the Achaemenid dynasty under Cyrus the Great forty years earlier. The second is in Akkadian (in particular, in the variety known as Babylonian), which was the usual language of administration and international affairs in the Near East from 1500 to 500 BCE (for instance, the fourteenth-century BCE correspondence between the renegade Egyptian Pharaoh Akhenaten and the rulers of the Hittites and the Mitanni was in Akkadian). The third version is in Old Persian, Darius's native language, and here written in its own semi-syllabic cuneiform script, which the king claims to have invented.[2] Old Persian is written on a number of other, less extensive, inscriptions erected by Darius. It continued in use by the later Achaemenids up until the mid-fourth century BCE, although the false archaisms and corruptions of the texts written in the reigns of Artaxerxes II (404–358 BCE) and Artaxerxes III (358–338 BCE) show a loosening grip on the language. Old Persian is also found written on prestige objects such as seals and alabaster bowls and in texts on precious metals buried under the foundations of buildings, when it is nearly always

---

[1] DB §15, translation from Kuhrt (2007 I 144).
[2] DB §70 'this (is) the form of writing, which I have made, besides in Aryan' (Kuhrt 2007 I 159, with 157 n. 115).

accompanied by parallel versions in other languages, including in some cases another international language, hieroglyphic Egyptian.[3]

The Achaemenids also made extensive use of written records in administration: over 20,000 clay tablets from the period of Darius's reign were excavated from Persepolis, the chief ceremonial capital of the Persians, by a team from the Chicago Oriental Institute in the 1930s.[4] Although fewer than a quarter of these have so far been published, the language composition of the tablets is known. Of those which have any writing on them, the majority relate to mundane palace business: ration lists, letter orders, accounts (together with yearly summaries) and the like written in Elamite; a smaller proportion (around 5 per cent) in Aramaic, a West Semitic variety which would later become the administrative lingua franca of the Near East and Iran; and around 100 documents which have both Elamite and Aramaic on the same tablet (the first written with a stylus in wet clay, the second in pen and ink). Four other languages are attested in the archive: one tablet is a private legal document written in Babylonian, which seems to have been included by error among the state files; another is a barely understood document apparently in Phrygian; a third short tablet is written in Greek, and records two measures of wine (we know from corresponding Elamite summaries that this account was entered into the yearly list) (Lewis 1994: 21 and 30); a fourth, fragmentary text, identified only in 2006, is written in Old Persian and contains what appears to be an account of rations for five villages (Stolper and Tavernier 2007).

Before the discovery of this Old Persian archival document, the language situation in Persepolis and the rest of the Achaemenid Empire seemed fairly clear-cut. The language of state administration was Elamite, giving way eventually to Aramaic, perhaps as scribes preferred the less friable medium of papyrus or leather to clay, and the pen and ink to the stylus. Old Persian was merely a prestige script, of limited function, with hardly anyone bothering to learn it. One scholar reckoned that only twenty people in history had ever learnt to write the script.[5] But the existence of this single tablet means the story must be more complex. There does not seem to have been any official drive to implement Old Persian as the administrative language (the Old Persian tablet appears to date to the twenty-second year of Darius's reign, the bulk of the dated

[3] See Schmitt (2004) for a survey article on Old Persian. Most of the texts are gathered in Kent (1953).
[4] Jones and Stolper (2008). Lewis (1994) gives an overview of the place of language and script in the Achaemenid administration.
[5] Gershevitch (1979).

Elamite texts to between the twenty-second and twenty-sixth), but it was clearly well enough known that it could be kept in a multilingual archive without any (as yet unearthed) need for an Elamite or Aramaic equivalent. The ordinariness of the tablet's contents argues strongly for the regular use of the language on administrative documents of this sort; it may be that another part of the Persepolis archive, now lost, or even archives in other Achaemenid cities, housed a greater number of records in Old Persian.

Achaemenid scribes, like those in the other palace economies of the ancient Near East, were clearly at ease with a multilingual administration, and their rulers were also aware of the function of written language as a display of power and state control. Darius's relation of his own 'history' on the Bisitun inscription acts as the legitimation of his claim to the throne; a message that was symbolically proclaimed in the national and international languages of the day. In the Greek and Roman worlds, there is no other documented example of a historical individual who created a new script for his own tongue in order to reinforce political power. But the example of Old Persian also shows that written languages may quickly develop functions beyond those for which they are designed, while the interaction of states and languages is never straightforward. This chapter is devoted to the political and administrative uses of language in the ancient world, and the promotion and development of specific linguistic varieties by various different states at different times. The focus is naturally on written forms of language because our evidence is solely from texts and documents. Moreover, committing speech to script can be a lengthy process and the result is usually intended to be permanent. Time and the desire for immortality lead to deliberate choices of form and style.

Standard and national languages

Old Persian in many ways corresponds to what was termed a 'standard' language in Chapter 1. To recap, standard languages are the varieties, codified in writing, which are taught in schools and employed in the government, media, and often the cultural life of a state. Standard languages in the modern world have been specifically associated with nation-states, to the extent that the distillation or even creation of a national standard language has been an integral part of awakening national identities and the formation of nation-states in the last two centuries. Thus Mustafa Kemal Atatürk, the first president of Turkey, attended the meetings of the two committees of the new Language Commission (*Dil Encümeni*) set up in 1928 in order to inaugurate a new orthography in an adapted Latin alphabet, and to 'modernize' the Turkish language, purging it of Arabic loanwords (Lewis 1999: 33); the enterprise was so successful that texts in Ottoman Turkish, the earlier form of the language written in Arabic script, are now incomprehensible to modern speakers of the language (Lewis 1999: 4). But in earlier centuries, the formation of the standard languages of many western states was due to the efforts or prestige of individual figures (including writers, scholars, priests, aristocrats and monarchs), para-state institutions (such as universities or academies), and even the arbitrary decisions of printers and publishers, as much as any input from the government of the day. In both cases, standard languages have been built up by accretion; over time, users have expanded the vocabulary to encompass a range of technical, legal and scientific vocabulary, and developed stylistic and syntactic means for expressing such features as reported speech.

Although Old Persian existed in written form for fewer than 200 years, it matches some of the features of its modern counterparts. Instigated in written form by the king, it shows hardly any variation over time or place, and was capable in at least one instance of being employed in administrative documents as well as royal proclamations. But documented Old Persian is also very unlike modern standard languages. It is unlikely to have been known by as few as twenty people, but Old Persian texts certainly never had a large readership, whereas written modern standard languages are accessible to millions, and generally reinforced through near-universal education and literacy and disseminated by mass media. Print and digital editions mean that we can access millions of words of standard English with ease; the only text of any length composed in Old Persian was situated a hundred metres up a cliff-face. Many modern standard languages are codified by official bodies and sanctioned by law: the recent German spelling reform (*Rechtschreibreform*), for example, was proposed by a council of forty members drawn from six German-speaking countries, debated in German courts, and defeated in a referendum in the *Land* of Schleswig-Holstein. There was no ancient equivalent to the spell-checker or even standard dictionaries or grammars for Old Persian,[6] or indeed for any ancient language. Finally, although Old Persian was clearly intended as symbolic of the Persian Empire and national pride (if that term is not too anachronistic), it existed alongside several other languages within the state.

The difference between ancient languages such as Old Persian and the modern standard may call into question the utility of the definition of a

---

[6] Modern scholarship has filled the gap: see Kent (1953), and Brandenstein and Mayrhofer (1964).

standard. Indeed, even in the modern and early modern world standard languages can differ so much between one another that it is hard to generalize what the essential features of a standard language are. Linguists have therefore tended to define standard languages in terms of a shared process of becoming, rather than any essential features of their nature. A standard language hence is best described as a form of language that has undergone the processes of standardization. Standardization is usually reckoned to have several different elements, which may proceed in orderly chronological fashion, but which frequently co-occur at any given point in the process:[7] first, the choice of a particular variety as the basis of the standard, whether made by an individual or by a committee, or whether it arises through a concatenation of independent events; secondly, the distillation of that variety into an agreed and accepted written form, its promulgation through education and official texts, and its concomitant codification in descriptive and prescriptive grammatical texts; thirdly, the growing use of the standard for texts of all different types by private individuals as well as by the state, for example as the medium of literature and scientific writing. This expansion of function may lead to an expansion in the vocabulary of the standard, as technical terms are created which have no direct equivalent in the vernacular. The final stage in standardization is the adoption and acceptance of the standard language by the entire speech community, who identify it as the basic form of the language. In many cases not only does the standard language thereby become a written variety, but the norms of the written form are seen as the correct forms of language, which language-users aim to reproduce in speech as well as writing.

Classical Latin as a standard

For Old Persian, there are clearly points of contact with some of these processes of standardization, but the present state of knowledge gives little insight into how the stages of selection or codification of the written form came about, and none at all into the extension of the standard into private documents or literature, if this indeed ever occurred. Classical Latin, which affords a far greater range of evidence, has sometimes been seen to fit neatly into the model created for modern standard language.[8] Something akin to standardization of Latin took place between 200 BCE and 100 CE, and can,

---

[7] For standardization, see Joseph (1987, especially 58–103), Wardhaugh (2010: 31–40).
[8] Neumann (1977) and Clackson (2011a). See Untermann (1977) for healthy scepticism about the extension of ideas about language norms to an age before printing.

in part, be traced, despite the near complete loss of most of the second-century BCE sources, owing to the wealth of references in sources such as Cicero and Quintilian. It is known that already in the middle of the second century BCE, literary figures such as Lucilius and Accius had formulated orthographic rules and proposals, and had also instituted a vocabulary for referring to mistakes and faults in Latin, testifying to an ongoing debate about which words and forms should be judged 'correct'. The wrangle over the nature of what came to be called *Latinitas*, 'Latinity' or simply 'Latin', continued into the Imperial period and is still alive in Quintilian, see for example 1.5.58-64 in relation to acceptable ways of declining Greek words in Latin. From a twenty-first-century perspective, the Latin texts of the Imperial age (particularly as they appear in modern printed editions) may seem to show that a standardized version of the language has won out, since there is an avoidance of certain archaic terms and an apparent regularity in rules of syntax, declensions of nouns and conjugation of verbs. But it is well to remember that we do not have the original texts from the hands of authors such as Cicero, Caesar and others, and the rigid rules of Lain grammarians may have become incorporated into our classical texts at a later date.

The codification of Classical Latin was entwined with these debates about the 'correct' forms of the language. Although there was an upsurge in Roman grammatical activity during this time (the largest extant remains of which are the surviving sections of Varro's *De lingua latina*), with considerable attention to interpreting and incorporating Greek grammatical ideas, the spread of a standard form was brought about as much by example as by prescription. Hence the writings of Cicero and Julius Caesar eventually became models of correct Latinity, and their vocabulary choice (and a shared preference for the diction of the second-century BCE comic poet Terence) influenced the style of subsequent writers. An earlier tolerance for variant forms appears to have been ironed out of most prose genres by the middle of the first century CE, as writers imitated the practice of either Cicero or Caesar. For example, in Republican Latin, authors could express the verb meaning 'they have loved' in up to four different ways: *amāuēre, amāuerunt, amāuērunt* or *amārunt*; in later centuries, *amāuērunt* became the favoured form in the written language, as far as it is possible to tell (although the evidence of the Romance languages suggests that in speech *amāuerunt* won out). There was also a gradual narrowing of the choice of different syntactic constructions, and some vocabulary items, such as the word *bellus* 'fine, pretty' were largely avoided in Classical Latin literary prose and poetry, stigmatized as being of an insufficiently elegant register (see Clackson 2011a for details).

The works of Cicero also allow us to trace the phase of the expansion of Latin vocabulary, through his coinages, translations and adaptations of Greek terms in his own philosophical and rhetorical works. At one place in his correspondence with his friend Titus Pomponius Atticus (a Roman resident at Athens, who was so thoroughly immersed in Greek culture that he acquired the cognomen *Atticus* 'the Athenian'), Cicero opens a window into the discourse that surrounded this process of lexical enrichment of Latin. Cicero gives his reasons for preferring the Latin *sustinere* 'to hold up' for a Greek term (*epékhō*) in the philosophical sense of 'suspend judgement' to the alternative suggested by Atticus, *inhibere* 'to hold back' (*Ad Atticum* 13.21.3). Cicero's reasons for the choice relate to technical senses both words already had in Latin, as applied to vehicles in motion. Only after observing oarsmen rowing backwards when told to *inhibere* does Cicero realize that this word does not have the appropriate meaning; on the other hand, he finds literary parallels for the use of *sustinere* to refer to drivers bringing chariots to a stop. The debate over this single term may have been indicative of some of the Roman debates about the most appropriate Latin vocabulary for rendering Greek language. We can also see different processes of lexical creation employed by slightly later Roman authors, in the development of Latin medical terminology during the Empire (during the Republic and early Empire, most medical text books were written in Greek by Greeks). Different writers helped to create a Latin repertoire of names for diseases, medical treatments and body parts through the selective employment of suffixes borrowed from Greek, or through metaphorical extensions of existing Latin words (Langslow 2000).

The fourth component of modern accounts of standardization is perhaps the most clearly illustrated for the Roman case. Speakers' internalization of the notion of a 'correct' Latin, and their attempt to employ this form in their own speech, can be seen in the increased incidence of comments about the linguistic solecisms of others in the late Republic and early Empire. Educated Romans seem to have been highly conscious and critical of both spoken and written language, and the presence of anything that could be presented as a 'mistake' of diction, or a badly chosen word in the speech of a rival, could be taken as an indication not only of the deficiency of his education, but also his lack of good breeding, intelligence and moral probity (the restriction to the male case is here deliberate; we shall address the issue of women's speech in chapter 5). Examples of Roman linguistic snobbery include Catullus' poem (84) about Arrius, who misplaced *h* at the beginning of words, and thereby betrayed his family's servile connections (cited in Chapter 4); or Suetonius' statement about the

senator Florus who corrected the emperor Vespasian's pronunciation of
the Latin word for 'wagon' (the emperor pronounced the lower register
form *plostrum* rather than *plaustrum*, Suetonius *Vespasian* 22). There are
numerous examples in Cicero of language as a vehicle for one-upmanship.
Take for example Cicero's criticism of Mark Antony's vocabulary in the
Philippics (3.22):

> 'nulla contumelia est quam facit dignus.' primum quid est dignus? nam
> etiam malo multi digni, sicut ipse. an quam facit is qui cum dignitate est?
> quae autem potest esse maior? quid est porro facere contumeliam? quis sic
> loquitur?
> 'An insult made by the worthy is no insult.' First, what is 'worthy?' For
> many folk are worthy of evil, as is he himself. Or does he mean an insult made
> by someone who possesses worth? Can any insult be greater? And further,
> what is 'making an insult'? Who talks like that? (translation D. R. Shackleton
> Bailey, Loeb Classical Library)

Cicero continues to insult Mark Antony's teacher, who had been rewarded
with a state pension. However, even Cicero's distaste for the locution
contumeliam facere 'to do an insult', did not mean that the phrase was
excluded from polite society thereafter (it already occurs in literature before
Cicero in the Latin comic poets and the speeches of Cato). Quintilian
(9.4.13), writing in the second half of the first century CE, implies that the
phrase was perfectly acceptable in his day.[9] Moreover, Cicero himself
makes use of a similar periphrasis *conuicium facere* 'to make a reproach',
as at *Pro Cluentio* 74, where he employs the phrase in order to highlight the
associated adjective *maximum* 'greatest'.[10]

   In the Republican period, Classical Latin functioned as the language of
the state, to such an extent that later authors reported that Roman
magistrates were expected to speak only Latin in their official capacity.[11]
In the Empire, Latin was still very much the state language, and indeed
continued to be seen as such even under the Byzantine Empire, when Latin
was retained as the language of law and in certain contexts in administration. However, by the time of the reign of Hadrian (117–38 CE), Latin was
certainly not the only 'state' language of the Empire. Greek was permitted
in the Senate, was in common use as the major administrative language
in the eastern Empire, and even in Rome the emperor might make a
speech in Greek in the Senate. The Romans never developed a coherent
policy with respect to language-use in the provinces, neither forbidding

---

[9] Manuwald (2007: 403–4).   [10] I owe this observation to Jim Adams.
[11] Rochette (2011), whose account I have largely followed in the rest of this paragraph.

other languages nor requiring citizens to learn Latin (although one anecdote does involve the emperor Claudius stripping a Greek of his citizenship because he did not know Latin, Suetonius *Claudius* 16.2). Even in Roman law the Latin language was not always necessary: oral contracts (*stipulationes*), for which there were precise Latin forms of words, could also be made in Greek (Gaius *Institutes* 3.93).[12] Latin thus appears to fit the criteria for a standard language well, but it was not also a national language, i.e. one which all citizens of the state are required to speak or write, at least in official functions or legal transactions.

Standard Greek? Linear B

If Latin broadly corresponds to modern standard languages, the case of Greek and the Greek dialects is far more complex. Unlike Latin, Greek has had a number of different standard forms throughout its history. It can be argued that the very first occurrence of a Greek standard was the variety now known as Mycenaean Greek, the language encoded on the Linear B tablets, which held the accounting records in the Mycenaean palaces of Greece and Crete in the second millennium BCE. Unlike Elamite or Old Persian, there is no evidence that Linear B was ever employed in inscriptions intended for display, either in monumental inscriptions or on prestige items. Other than on clay tablets, Linear B is found painted on nearly 180 stirrup-jars, containers for oil or perfume, but here its function seems to be to record the name and origin of the producer, owner, or collector.[13] Linear B is a resolutely bureaucratic instrument. In general, Linear B texts display a very high degree of consistency in spellings, morphological forms and formulae for different types of record, which is surprising considering both the fact that the tablets cover a time span of over 200 years,[14] and that they have been found across a wide geographical range: at Knossos and Khania on Crete, Pylos and nearby Iklaina, Ayios Vasilios, Mycenae and Tiryns in the Peloponnese, and Boeotian Thebes and Volos in Thessaly, with stirrup-jars and sealings more widely scattered. Indeed, later inhabitants of these areas would speak a range of different Greek dialects: Doric in Crete, the Peloponnese and the Argolid, and Aeolic in Boeotia and Thessaly. Even given the shortcomings of the Linear B writing system for encoding the Greek language, there is no comparable example of similar linguistic uniformity of written forms of Greek for the next 3,000 years.

---

[12] The particular case of the oral legacies known as *fideicommissa* will be discussed in Chapter 3.
[13] van Alfen (2008).   [14] Driessen (2008).

What is more, it can easily be shown that the variety encoded in the Linear B texts is not some linguistic equivalent of the golden age, offering an uncorrupted state of Greek which was to become debased over time to become the various dialects familiar from later literature and inscriptions. Mycenaean Greek cannot be the direct ancestor of the Doric dialect of Greek, since it has undergone changes that never took place in Doric. For example, in Doric Greek the verb *ékhonti* means 'they have', and we know that this keeps the shape of the earliest form of the verb. In Linear B 'they have' is written out in three signs: *e-ko-si*, which most likely represents something like /*ékhonsi*/ in speech. The final *-ti* has changed to *-si*, a change paralleled in many languages of the world (compare the way the French pronounce the word *nation*), whereas the opposite shift from *-si* to *-ti* would be highly unusual. Mycenaean Greek therefore has gone one stage further than Doric. In most societies, including ancient Greece, speakers have no access to their linguistic history, and changes such as this are not usually undone.[15]

Does the apparent lack of variation in the Mycenaean corpus indicate a standardized bureaucratic dialect in use across the Mycenaean palaces, perhaps even reflecting the Greek once spoken by Minoan officials in Crete, and spread from there to Mycenaean palaces on the mainland?[16] Or is the almost uniform nature of the language of the documents rather an indication of a tightly controlled scribal education, and not a reflection of the real spoken variation at all? One place to look for answers to these questions is through closer examination of the small number of cases where there is identifiable variation in the texts. For example, the name of the goddess Artemis is once spelt *a-te-mi-to* (corresponding to a later Greek genitive *Artémitos*) and once *a-ti-mi-ti* (corresponding to what would have been the dative case *Artímiti*, with a different vowel in the middle of the word than is found in later Greek).[17] The fluctuation between *e* and *i* is also found in other words and names, generally next to an *m* or a *p*; in general, spellings of this type with *e* are less common in the Mycenaean texts (although these also tend to be the forms preserved by later Greek dialects, as in the name of the goddess). Variation is also evident in one grammatical ending, the dative singular of third declension nouns, where again there is a

---

[15] *Pace* Thompson (2008b), who suggests that Doric speakers may have reversed the change of *–ti* to *–si* by analogy to other verb forms.
[16] Chadwick (1976).
[17] See Beekes (2010: 142) on Lydian and Lycian forms of the name of the goddess and possible etymologies.

fluctuation between writings with *-e* and *-i*, except this time the forms ending with *-i* are less frequent than those ending in *-e*.

Following the lead of Risch (1966), scholars have attempted to group the few variables in the Linear B texts together to isolate two distinct dialects of Mycenaean Greek, dubbed *normal* (those of more frequent occurrence) and *special* Mycenaean. However, special features do not normally cluster together in the same word, as the example of *a-ti-mi-ti* shows, with one special feature (here the dative in *-i*) and one normal (the spelling *a-ti-mi-* rather than *a-te-mi-*). Indeed, it is possible to identify individual Mycenaean scribes through their handwriting, and analysis of the documents from Knossos shows that no Mycenaean scribe there ever employs more than one of the special features, although there is some evidence that some clusters of scribes, working in the same division of the archives, favour the special spellings (Woodard 1986). At Pylos, the only other Mycenaean palace from which a large archive of tablets survives, one scribe ('hand 24') managed to fit in two, possibly three, of the non-standard writings in the three tablets he wrote (Palaima 2002). If the idea that the special features actually represent a separate dialect can be made to fit this evidence, we have to assume that the special features were somehow the disfavoured alternatives, which sneaked into documents either as oversights or slips, or because the scribe concerned had been less well-trained. Chadwick (1976) suggested that the special dialect corresponded more closely to the speech of those living and working outside the palatial complexes, and further argued that the Doric dialects of later Crete and Messenia were continuations of these forms of speech. Most linguists have been reluctant to follow Chadwick this far, although Palaima (2002) has resurrected the idea in his discussion of hand 24, whom he assumes to be an official from a regional centre away from the palace. An alternative view is that the existence of two distinct dialects is a mirage, and that the variation can be better explained by the hypothesis that the scribes were attempting to do the best they could to fit a changing spoken language to an unwieldy script (Thompson 1999; 2002; 2008a).

It is probably anachronistic to imagine Linear B scribes either as minding their *ps* and *qs* and carefully avoiding a slide into the vernacular, or as careful observers of the changing linguistic forms of speech. As far as we can tell, in the Mycenaean palaces writing played no part in prestige display or in the recording of any information other than bureaucratic accounts and stock-taking. The Linear B tablets most likely functioned as aide-mémoires in a largely oral culture, and were not intended to be read by anyone other than their composer (Palaima 2011). Corrections of special Mycenaean forms to normal Mycenaean on the tablets are rare; Palaima (2002: 217) gives an apparent example of a tablet from Pylos where a scribe corrects a personal name from the spelling *e-pa-sa-na-ti* to *i-pa-sa-na-ti*, but the same scribe also spells the name with an *e* elsewhere, as does the prolific Pylian scribe known as hand 1, who otherwise largely uses normal Mycenaean forms. The apparent consistency of Linear B writing across time and space is most likely due to shared traditions of literacy and scribal training, and it is doubtful how closely scribes would have felt the need to reflect accurately their current speech. Thompson (2008a) has shown that scribes tend to write the same word with the same spelling consistently, even if they show variation across different words, probably reflecting their education rather than anything else. Moreover, although there are indications of dialectal differences between Knossos and Pylos, even these are hardly evident in the script (Meißner 2007). Rather than representing a Mycenaean standard or a common palace dialect, Linear B is more likely to show the extension of a shared written form over a very limited body of clerks (whose social position is unfortunately almost completely irrecoverable). In cases such as this, where literacy is so restricted both in extent and in function, notions of a standard language add little to our understanding of a complex situation.

Greek in the Archaic and Classical periods

If Linear B seems to show too little variation, Greek recorded in alphabetic script appears to show too much. In the archaic Greek world there is not even a single alphabet to write the language, but a diverse range of scripts, differing in number of letters, letter-forms and the values accorded to the various signs. Map 2.1 gives a schema for four major groupings of the Greek alphabet, labelled since Kirchhoff (1863) as the Green, Red, Blue and Light Blue, but it is important to remember that within these families there are further divisions into *genera* and *species*, allowing modern specialists to pinpoint the provenance of an inscription accurately from the letter-forms alone. The earliest Greek written texts to have survived are not just written in different alphabets,[18] they also show a dizzying variation in spelling, vocabulary and grammar. Not only is there variation over geographical space, with dialectal features associated with different city-states (*poleis*), but also, from the earliest inscriptions continuing through the history of

---

[18] *LSAG* is the standard work on the early varieties of the Greek alphabet; Powell (1991) handily gathers sixty-eight of the surviving Greek inscriptions before 650 BCE, which are reproduced as line-drawings.

Greek, linguistic choices are associated with the genre and function of the inscription, and also with the geographical background of the writer.

When Greeks of the Archaic and Classical periods inscribed texts (other than those composed in a verse metre), they chose to communicate in their own local speech varieties, termed the *epichoric* dialects, and did not accommodate to the speech of other dialect speakers. Inscriptions made on behalf of the *polis* or of religious groups reflect the local dialect of the region and use the local script, as do dedications and inscriptions by individuals. In cases where an inscription is set up by a state or a person in a different *polis* or in a Panhellenic sanctuary, for example a dedication at Olympia, Delphi or Delos, the alphabet and dialect of the hometown are also standard. Artists, if they sign their works, generally do so in their local dialect, leading to cases where a dedicated object may carry two texts in different regional varieties, one of the dedicator, and the other of the maker. Sometimes peripatetic craftsmen may leave records that combine linguistic features of their place of origin and their place of residence.[19] Monuments or honorary decrees commemorating foreigners were erected in the language and script of those paying for the monument, with only occasional examples showing any regard to the regional variety spoken by the honorand (Buck 1913: 147–50). Records of interstate arbitration were in the dialect of the third party who settled the dispute (Buck 1913: 150–2). Treaties made between *poleis* sometimes included clauses requiring that pillars inscribed with the treaty were to be set up in each *polis* and in sanctuaries (for example, Thucydides 5.18.10 records the terms of the treaty between Athens and Sparta in 421 BCE, which requires the erection of inscriptions at Olympia, Delphi, the Isthmus, on the Athenian acropolis and in the temple of Apollo at Amyklai in Sparta). Examples of such inscriptions that survive show that these were written in the dialect of each respective party (Buck 1913: 152–9).[20]

In some literary works, speakers from different dialect areas are sometimes represented speaking their own varieties when in communication with each other. For example, in Aristophanes' *Acharnians* and *Lysistrata*, Megarians, Boeotians and Spartans speak their own dialects (or approximations of them) in the city of Athens in a variety of different situations, from market traders in the *Acharnians* to Spartan envoys in the *Lysistrata*,

---

[19] Buck (1913: 140) gives the example of the dedication by the sons of the Parian artist Kharopinos (*SIG³* 16a and 16b) written with both Parian and Phocian features.

[20] A possible exception to this may be the treaties between the Spartans and Argives recorded at Thucydides 5.77 and 79. Thucydides records the words of the treaties, which appear to be in Doric, but not in the specific dialect of either Sparta or Argos. Unfortunately, the text seems to have been altered during transmission, making any conclusion uncertain (Colvin 1999: 65–7).

and this seems to be the general practice in Old Comedy (Colvin 1999: 281). But in tragedy and historical or forensic narratives, all Greeks generally speak the same dialect as in the rest of the text. Hence in Herodotus everyone speaks Ionic, in Thucydides literary Attic, and in Plato and oratory the less elevated register of Attic. The historian Xenophon reproduces the dialect text of a letter sent by the Spartan vice-admiral Hippocrates after the defeat at the Battle of Cyzicus in 410 BCE (*Hellenica* 1.1.23), but depicts conversations between Spartans in Attic (e.g. *Hellenica* 3.3.2–3). In Aeschylus' *Choephoroe* (563–4) Orestes declares that he and Pylades will imitate the Phocian dialect, which the audience then has to imagine through their otherwise unchanged tragic diction. This literary flattening of dialectal variation in narrative appears to have been an accepted convention, and continues throughout the history of Greek; Pausanias, writing in the later second century CE, silently adapts or omits dialect forms in inscriptions he cites (as at 5.24.3, discussed by Karali 2007: 977, Kaczko 2009: 97). The tacit avoidance of discordant dialectal features parallels the normal assumption that the audience will understand that different languages or interpreters were involved when barbarians speak to each other (as discussed in Chapter 1). Indeed, after a wider analysis of cited direct speech in Attic oratory and drama, Bers (1997) concluded that the Greeks generally made little attempt to distinguish the voice of another speaker in narrative. The jangle of different dialects given in comic drama is most likely to reproduce the sound of the Athenian streets, and other testimonia, such as Socrates' plea to be treated in a law court as if he were a foreigner speaking in his native dialect (*Apology* 17d), suggest that it was accepted practice to use vernaculars even in highly formal surroundings.

The Greek epichoric dialects have provided linguists and classical philologists with material for concentrated study since ancient times, and there are numerous grammars and descriptions of the language of the dialects. However, as Bile *et al.* pointed out (1984), Greek dialect studies can give a false impression of scholarly omniscience, when in many cases our evidence for an individual dialect comes from a small collection of inscriptions, often inscribed over a considerable time span, and sometimes still imperfectly edited or understood. Our knowledge of the Laconian dialect of Sparta, for example, is based on a very small corpus, which is itself internally inconsistent.[21] Many of the Laconian dialect texts themselves belong to a period between the second century BCE and second century CE and are associated with the cult of Artemis Orthia; they may have incorporated

---

[21] See Bourguet (1927) for a grammar of the Laconian dialect.

archaic forms in order to heighten the distancing effect of the dialect, which was no longer the spoken idiom (Kennell 1995: 87–94, Prauscello 2009: 176). Furthermore, all our knowledge of these local dialects comes from written sources, which are, consequently, very different from what a speaker of a modern language, or a modern dialectologist, might consider as a dialect. In modern speech communities, dialect forms and expressions are often not written down; indeed, they are usually at odds with the written registers of the language. Despite these caveats, scholars are agreed that it is possible to divide the epichoric dialects of Greek into four different groups, distinguished by different sound changes (we have already mentioned the characteristic change of -*ti* > -*si* which most of the Greek dialects, apart from Doric, have undergone), or by innovation of different verbal or nominal endings, or by variation in vocabulary.

The different dialect groups, as hypothesized for the fifth century BCE (projecting back from later information in many cases) can be plotted on a map (Map 2.2). The distribution of dialects over space is in some ways unexpected – most particularly for the group labelled Arcado-Cypriot, the only dialectal group which extends over a non-contiguous area. Cyprus is of course on the periphery of the Greek world, and, as we saw in Chapter 1, we have good evidence to suggest that other languages were spoken there before Greek. Arcadian is surrounded in the Peloponnese by unrelated Doric dialects. By inspection of the map alone it is clear that Arcado-Cypriot has been pushed out to peripheral areas, and it might be hypothesized that the dialect once occupied a more central role. This conclusion accords well with linguistic research on Arcado-Cypriot, which suggests that it is the closest Greek dialect to the idiom recorded in the Linear B tablets (Morpurgo Davies 1992). But were the speakers of Arcadian and Cypriot driven back by a wave of invaders from the north? Or could the dialects that replaced them have been the speech of an underclass, able to throw off the yoke of oppression only after the collapse of the Mycenaean palatial economy? The theory of a Dorian invasion of Greece in the dark age period between 1100 and 800 BCE is largely a construct of nineteenth-century German romanticism, based on late Greek sources which conflated earlier tales about the returns of the descendants of Heracles to Greece (Hall 1997: 56–66), but it exerted a powerful hold on scholarship for much of the twentieth century. Although the dialect map of Greece appears to support the invasion hypothesis, the linguistic evidence is inconclusive: Doric dialects share almost all the same vocabulary, including loanwords, as the other Greek varieties, and have undergone several prehistoric changes in common with them. The idea that the ancestors of the later

Dorians were present in the same regions as their later descendants in Mycenaean times is supported by Chadwick's (1976) theory, mentioned above, that the Linear B documents contain isolated glimpses of a stigmatized Doric dialect. But, as Risch (1979) pointed out, the 'special' Mycenaean features are found in pretty much every later Greek dialect, and are not specifically Doric; furthermore, we find very few names which are specifically Doric in the extensive Linear B lists of personnel. It seems that the Dorians were beyond the reach of the palatial economies, since they were either inhabiting different parts of Greece, or living at a lower social level (see discussion of Horrocks 2010: 20–4).

Alongside the epichoric dialects, which are inescapably linked with a specific region through the presence of inscriptions on the ground, there is another stratum of Greek language variation that is not geographically bounded. Poets and prose authors of the archaic and classical periods compose literary works in dialects which are not those of their home town; for example Hesiod and Pindar do not use the Boeotian dialect (one of the constituents of the Aeolic group), Tyrtaeus of Sparta does not write in Laconian, but in Ionic (albeit with some scattered Laconian features), the same variety as the Athenian Solon and the Megarian Theognis (Horrocks 2010: 49). Although Sappho and Alcaeus write in Lesbian, and Page thought that Alcman wrote in the Laconian vernacular (Page 1951: 163), in fact these literary forms are not the same as the epichoric dialects (Tribulato 2010 for Sappho and Alcaeus, Hinge 2006 for Alcman). Indeed, most varieties of literary Greek correspond to no single Greek dialect, and reproduce varieties that can never have been the everyday spoken vernacular of any individual. Here it is important to note some ambiguity in the terminology used to refer to Greek dialects. Ancient authorities employed supra-regional or ethnic terms, such as Ionic, Doric or Aeolic to refer to literary varieties (Morpurgo Davies 1987). This is followed in modern works, where the same terms are also understood to refer to higher-order groupings of epichoric dialects (Arcado-Cypriot and North-West Greek, the latter sometimes considered a variety of Doric, are modern terms and have no ancient counterparts).

It is thus perfectly possible both to speak of Laconian and Cretan as Doric dialects, and to refer to the choral Doric of Pindar, but in the two cases the significance of Doric is slightly different. Pindar's Doric shares some features with the majority of epichoric dialects, but his language also includes some features not found in any Greek epichoric dialect. Or consider the language of Homer, which may be superficially classed as Ionic. Every Greek beginner who reads Homer knows that it is not enough to learn a single paradigm of a noun declension or verbal conjugation, but that variant forms exist alongside each other, and something so apparently simple as the infinitive of the verb 'to be' may have more different forms than is convenient to hold in the head: *eînai, émmen, émen, émmenai* and *émenai*. Some of these different forms correspond to epichoric forms: thus *eînai* is the form proper to the group of epichoric dialects spoken in the Aegean collectively labelled Ionic. Others are found in epichoric dialects outside Ionia: *émmen* and *émmenai* occur in inscriptions from Lesbos, whose dialect is traditionally grouped with Thessalian and Boeotian to form the Aeolic dialect group. Furthermore, two forms do not occur in any epichoric dialect: *émen*, and *émenai*. These infinitives are artificial creations of the epic language, as passed down by word of mouth through generations of bards. The singers of the Homeric epics adapted or borrowed different dialectal words to fit the metre of the poetry, and to allow them to construct a range of poetic formulae. Sometimes, the bards created new material through the extension of existing patterns by a process known to linguists as 'analogy'. Analogy is the explanation for why some English speakers derive a past tense *I dove* from the verb *I dive*, repeating the pattern of existing *I drive* and *I drove*. Hence *émen* derives from the participle *eón* 'being' by analogy to pairs such as *lúmen* 'to free' and *lúōn* 'freeing'. The form *émenai*, which does not have any life outside literary varieties, is apparently created by merging together the two different dialectal variants, Aeolic *émmen* and Ionic *eînai*.

Greek literary idioms we are familiar with from Homer and other authors have a parallel in early Greek verse inscriptions.[22] Nearly all verse inscriptions before 400 BCE that have an identifiable metre are written in hexameters, or, from 500 BCE on, in elegiac couplets. The shared metre, formulaic and lexical borrowing, and allusion to the Homeric epics show that there was a shared literary culture across the Greek world. However, as Mickey demonstrated (Mickey 1981a, 1981b), there is no compulsion for inscriptional verse to adopt what we think of as defining elements of the Homeric language. Verse inscriptions from Doric areas do not adopt Ionic peculiarities, or the special forms of the Homeric epics, but keep a Doric cast. For example, verse inscriptions regularly retain dialectal *sâma* 'monument' and *mnâma* 'memorial' where Homer and Ionic have *sêma* and *mnêma*, with the characteristic Ionic feature of the vowel *ē*

---

[22] Greek verse inscriptions are collected and edited in Peek (1955–7) and Hansen (1983) and (1989) (=*CEG* 1 and 2).

where Doric has *ā*; an inscription from Troizen peninsula in the east Peloponnese from around 600 BCE (Peek 158, *CEG* 137) has both *sâma* 'monument' and *mnâma* as well as the Doric infinitive *êmen* 'to be',[23] rather than any of the five different alternatives in Homer (two of which, *eînai* and *émmen*, would fit the metre). Nor do these verse inscriptions show a predilection for archaic elements of speech that are characteristic of Homer, such as omitting the prefix *e-* (called the augment) before past tense verbs. However, verse inscriptions do appear to tone down the peculiarities of their own dialect (even though they make no concessions with their local variety of the Greek alphabet!). They avoid forms which are specific to only a small locality, or which might not be widely recognized, even where these forms are close to ones that occur in Homer. Thus dialect inscriptions from Thessaly appear to avoid using the peculiar Thessalian genitive ending *-oi*, even though it is close to the Homeric *-oio*. This move to iron out idiosyncratic differences is also occasionally found in prose inscriptions: the serpent column from Delphi dedicated by the Spartans and other Hellenes after the Battle of Plataea in 479 BCE avoids the specifically Laconian form *epolémion* 'they waged war' in favour of the more widespread *epolémeon* in the heading of the list of those taking part in the battle, and is set up in the Phocian script appropriate to Delphi.[24]

In Archaic and Classical Greece then, there is nothing that can be usefully called a 'standard language' for all Greek speakers. Even literary dialects were mutable according to local usages and standards. It is not surprising in this linguistic milieu that Greeks sometimes had trouble understanding each other. Thucydides (3.94) characterizes the Eurytanians, the largest tribe of the Aetolians, as 'most unintelligible of language (*agnōstótatoi glôssan*)' as well as being eaters of uncooked meat. But they do seem to have recognized that, in some sense, all Greeks spoke a shared language. This is evident from the famous Herodotean passage where the Athenians assure the Spartans that their shared Greekness will prevent them from allying with the barbarian: 'there is the fact of our being Greek – our common blood and common language, common altars and sacrifices to the gods, and identical folkways' (Herodotus 8.144.2, translation from Cartledge 2007: 312); other statements in Classical authors lend further support.[25] It is significant that the

---

[23] The local script writes this EMEN, using the same sign for both the long *ē* and the short *e*; the first vowel is revealed to be long by the metre.

[24] Inscription no. 27 in Meiggs and Lewis (1988), cited by Buck (1913: 134) and Morpurgo Davies (1993: 293).

[25] See Morpurgo Davies (1987), Willi (2002b: 136) and Cartledge (2007) for further passages from ancient sources.

incomprehensible Eurytanians are also culturally removed from ideas of what Greeks are by their dietary habits. It is clear also, to judge from the avoidance of peculiar local forms in verse inscriptions, that Greek speakers did have an awareness of what was distinctive about particular dialects, a point which is also highlighted by Aristophanes' representations of different dialects, which note some local oddities while ignoring others (Colvin 1999: 297–9). Greeks also employed a distinction between speaking a different Greek dialect and speaking a different language, using the verb *xenízein* for the first but *barbarízein* for the second, matching the distinction between a *xénos* 'stranger' (someone to whom there was a duty of hospitality) and *bárbaros* 'barbarian, non-Greek'. (Although in Plato's *Protagoras* the Lesbian dialect is termed 'barbarous' (*Protagoras* 341c), this is best taken to be a joke rather than a linguistic classification.)

There was thus a rather fuzzy notion of what Greek as a whole was, and an acceptance that different varieties of Greek were appropriate in certain literary or religious contexts. However, within this broad spectrum, there were, increasingly from the sixth century BCE onwards, movements towards what can be seen as standardized varieties of Greek, especially in areas under a central political or administrative control, or where there was a shared culture and commerce. The first traces of this process appear in the Ionian *poleis* of the eastern Aegean where, judging from the scanty epigraphic remains and the survival of literary prose works of the fifth century BCE, the variation between the spoken varieties (as mentioned by Herodotus I. 142–3) appears to have been largely levelled out in the written language. This idiom appears to have spread as the cultured and modern literary style of newly emerging disciplines such as philosophy, history, science and ethnography.[26]

However, our evidence for the early Ionic is severely limited. We can best track the process of selection of a single dialect variant for both the administrative and the literary productions of a city-state in the case of Athens, where we do not lack for surviving linguistic data, from both inscriptions and a range of literary works. No other city can equal Athens for the wealth of material or its later cultural significance, but some evidence suggests that Athens was not unusual in the fifth century BCE for its tolerance of a range of literary varieties; for example, at Syracuse Epicharmus composed his comedies in the local vernacular while conscious

---

[26] See Tribulato (2010: 392), and Stüber (1996) for detailed discussion of the inscriptions. Stüber shows that, although the inscriptional evidence does not support Herodotus' statement (1.142.3) on the dialectal array of East Ionic, local variations do persist (see her conclusion at 1996: 141).

of, and occasionally employing, forms from a more prestigious literary idiom (Willi 2008: 119–61). Official inscriptions (and coinage) from Athens employ the local variety of Attic, which was distinguished from Ionic by a number of special aspects of pronunciation, word-endings and vocabulary. In the mid-fifth century, this variety is noticeably different from the literary idioms of the contemporary playwrights Aeschylus and Sophocles. The language of Athenian drama is of course far removed from administrative prose in its employment of recondite vocabulary, metaphors and metonyms in place of everyday language, and syntactic ellipsis (i.e. omission of verbs or other key elements of the sentence) and marked displacements of word order.[27] Moreover, the dramatists compose in two different literary varieties, depending on the mode of performance: sung portions of the play, set in lyric metres, are written in the literary Doric dialect associated with choral lyric; whereas the spoken passages, especially those of dialogue, in iambic or other stichic metres (i.e. those where each line repeats the same metre) are composed in what can best be described as literary Attic. In this literary version of the Attic language, the poets avoided what were seen as parochial forms, i.e. those features of pronunciation and grammar which were shared with nearby dialects such as Boeotian, and incorporated Ionic forms in their place (indeed, their practice mirrors that of the composers of Greek verse epitaphs, who also avoided what were felt to be vernacular forms of very limited reach). Thucydides, among the first extant writers of prose in Attic, adopted largely the idiom of literary Attic from the dramatists, but Athenian orators, who were mostly writing for audiences within the city of Athens rather than for wider consumption, selected the local vernacular instead. In this they were in step with the language of Attic comedy, and Plato also adopted this Attic variety in his dialogues. Four of the distinctive features of the different literary dialects (with the Attic forms divided between 'literary Attic' and 'conservative Attic', following the labels given by Horrocks 2010: 64) are given in Table 2.1. It can be seen that, although literary Attic agrees with literary Ionic on many points, it does not always avoid a local variety in the interest of having the same form as literary Ionic, as in the case of the outcome of an original long $\bar{a}$ vowel after an e, i or r, where it agrees with the conservative Attic form. The justification for this can be seen from the fact that here the literary Attic form agrees with what is normal in literary

---

[27] See for example Aristotle *Poetics* 1457c on the impossibility of using the tragic word order with preposition after its noun in everyday speech.

Table 2.1 *Varieties of Attic and literary languages*

Early Greek	Literary Ionic	Literary Attic	Conservative Attic Prose	Literary Doric
(* indicates a hypothetical form not actually attested)	(e.g. Herodotus)	(e.g. tragedy and Thucydides)	(e.g. inscriptions, orators and Plato)	(e.g. choral lyric)
mā́tēr 'mother'	*mḗtēr*	*mḗtēr*	*mḗtēr*	*mā́tēr*
ā after *e, i,* or *r*	*ē̆*	*ā*	*ā*	*ā*
sophiā́ 'wisdom'	*sophiḗ*	*sophiā́*	*sophiā́*	*sophiā́*
khṓrā 'country'	*khṓrē*	*khṓrā*	*khṓrā*	*khṓrā*
*thálakya 'sea'	*thálassa*	*thálassa*	*thálatta*	*thálassa*
*prā́k-yō 'I make'	*prḗssō*	*prā́ssō*	*prā́ttō*	*prā́ssō*
arsēn 'male'	*arsḗn*	*arsḗn*	*arrḗn*	*arsḗn*

Doric, and so has some sanction in the literary language. But where the local Attic variant is not already enshrined in any literary language, as is the case for the *-tt-* in words such as *thálatta* 'sea', it is largely absent from literary Attic.

Literary Attic and conservative Attic were of course not fixed absolutes, and variation is apparent within the two different standards. Literary Attic, with its incorporation of Ionic forms, seems also to have corresponded in some degree to the spoken language of some of the Athenians who had a more 'international' outlook, who traded or practised a profession over an area wider than Attica itself, and also probably to the speech of incomers to Athens from the Aegean islands or elsewhere (Horrocks 2010: 73–7). Some fifth-century Athenian texts witness the presence of a tension, or at least an awareness, about different variants of spoken Attic, or deplore the creeping loss of vernacular terms in favour of less parochial ones. A fragment of Aristophanes (fr. 706 *PCG*) contrasts the 'womanish' or 'feminized' language of the urbane, and the 'slavish' language of the countryside, and recommends a middle path. The unknown author of the tract now known as the *Constitution of Athens*, whose anti-democratic views have given him the modern sobriquet of 'the Old Oligarch', found fault with the language of the Athenians of his day (probably the 420s or 410s, Osborne 2004: 18):

> Again, they listen to every kind of dialect, and take something from one, something from another. The Greeks in general tend to keep to their own dialect, way of life, and dress, whereas the Athenians mix theirs from all the Greeks and barbarians. (Ps. Xen. *Const. Ath.* 2.8, translation from Osborne 2004: 22)

The Old Oligarch's complaint about linguistic change is in keeping with his generally negative attitude towards any kind of novelty, and he may not have had any definite features in mind, but it is at least possible that he had noticed a creeping Ionicization of some Attic speech. The gradual loss of some older Attic forms in favour of Ionic ones can be seen in some inscriptional texts. López Eire (1993, 1999) drew attention to the inscriptional record of a treaty between Athens and the Euboean city of Chalcis (*IG* I³ 40), dated to 446 BCE, where the official administrative text contains a variant of conservative Attic, but clauses added by independent Athenian citizens move towards the language of literary Attic, replacing the prefix *xun-* (written *khsun*) with *sun-* and dative plurals ending in *-oisi* with the ending *-ois*.

Greek dialects in the Hellenistic and Roman periods

Over time, the tension, if this is not too emphatic a word, between the conservative and the literary varieties of Attic appears to have eased, and, in speech (although not in all literary forms) a compromise between the two forms evolved which became spoken over a wide area of both Attica and the central Aegean. This variety, now often termed 'Great Attic' (although there is no ancient sanction for this name), avoided the localized forms of Attic (such as the words with *-tt-*), preferring the Ionicized versions; it avoided some of the peculiarities of Attic grammar (such as the continued existence of a dual number, marking a pair of objects as distinct from a singular and plural); regularized verbal conjugations and nominal declensions; and avoided specifically Attic oddities of morphology. This was the variety which was adopted by the Macedonian court of Philip and Alexander, and the form which spread to the new Greek territories to the east after Alexander's conquests. Great Attic was the basis for what became known as the *koiné*, the language of administration and technical and other works (including the 'New Testament' of the Christian Bible) written after Alexander (Horrocks 2010: 73–83). Papyrus finds from Egypt mean that we can track the *koiné*'s rapid encroachment upon local dialects spoken by incomers from the Greek mainland to the newly wealthy Hellenized cities of Egypt. Theocritus, in Idyll 15, represents Doric spoken both by two women from Syracuse and by the people they meet at Alexandria, but this may be because his dialect choice is based on literary considerations rather than verisimilitude (see the discussion in Willi 2012). Papyri further reveal that the *koiné* was the form of Greek which speakers of

Egyptian Demotic acquired when they learnt Greek. The *koinē* was the language of trade, business and administration, and both local elites and merchants of mainland Greece and the western colonies gradually adopted it in place of their former vernaculars. From the third century BCE on, both public and private inscriptions all over the Greek world increasingly show the influence of the *koinē*, if they are not written entirely in the language. Modern Greek and its dialects, including those spoken in isolated parts of southern Italy and Asia Minor, all derive from the *koinē* (the only exception is the Tsakonian dialect of the south-eastern Peloponnese, which partly continues ancient Laconian, Horrocks 2010: 382). In later literary accounts or fictions, speakers of Greek in different regions are usually represented speaking the *koinē*, although sometimes with a qualification such as 'with a Doric accent' (*dōrízōn*). For example, in Dio Chrysostom's *Orations* (written in the latter half of the first century CE) he relates several encounters in Greek backwaters: an old priestess in the Peloponnesian countryside between Heraea and Pisa (1. 50–84); a huntsman in Euboea after a shipwreck (7); and the semi-barbarized Greeks of Olbia in the Black Sea (36). In line with the normal Greek convention, their utterances are recorded in language that is the same as that of the surrounding text, even though the priestess is described as speaking Doric, but Dio makes it clear that he has no difficulty in understanding any of them, and mutual intelligibility is never in doubt.[28]

The Syracusan mathematician Archimedes (third century BCE) wrote in Doric, but after him *koinē* became the norm for Hellenistic technical prose writings such as medical, mathematical or grammar texts, or in low-level texts such as the Greek New Testament and the *Discourses* of Epictetus (itself supposedly a transcription of Epictetus' sayings by his pupil Arrian, rather than a literary composition). However, poetry is not written in the *koinē*, and the surviving literary uses are mostly for histories (Polybius, Diodorus Siculus), geographical or ethnographic work (Strabo), and biographies or essays (Plutarch). Other authors set themselves apart from the *koinē*: the fourth-century BCE historians Cratippus (if he is the author of the *Hellenica Oxyrhynchia*) and Theopompus (born in Ionic Chios not

---

[28] A possible exception is the biblical passage in Acts 2:4–11, cited in Chapter 1, where peoples probably speaking Greek at this date, such as Cretans, Cappadocians and the visitors from Pontus are mentioned among those who are able to understand one another miraculously. See also Langslow (1988: 201) for other possible examples of local Greek vernaculars which were unintelligible during the Roman period.

Athens) consciously employ forms with -tt- and -rr-, in place of the
koinế's -ss- and -rs-, even though they continue in the tradition of
Herodotus and Thucydides (both of whom selected the latter spellings).
Although the Athenian Menander's comedies, written at the end of the
fourth century, mirror some of the linguistic developments of the earlier
Attic of Aristophanes, and employ some koinế forms, his characters also
continue to say práttō and arrến, not prássō and arsến. Hellenistic and later
poets extend the range of existing literary dialects to new forms (or to
erudite pastiches of earlier genres). As in earlier centuries, high-style literary
composition was viewed as something separate from the language of the
everyday. Now however, the varieties seen to be removed from the parochial are in some cases the same which were viewed as too parochial for
high style. Thus authors seek out the distinctly Attic forms of Plato or
Lysias in order to set themselves apart from the spoken koinế, much as at an
earlier period Thucydides' literary Attic distinguished his prose from the
everyday language of the city.

The koinế is, in some respects, the Greek equivalent to a standard
language in the Hellenistic and the Roman periods. It is codified in the
grammar of Dionysius Thrax,[29] and papyrus school texts surviving from
Egypt show that the first variety of Greek to be taught, and the one through
which the more recondite literary texts were explained, was the koinế
(Cribiore 2001: 185–219). It is the variety used in the administration of
the Ptolemies, and later in the administration of the eastern provinces of
the Roman Empire. It was the only Greek dialect to acquire a fully
developed technical vocabulary, and the means of expressing complex
ideas in medicine and maths (Schironi 2010). When educated Romans
such as Cicero switched into Greek, they generally spoke koinế rather than
any of the earlier dialects, except to allude to a literary text (Swain 2002:
146–7). However, the fourth stage of standardization, *acceptance*, was never
quite reached. Partly owing to the fact that the literary dialects continued
to be accorded prestige, the koinế never attained a status as anything other
than one particular variety of Greek. When Valerius Maximus, writing in
the early days of the Roman Empire, reports the linguistic abilities of
Publius Crassus Mucianus (who was proconsul in Asia Minor in 131
BCE), he reports that he was proficient in 'all five branches of Greek'
(V. Max. 8.7.6). The fivefold division of Greek encompasses the four

---

[29] Dionysius Thrax lived in the second century BCE, but his grammar is likely to have been reworked
many times over the next 600 years; see the discussion of Lallot (1998: 20–6).

recognized literary dialects: Attic, Ionic, Aeolic and Doric, and the *koiné*, which is not seen as superordinate or even of a different nature than the others. This division is held equally by the later Greek grammarians, who curiously cited Pindar as an example of an author who wrote in the *koiné* (Morpurgo Davies 1987). Of course the variety did not come into existence until the fourth century BCE, but the mixture of different dialect forms in Pindar was so extreme that there was no other slot for him.

Far from becoming accepted, the *koiné* actually began to lose prestige during a literary movement now known as the Second Sophistic, which was at its peak during the second century CE. Authors associated with the Second Sophistic made a concerted effort to write in a more 'pure' Attic, and strove to purge their works of anything which was not established in fifth-century BCE Athenian authors. Lucian's humorous skit, written around this time, entitled *Trial in the Court of Vowels*, represents an unhappy letter sigma (s), complaining of the depredations the letter tau (t) has done to his property:

> He has expelled me from all Thessaly, deeming it Thettaly, and he has established an exclusion zone over the whole sea [i.e. *thálassa/thálatta* 'sea']. (Lucian, *Trial in the Court of Vowels* 9)[30]

It is significant that the letter sigma recounts that he was first aware of tau's acquisitiveness when staying in Cybelus (an invented place-name, although it is 'said to be an Athenian colony'), where his host was one Lysimachus, who affected to be from inner Attica but actually was a Boeotian. Lucian is mocking the claim to Attic pedigree among people and even places, as well as among letters, while also alluding to the fact that the ancient Boeotian dialect (probably no longer spoken in his day, but known from Aristophanes and grammarians) shared with the pure Attic variety double -*tt*- spellings in place of double -*ss*-, and even showed -*tt*- in words such as *méttos* 'middle' where Attic and *koiné* had single -*s*-: *mésos*. The Atticists (as the proponents of the conservative Attic are known) were also concerned with the morphology, syntax and vocabulary of Greek, recommending the use of categories such as the dual number, which had long been absent from the spoken language. Atticists such as Phrynichus, Moeris and Pollux compiled dictionaries of recommended Attic vocabulary, and listed words that should be avoided.[31] The

---

[30] Translation after the commentary of Hopkinson (2008).
[31] Lee (2013) gives an overview of Atticist grammarians, and samples of their work.

results of extreme Atticism are again mocked by Lucian in his *Lexiphanes*, where the pedantic critic Lexiphanes is twitted for producing Greek which is less intelligible than that of barbarians. But a 'moderate' Atticism came to be seen as something to be aimed at. Philostratus, for example, recommends that a good epistolary style should be 'more Attic than everyday speech, but more everyday than Atticism' (in the formulation of the *De forma epistolari* attributed to Libanius, 48, translation from Trapp 2003: 191).

The general lack of acceptance of the *koinē* as the 'correct' variant of Greek is revealing, as are the efforts to avoid or purge *koinē* forms from the literary language; the language situation in ancient Greece has no clear modern counterpart. The Greeks never arrived at a sense of having a single correct form of their language, and the choices authors make in their selection of an idiom when composing literary works, or even erecting commemorative inscriptions, are usually revealing about the written traditions and spoken varieties to which they wanted to align themselves. Even so, it is possible to trace a gradual change in attitude towards language variation over the history of Greek. Aristotle, in *Poetics* (1457b), shows a relativist approach to variation in vocabulary: 'the same word may be at once an unusual term[32] and a current one, but not in relation to the same people; the word *sígunon* ['lance'] is to the Cypriots a current term but to us an unusual one.' Compare this with statements by Atticist grammarians, some of whom do not even accept lexical variants as Greek. For example, Phrynicus 306 discusses the Greek word for 'flea': '[The form] *psúllos* (masculine) is barbarous; but *psúlla* (feminine) is approved because it is also ancient' (translation from Lee 2013: 286). Here a Greek word, which turns up in authors including Epicharmus and Aristotle, and which survived in the spoken language into Modern Greek, is termed 'barbarous', i.e. non-Greek. Phrynicus here presents a polar opposition between a single form of Greek, which is what he judges to be correct, and everything else. In this he is following in the same steps as some Roman writers on language, who would characterize what they thought of as correct as 'Latin', and disparage deviations from this as non-Latin (see Clackson 2011a: 242 for examples).

---

[32] The Greek word here translated as 'an unusual term' is *glõssa*, which also means 'tongue', and 'language'.

Linguistic negotiations and the meaning of Greek dialect

Greek thus existed in many different forms. Speakers and writers at all periods potentially had access to different varieties of Greek, and audiences appear to have been largely competent in understanding varieties far different from the ones they most commonly heard. Speaking or writing in a dialect different from one's usual variety could have different meanings, but it is impossible to generalize any straightforward correlations between dialect and social situation or political intent. At the level of individual speakers, we have no record of switching between different dialects in everyday conversation ('code-switching' in linguistic parlance), and the indications from the Classical period are that speakers would retain their own dialect when conversing with others. We have already mentioned above Aristophanes' representation of cross-dialectal dialogues among Greeks from different regions and Socrates' implication (at Plato *Apology* 17d–18a) that non-Attic speakers would not feel the need to accommodate to the language of their jurors. In the Hellenistic and Roman periods the associations and connotations of different literary dialects were available to authors. The poet Theocritus was thus able to select the dialect appropriate to the genre of his poetry: Doric for idylls set in Sicily, with a more mitigated version for idylls set elsewhere (Idylls 14 and 15), but Aeolic for poems in Aeolic metres. Iulia Balbilla, a Roman noblewoman who accompanied Hadrian on his tour to Egypt in 130 CE, left four epigrams in Aeolic dialect inscribed on the left ankle and foot of the Colossus of Memnon (actually one of twin statues of the Pharaoh Amenhotep III), in implicit emulation of the Greek poetess *par excellence*, Sappho (Brennan 1998: 218, Cirio 2011: 51–2).

At the level of the speech community, whether a small town or larger region, the political role played by dialect appears to vary. A case in point was the town of Oropos, situated in the ancient contested borderland between Attica and Boeotia. Between the fifth and third centuries BCE Oropos vacillated between the control of Athens and the Boeotian confederation (or at times Thebes), and independence. The inscriptional record from Oropos is not large, but it is enough to allow us to trace the linguistic history of the town (Morpurgo Davies 1993). It is possible that Oropos was originally a colony from Eretria, a Euboean *polis* lying on the other side of the Euripos strait, and the scanty epigraphic records from the early fourth century support the notion that Eretrian, an Ionic dialect with many similar features to Attic, was originally the idiom of the town. But in the years after the initial Athenian domination, to which the bulk of our evidence dates, documents from Oropos switch to Attic, even at periods when it is independent of Athens, part of a Boeotian league or participating in Boeotian festivals. Morpurgo Davies (1993) contrasts what she sees as a dominating use of Attic dialect under Athenian power with a more tolerant linguistic attitude from the Boeotians. However, it is difficult to draw secure conclusions, since Oropos's adoption of Attic is in line with the spread of Great Attic through the Aegean at this time, which may have been motivated as much by commercial as by political considerations. Moreover, there is little other direct evidence for the Athenians imposing their language on other Greeks in the same way that they tried to enforce the circulation of Athenian silver coinage and certain Athenian cults during their period of dominance of the federation of Greek city-states known as the Delian league.

Over time, the meanings of the Greek dialects changed. We have seen how Attic became a cultural signifier in the period of the Second Sophistic, rather than a regional one. In some areas local vernaculars still appear on inscriptions in the Hellenistic and Roman periods, when it is likely that

Fig. 2.1 Line drawing of inscription number 50 'Stele of Philokhareinos', c. 150 CE. Reproduced from Woodward (1929: 323) by kind permission of The Society for the Promotion of Hellenic Studies.

they were no longer widely spoken. A case in point is the survival of what appears to be the local Spartan dialect alongside the *koiné* in dedications at the sanctuary of Artemis Orthia, made by successful contestants in the boys' athletic and musical contests. The presence of regional varieties in Sparta takes on added significance when we recall that the one area in which ancient Greek dialect may have lived on into the modern world is the south-eastern Peloponnese. It is an appealing notion that young Spartans may have managed to smuggle their own vernacular speech forms into the dedications, much as the Spartan boy in the story hid a live fox under his cloak (Plutarch *Lycurgus* 18.1), but the truth may be more prosaic. In the absence of a substantial control corpus of Laconian inscriptions, it is difficult to decide whether this is really a revival of the ancient dialect and resurgence of local linguistic pride, or reflects attempts to manufacture a marked code language for the purposes of religious cult, or indeed whether it is just an indication of the incompetence of the stone-cutters and composers. The most striking thing about the dedications to Artemis Orthia is the wide variation in spellings and letter-forms across different inscriptions (compare the roughly contemporary inscriptions reproduced as Fig. 2.1 and Fig. 2.2), even in the

Fig. 2.2 Plate of inscription number 51 (Fig. 140) 'Stele of Damokrates', *c.* 150 CE. Reproduced from Woodward (1929: 324) by kind permission of the Society for the Promotion of Hellenic Studies.

simplest formulae such as the name of the goddess. This, as much as anything, reveals that these texts are not associated with any systematic civic- or state-sanctioned linguistic practice.[33] The next three chapters will look more closely at individuals' choice of words to signal their own identity.

---

[33] Woodward (1929) gives images or reproductions of the letter-forms on most of the dedications.

CHAPTER 3

Language and identity

Introduction

In modern nation-states language can function as a marker of individual or political identity. This is particularly true in cases where there is more than one officially recognized language in the community: the choice of which language to speak or write down may reveal not only individuals' relations with and expectations of their audience, but also their self-ascribed political identity and their place within or attitude towards larger power structures, including government or religious groups. The sociolinguistic literature is well served by examples of the various ways in which language in the modern world overlaps with ethnic, cultural or national identities. Language is widely recognized to be a potential marker of identity: groups of speakers or societies may select a shared competency in a particular language as part of the 'stuff' out of which their identity is constructed. However, a shared language is not a necessary feature of an ethnic or cultural identity, and there are many examples where identity construction cuts across linguistic divisions. Furthermore, spoken and written forms of the same language may function in different ways in the formation of identities.

British citizens are generally not well known for their command of more than a single language, but even so, the constituent parts of the United Kingdom can provide some useful examples of the intersections between language and identity. Consider, for instance, the National Assembly of Wales. Since its inception in 1989, the National Assembly has allowed elected members to speak either Welsh or English in its formal sessions. No member of the Assembly is unable to speak English fluently, but speeches and questions to ministers are regularly made in Welsh by members of all political parties, not just the Welsh nationalist party Plaid Cymru. Moreover, the nationalist members of the Assembly do not all necessarily speak Welsh inside or even outside the Assembly. Welsh is not used in order for members to communicate better, or to discuss matters for which English would be inadequate; rather, it functions as one of the ways in which Welsh politicians advertise their allegiance to their homeland.

In the province of Northern Ireland, there has been a long-standing sectarian divide between two communities, one nationalist and predominately Roman Catholic, and the other unionist and Protestant. Unlike Wales, where roughly 20 per cent of the population have a fluency in Welsh,[1] Northern Ireland is an essentially monoglot province, with English the main language for 97 per cent of the population, across the sectarian divide.[2] However, written versions of two different minority languages, Gaelic and Ulster Scots, are in official use here, each with a largely symbolic significance.[3] In the Republic of Ireland, Irish (also called Gaelic) is one of the two official languages of the state, and is still spoken in some regions, known as the Gaeltacht. Members of the nationalist community in the north, who are in favour of unification with the Republic of Ireland, have pressed for Gaelic to have a presence in Northern Ireland, leading to the production of census forms, street signs (in some neighbourhoods), and official publications and websites in Irish as well as English. The recognition of Irish, however, has produced a reaction among members of the unionist community, who seek to maintain Northern Ireland as a province of the United Kingdom. Some unionists have worked to achieve equal recognition for Ulster Scots, the Scots dialect of English brought by the settlers of Ulster in the seventeenth century. Ulster Scots has accordingly been given parity status with Irish, and is likewise a medium for government publications and documentation, even though there has been scarcely any literary tradition or codification of the written variety. In the case of Northern Ireland, political pressures have thus led to the resurrection (if not the actual creation) of a written form of language, even though it scarcely has an independent spoken existence.[4]

The Northern Irish and Welsh examples show two of the ways in which minority languages can interact with the dominant language of the state.

[1] 22.8 per cent claimed to understand spoken Welsh and 15.6 per cent to be able to write in Welsh in the 2011 census, with the proportions of those able to speak and read Welsh falling in between (source: www.neighbourhood.statistics.gov.uk).
[2] Figure from the 2011 census (source: http://www.nisra.gov.uk).
[3] 10.65 per cent of the population claimed to 'have some ability in Irish' in the 2011 census, while 8.08 per cent claimed to have some ability in Ulster Scots. Smaller numbers claimed to be able to speak, read and write either language (3.74 per cent Irish, 0.94 per cent Ulster Scots).
[4] Bispham (2007: 144–6) also discusses the example of Irish in Northern Ireland as a politically motivated use of language, and compares it with the case of the use of Oscan in Italy, which we will discuss later in this chapter.

They reveal that both spoken and written languages can have a symbolic value, and can constitute parts of the construction of ethnic or political identity of groups or individuals. For the ancient world, language choice has also been seen as significant, and many recent works on bilingualism or multilingualism in the ancient world have stressed the relevance of identity to deconstructing the meaning of a text or inscription set up in more than one language, or a language other than the dominant language of the region or the ruling state. In the rest of this chapter we shall examine a number of case studies of the different ways in which the linguistic choices of communities or individuals have been seen as part of their construction of identity.

Languages in the face of colonization and conquest

The array of languages spoken around the Mediterranean and in Europe (as shown in Map 1.1) was to undergo profound changes during the years 500 BCE – 500 CE. As Greek colonists and traders, and later Roman soldiers and settlers, spread to new territories, they imported their languages with them, and Greek and Latin spread around the shores of the Mediterranean and further afield, replacing nearly all of the indigenous languages of the west and of Asia Minor and much of North Africa. We discussed in Chapter 1 how many of these earlier languages probably perished without leaving any written record, or even without any record of their existence surviving in any ancient account. But even so, we have written evidence for a considerable number of local languages written by their own indigenous speakers. One of the paradoxes of the linguistic history of Europe and the Near East is that many of the ancient languages which were lost over time as former speakers switched to Latin and Greek are known to us only through their written records transmitted in scripts which were introduced by the Greeks and Romans.

One such case is the language of ancient Gaul, called Gaulish, which is recorded in France from the second century BCE onwards in two different scripts:[5] first, in the Greek alphabet, after a long period of contact between Gaulish speakers and the Greek colonies of Mediterranean France, and then, from the first century BCE, in Latin script, following the Roman conquests in Gaul culminating in Julius Caesar's victory at the Battle of

---

[5] See Mullen (2013: 106–10) for the dating and circumstances of the first writing of Gaulish in Greek script in southern France. Gaulish is also recorded outside France in Switzerland and northern Italy; see Lambert (2003) for an introduction to the language and selected texts.

Alesia in 52 BCE. But, as the local elites adopted Roman dress and cultural habits, and became incorporated into the Roman power structures, they also seem to have adopted the Latin language. The epigraphic record shows the steady loss of the tradition of writing Gaulish in Greek script after the Roman conquest of the Tres Galliae, and few public monuments bearing Gaulish inscriptions written in Latin script. At the same time, under Roman rule, members of the elite increasingly left stone funerary memorials written in both Latin and (especially in the South) Greek. Woolf (1998: 99–100) estimates that around 20–30 per cent of the population of the southern province of Gallia Narbonensis (an area roughly corresponding to the modern region Provence) were commemorated with Latin epitaphs in the first three centuries CE.

As Latin replaced Gaulish as the language of the Gaulish elite, we might ask what effect this had on the notion of Gaulish identity, or indeed whether it is possible to speak about 'Gaulish' identity in this context. Ancient attitudes towards language use, inasmuch as we can access them through surviving geographical and ethnographical works, often make an unproblematic correlation between ethnicity and language. Thus, ancient peoples who were characterized as exceptional in cultural terms were also linguistically at odds. For example, the Etruscans were characterized by the Greek Dionysius of Halicarnassus (1.30) as being like no other nation either in language or their customs. And peoples whose ethnic identity was mixed could also be seen as departing from the purity of their inherited language, such as the Greeks of Borysthenes in Pontus on the southern coast of the Black Sea, who had become semi-barbarized in dress, wearing Scythian trousers and capes, and are described by Dio Chrysostom as having become barbarized in their speech as well (Dio Chrysostom 36.9).

We might expect therefore that speakers of vernacular languages, such as the Gauls, who switched to speaking Latin or Greek, straightforwardly became Roman or Greek. Unfortunately, here the simplistic equation between language and identity starts to break down. In the Roman Empire, both languages were employed in ways that transcend a simple categorization of ethnic identity (as we shall see in more detail later in this chapter). By the end of the first century CE it was accepted that the Roman Empire was essentially bilingual, in the sense that both Latin and Greek were recognized: 'both of our languages' as the emperor Claudius succinctly put it.[6] Competence in one or both of Latin and Greek could enable the speaker to claim an identity as a Roman. Indeed, the case of the

---

[6] Suetonius *Claudius* 42: *utroque sermone nostro.*

philosopher, orator and sophist Favorinus provides a telling example of the intersections between language and cultural identity. Favorinus was born in Arles (ancient Arelate) in the province of Gallia Narbonensis in the first half of the second century CE. He later travelled throughout the Roman Empire, gave speeches and wrote works in Greek, some of which survive. In his *Oration to the Corinthians* ([Dio Chrysostom] 37.25), Favorinus is able to characterize himself as both Roman, and someone who has attained the right to be Greek as well, through his mastery of Greek eloquence.

> Well, if someone who is not a Lucanian but a Roman, not one of the masses but of the equestrian order, one who has affected, not merely the language, but also the thought and manners and dress of the Greeks, and that too with such mastery and manifest success as no one among the Romans of early days or the Greeks of his own time, I must say, has achieved – for while the best of the Greeks over there may be seen inclining toward Roman ways, he inclines toward the Greek and to that end is sacrificing both his property and his political standing and absolutely everything, aiming to achieve one thing at the cost of all else, namely, not only to seem Greek but to be Greek too – taking all this into consideration, ought he not to have a bronze statue here in Corinth? (Favorinus *Oration to the Corinthians* 25, translation H. Lamar Crosby, Loeb Classical Library)

Shortly after this passage Favorinus presents himself furthermore as a model to Celts (i.e. Gauls), as an example that even barbarians can reach the heights of Greek cultural life. Favorinus demonstrates that, at this time, a Greek identity can be seen as supplementary to a Roman one, and that he thus can have something approaching a triple identity, at once both Roman and Greek, but with a Celtic ancestry.[7] The archaeological and inscriptional record from Gaul implies that Favorinus was not alone in his unquestioning assertion that he was a Roman; large sections of Gaulish society readily adopted Roman material culture and religious practice as well as Latin literary and linguistic norms. As Woolf (1998) has argued, there is no need to see Roman culture under the Empire as a 'thin veneer' covering an underlying stratum of a surviving native culture. Gauls themselves came to forge a new Roman or Gallo-Roman identity, and the Gaulish language generally did not play a part in this (we shall discuss some exceptions below). In the ancient Greek or Roman literary sources, there is little acknowledgement or attention paid to the native language of

---

[7] See Whitmarsh (2004: 175–6) for discussion of the cultural precedents and political context of this speech.

Gaul, and certainly nothing approaching scholarly interest in Gaulish vocabulary or surviving inscriptions for their own sake. There was no move to recognize the language through the types of symbolic or cultural displays that we saw taking place with the minority languages of the UK in the introduction to this chapter.

However, Gaulish clearly did survive the Roman conquest, both as a written language, and as a spoken idiom. The written record is limited mainly to some domestic and religious contexts, and stops almost completely by 300 CE, but chance remarks from some Classical authors suggest that the language continued to be spoken well into the fourth century CE (perhaps later). For example, Jerome (347–420 CE), in his commentary on St Paul's second epistle to the Galatians (Migne *PL* 36,357), claims: 'Leaving aside Greek, which all the east speaks, the Galatians have their own language which is almost the same as that which the Treveri speak . . . ' Jerome implies that Gaulish, a Celtic language like that of the Galatians in Asia Minor, was still spoken by the Treveri, i.e. the people of Trier (Augusta Treverorum) in the Rhineland, even though there is no direct inscriptional evidence for Gaulish at Trier anything like this late (but see Meißner 2009–10 for possible onomastic evidence).

Jerome's statement about Gaulish also has implications for the survival of a vernacular language elsewhere in the Empire, since he states that the Galatians had their own language. Other sources corroborate the existence of the Galatian language in Asia Minor, although it was never a written language (Freeman 2001). We also have inscriptional evidence for another ancient language of Asia Minor, Phrygian, well into the period of the Roman Empire.[8] In North Africa, the Punic language remained in use until the fifth century (see further Chapter 6), and it is possible that the language of the Berbers was also spoken in North Africa in ancient times.[9] Other languages which do not appear directly in the inscriptional record but which survive to the modern day, such as Basque and Albanian, probably were also spoken within the bounds of the Roman Empire in ancient times. The existence of these (and other) linguistic survivals in the face of the spread of Latin and Greek in the ancient world has been the subject of some discussion in the scholarly literature, as we shall see in the next section.

---

[8] Brixhe (1987: 11) is of the opinion that Phrygian was still in use in the fifth century CE, but the inscriptional evidence only extends into the third.

[9] For Punic and Berber in North Africa, see Millar (1968), and note Adams's scepticism about Berber borrowings from Latin in ancient times (Adams 2003a: 245–7).

Linguistic survivals and counter-attacks?

In an article published in 1966, Ramsay MacMullen identified a surge of renewed interest, and an extended written use of vernacular languages, from the second to the fourth centuries CE. This was perhaps most evident in Roman Egypt, where the last phase of Ancient Egyptian was written for the first time in Greek letters to give birth to a language and script now called Coptic, but MacMullen also identified Gaulish and Punic as revivified languages during this period. He thought this linguistic reawakening reflected the new-found wealth and burgeoning self-confidence of provincials, who had previously been largely excluded from access to elite Roman commerce and society through their ignorance of Latin. The extended functions of the local idiom were coupled with a new regional identity centred on language. MacMullen declared that there was 'a positive counter-attack' (against Latin and Greek) 'by two or three minority languages towards the close of the second century, demonstrating the height of its strength by the end of the fourth' (MacMullen 1966: 13).[10] In this model of language choice, the local language marks out a provincial identity, as opposed to that of the Roman centre.

MacMullen's view of the language situation in the Roman Empire can be challenged by the increased work on bilingualism in the last twenty years, however, in particular by Adams's monumental work on bilingualism and the Latin language (Adams 2003a), and by the publication of new texts, and reconstruction and publication of papyrological archives. It seems better now to see individual and societal negotiations of language choice as taking place in a more nuanced way than a simple black or white choice between either of two languages. In many situations in the modern world of immigration, colonization and culture change, there are long periods when two or more languages are employed concurrently by members of the same society (what is known in the literature as *stable bilingualism*, Fishman 1965: 67–8). Texts from the ancient world, many of which were first published after MacMullen's article, reveal that bilingualism was also present on a much wider scale in ancient society than MacMullen realized. Two examples from the first two centuries CE from opposite ends of the Mediterranean can illustrate the point. From ancient Palestine/Judaea, the ostraca (inscribed potsherds) and papyri from sites

---

[10] MacMullen's position has been followed by others, most notably Hopkins who argued that 'Coptic represents a cultural resistance of native Egyptian against the dominance of Greek speakers and writers' (Hopkins 1991: 147). See Millar (1968), Brunt (1976) and Woolf (1998) for more nuanced views, and, for Coptic, the discussion in Chapter 6.

including Nahal Hever show both Greek and Aramaic used in documents, contracts and letters from the same archive, with the same parties able to write both languages (Cotton and Yardeni 1997).[11] From the site of a Roman pottery factory, La Graufesenque in central southern France, extensive archives recording production and firing of ceramics have been published which reveal that Gaulish and Latin were used alongside each other by scribes and potters (discussed in Adams 2003a: 687–719; Mullen 2013). Neither of these sites corresponds to the locus that MacMullen saw as the arena for bilingualism, the large cities of Alexandria, Marseille or Beirut (1966: 1). Thus rather than a monolingual population robustly defending the mother tongue in the face of the onslaught of Latin, it seems better to envisage far more day-to-day bilingualism in the Roman Empire (and probably also at earlier periods of Greek colonization in the Mediterranean basin).

In modern societies with stable bilingualism, there is often an association of different languages with different areas of use, such as particular speech situations: a religious ritual, for instance; a casual conversation; a formal interview; or a particular venue such as the marketplace, the law court or the private home. In sociolinguistic parlance these are different *domains* of each language. Furthermore, in situations where two languages (or where two varieties of the same language) co-exist in the same society, it is often possible to identify one as the *High* language (often abbreviated to the *H* language), normally that which is associated with state institutions such as government and the law, the form taught in schools, and also often the forms employed in religion and in literary compositions, and the other as the *Low* (or *L*) language, usually the idiom of everyday conversation in the streets or at home. In many modern cases (such as Modern Standard Arabic as against the Arabic vernaculars, or Latin American Portuguese or Spanish as against native languages in South America) only the *H* variety exists in a codified written form, while the *L* variety is only rarely or in special circumstances committed to writing. It is possible to imagine that analogous situations existed in the ancient world, at least at some times and in some places.

Unfortunately, trying to posit the domains of language use, or even the existence of periods of stable bilingualism in the ancient world, is usually a frustrating exercise. If local varieties persisted alongside Latin or Greek as the *L* language next to the Classical *H*, they were very seldom written

---

[11] Hebrew and Latin are also found on these documents. See Chapter 6 for citation of a text from the Judaean desert in which the author apologizes for using Greek rather than a local language.

down, and most Classical texts did not even acknowledge their existence. Greek and Latin certainly occupied the position of *H* variants (we shall see later in this chapter the division of functions associated with Greek and Latin); they were codified as standard languages (as we saw in Chapter 2) and were the languages of administration, elite display and elite performance. Roman law relied upon oral contracts (*stipulationes*), and, as we saw in Chapter 2, these were permitted to be uttered in Latin or in Greek, but not in other languages,[12] whereas Ulpian does allow for the low-level legacies or trusts known as *fideicommissa* to be made in a language other than Latin or Greek (*Digest* 32.1.11): '*Fideicommissa* may be left in any language, not only Latin or Greek, but Punic, Gallic, or that of any other nation' (translation from Watson 1998). Ulpian's statement is remarkable in that he actually names languages other than Greek and Latin, but it is noteworthy that the Latin word which is here translated as 'Gallic' (and which probably refers to Gaulish), *gallicana*, stands in place of the usual term *gallica*.[13] Languages other than Latin and Greek are of such little importance to the lawyer that it is no small matter to identify them accurately.

Sometimes, however, we do get a glimpse of languages other than Latin and Greek in certain domains or used among certain groups of speakers. In Chapters 5 and 6 I shall discuss at more length the languages of the Near East and North Africa during the Roman Empire, including Aramaic, Coptic and Punic. But here I shall give a couple of examples from the west, Etruscan and Gaulish, and examine how they coincide with particular domains. First, consider the sphere of divination in Rome in the first century BCE, which has a strong cultural Etruscan background, and where language seems to have played a role. The Romans themselves referred to divination through examination of entrails (also known as haruspicy) and divination through observation of thunder and lightning (sometimes called brontoscopy) as *disciplina etrusca* 'the Etruscan science'. Moreover some surviving passages of prophecy were given added 'authenticity' by the claim that they were translations of Etruscan originals, a view that has continued in modern times: for example, the second prophecy of Vegoia (although Adams 2003a: 179–82 finds no grounds for supposing this is Etruscan translationese); and the brontoscopic calendar (which was used to explain the meaning of thunder on any particular day of the year),

---

[12] Gaius 3.93 and *Digest* 45.1.13 imply that other languages were invalid for formulating the *stipulationes*.

[13] Blom (2009) includes the Ulpian passage among a collection of the Latin citations referring to *lingua gallica*.

which is known only through the sixth-century CE Greek translation made by John the Lydian of a Latin version ascribed to the first-century BCE Roman polymath Nigidius Figulus (Turfa 2006). It would seem that diviners at Rome were familiar with the Etruscan language into the imperial period, to judge from Suetonius' account (*Augustus* 97) of their opinion after the first letter of the name *Caesar* on an inscription erected to Augustus was struck off by lightning. The soothsayers reportedly acclaimed this as an indication of the divine nature of Augustus, since, they said, *Aesar* was the Etruscan word for 'god', a meaning confirmed by research on surviving Etruscan where *ais* (plural *aisar*) is indeed the Etruscan word for god. Haruspicy is represented on Etruscan gems and bronze mirrors (de Grummond 2006); some of these depictions also have writing beside them, from which the Etruscan terminology for the profession can be partly worked out. Two other inscribed objects may also show the continued use of Etruscan by soothsayers in Roman environments in the late Republic. The first is one of the most unusual records of the Etruscan language: a bronze model of a sheep's liver, dated to *c.* 100 BCE and found near Piacenza in the Po valley of northern Italy (*ET* Pa 4.2, van der Meer 1987). The model liver is divided into forty-two sections, in each of which is written the name of a divinity, thereby giving the haruspex a practical guide for how to read entrails. Furthermore, the sixteen sections on the margin of the liver correspond to the divisions of the sky, as recorded by the fourth-century author Martianus Capella, showing the link between haruspicy and brontoscopy. There are very few surviving Etruscan records from the Po valley, and epigraphic analysis of the liver suggests it was made near Cortona, over 300 km to the south, leading to the theory that it was lost by an Etruscan haruspex in the employ of one of the Roman generals campaigning in the area in the first century BCE (van der Meer 1987: 18). The second record is a bilingual inscription, an impressive gravestone commemorating Lucius Cafatius, who is named and identified as both a haruspex and a lightning diviner (Latin *fulguriator*) in both Latin and Etruscan.[14] Cafatius' memorial was found near Pisaurum on the Adriatic coast, and also dates from *c.* 100 BCE. This is again outside the usual area of Etruscan speakers or Etruscan inscriptions, and the prominence given to the Latin text, written first and in larger letters, suggests that Cafatius moved in a Latin-speaking world but chose to leave an Etruscan

---

[14] *CIL* I² 2127 = *ET* Um 1.7, Benelli (1994) no. 1; an image of the inscription is reproduced at Clackson (2012b: 39).

text as well to establish his professional credentials rather than to determine any allegiance to a local community of Etruscan speakers.

Religion and cult may also have been a factor in the preservation of written forms of Gaulish. The longer Gaulish texts written in Latin script cannot all be translated with confidence, given our still patchy knowledge of Gaulish, but enough can be made out of them to reveal a connection with indigenous ritual and cultic practices. Furthermore, these inscriptions appear to be 'conscious attempts to produce public writing in a Celtic language by individuals familiar with similar texts in Latin' (Woolf 1998: 96). As we have just seen, a purported Etruscan brontoscopic calendar giving the meanings of thunder at different times of the year survives in a Greek translation, and once extensive Gaulish calendars survive in fragments from Coligny near Lyon, in France, and Villards d'Héria in the French Jura from the late second or early third centuries CE (published in *RIG* III). Even though these calendars show influence from Roman timekeeping practices (Stern 2012: 311), the retention of an indigenous time frame is probably linked to the need to celebrate festivals at the right time. Lead tablets from other sites in France, Chamalières (Puy-de-Dôme, *RIG* L-100) and Larzac (near Millau, *RIG* L-98), show magical texts written in Gaulish, and an inscribed tile from Châteaubleau (Brie), only discovered in 1997, may also contain a curse in Gaulish (Mees 2011).

Language and resistance to Rome

In the last section we saw that it was probably better to replace MacMullen's theory that there was a 'counter-attack' to Roman and Greek dominance through the rise of local languages in the Roman Empire with a model envisaging more widespread bilingualism, and local languages associated with certain domains. But what about earlier periods of history? What did it mean then if people under, or threatened by, Roman domination chose to speak a language other than Latin? To modern eyes it might seem as natural that those who were opposed to the growing power and annexation of land under the Romans would also reject the language of their oppressors, and make either real or symbolic moves to retain, or perhaps even revivify, local languages. However, hard and fast examples of linguistic resistance to Roman power are not so easy to come across. Adams (2003a: 280) gives Tacitus' account (Tacitus *Ann.* 4.45.2) of the Spanish assassin of the governor Piso, who when interrogated under torture refused to reveal his accomplices, crying out in his native tongue that they would get nothing from him. This may be a symbolic use of language, but it may also reveal the reversion to the first language under extreme stress. Another possible example is a late second-century BCE Etruscan funerary inscription from Tarquinia (as published in *ET* Ta 1.107):

> Felsnas. la. leθes / svalce. avil. CVI / murce. capue / tleχe. hanipaluscle.
>
> Felsna Laris son of (Felsna) Lethe lived 106 years. He lived (?) at Capua. He was enrolled in (the army) of Hannibal. (translation after Bonfante and Bonfante 2002: 176)

The subject of the commemoration might therefore have been one of the Italian allies who defected to Hannibal following the Roman defeat at the Battle of Cannae (Liv. 22.61), and it would be possible to interpret his use of a non-Latin language in his funerary inscription, at a time when the native language was losing ground to the Romans, as another indication of his anti-Roman feeling. However, Etruscan is used in Tarquinia until the first century BCE (although there are also some early Latin tomb inscriptions, Kaimio 1975: 196–200), so the selection of Etruscan in this text is not necessarily indicative of a conscious avoidance of Latin. Furthermore, not all scholars have been so confident in the ascription of meaning to the Etruscan verb *tleχe*, which can be grammatically identified (through its ending – *χe*) as a past tense form with a passive meaning 'he was x-ed', but the sense of the otherwise unattested root *tle-* is uncertain (Cristofani 1991: 141–2; Wallace 2008: 145–6). It is possible that the verb actually indicated that he fought on the Roman side rather than the Punic.

Perhaps the most frequently cited example of a local language chosen in opposition to Rome is Oscan, the language of central and southern Italy. During the 'Social War' of 91–88 BCE a number of tribes who had been formerly allied to Rome broke the alliance and formed a separate 'Italian league'. The Italians minted their own coinage, of which various designs and denominations survive, and which is conspicuous firstly for some of the iconography, with an Italian bull trampling or raping a Roman wolf, and also for the legend *Italia* on some of the coins, the first recorded use of the term as a political designation.[15] Willi (2009: 594) has argued that the choice of Oscan, rather than Latin, during the Social War was a conspicuous anti-Roman movement, and was intended to unify the allies, not all of whom had previously employed the Oscan language or its distinctive alphabet. Other scholars have also interpreted the appearance of Oscan in

---

[15] See Rutter (2001: 55–6) and Crawford et al. (2011 s.v. *Italia* 1) for the coinage.

first-century BCE inscriptions as a deliberate and symbolic counter to the dominance of Latin in the context of the Social War.[16]

Most of the evidence for Oscan as a language of resistance to Rome during the Social War comes from the town of Corfinium, which was the headquarters of the rebels. Corfinium was situated in the region of the Italic people known as the Paelignians, and lies 12 km to the north-west of Sulmo, the birthplace of the Roman poet Ovid, who declared that he would be known as the 'glory of the Paelignian people' (*Amores* 3.15.8). The epigraphic record shows that the local language, usually referred to as Paelignian, was still in use in the second and first centuries BCE in both Corfinium and Sulmo. All of our written remains of Paelignian (twenty-three inscriptions from Sulmo, thirty-five from Corfinium, and four from nearby Superaequum as recorded in Crawford et al. 2011) are in the Latin script, and most are very short, but enough survives to show that linguistically Paelignian differs only in certain specifics from Oscan. It was at Corfinium that the coinage of the Italian allies was struck during the Social War, and it is on this coinage that the Oscan script first makes its appearance in the area. The coins themselves bear the legend of Oscan commanders (including one, Gaius Papius Mutilus, who is described as **embratur**, the Oscan equivalent of Latin *imperator* 'general', in two silver issues).[17] Other issues of the Social War coinage include the Oscan equivalent to *Italia*, **víteliú**, and one has what appears to be the Oscan equivalent to Latin *Samnium*, **safinim**. However, the striking of Oscan legends on these coins cannot be considered as an adoption of a specifically Oscan identity by all the Italian allies, since there are parallel issues of coins with legends in Latin and in Latin script, including *C. Papius Mutilus, Imperator* 'Gaius Papius Mutilus, General'. The mint at Corfinium struck coins to pay the soldiers fighting on the Italian side, and the issues are in two languages since some were destined for the Oscan speakers of the south, and the rest for the northern allies, who either were completely Latin-speaking (such as probably the Marsians), or conversant with Latin (such as the Paelignians).[18]

The Social War coinage therefore tells us little about the language situation at Corfinium, and cannot support a hypothesis that language

---

[16] So for example Bispham (2007: 142–60) on the Oscan legal inscription the *Tabula Bantina*; see also Cooley (2002) for the inscriptions in Pompeii, with the further observations of Crawford (2011: 33–9), McDonald (2012) and Langslow (2012).

[17] Oscan words in the Oscan alphabet (and Umbrian words in the Umbrian alphabet) are conventionally transcribed in bold typeface.

[18] Dench (1995: 212–14), Rutter (2001: 55–6).

came to have a political function in the town. Potentially more interesting is the occurrence of two varieties of Paelignian in the inscriptional record. The longest Paelignian inscription known to date is a funerary epitaph of seven lines, although the writing on the top is mostly obliterated by the reuse of the stone in another function.[19] Written on white stone, with the chiselled Roman lettering picked out in red, the epitaph commemorates a priestess by the name of *Prismu Petiedu*. The commemoration of a female is not exceptional among the Paelignian funerary monuments, given that nearly half of the forty-plus Paelignian grave-markers record women, although in nearly all the other cases the name alone, or name and title, is given. However, only one other Paelignian epitaph comes near to Prismu's monument in style and length; this is a much shorter inscription to an individual described as a *casnar*, a word which is attested in a Latin gloss with the meaning 'old man' (Crawford et al. 2011: Corfinium 11). Both Prismu's epitaph and the Casnar inscription feature a high degree of alliteration, and in the first the expected word order seems to have been displaced as well (making the correct translation uncertain). Given the Greek and Roman traditions of using verse in funerary monuments, it is not unlikely that the composer of this text also tried to produce something in language removed from the everyday, extending this attempt also to the choice of word-endings and perhaps lexical forms, which are at odds with our other evidence for Paelignian. Thus Prismu's name itself, ending in *-u*, stands apart from those of all the other commemorated Paelignian priest-esses, whose names end in *-a*, for example, *brata ania / ancta c<e>riei(a)* 'Grata Ania, priestess of Ceres' (Crawford et al. 2011: Sulmo 4). Note further that the word for 'life', *aetatu*, seems to be in the same grammatical case (ablative singular) as *aetate* in the Casnar inscription, but here with a different ending.

   The epitaph of Prismu Petiedu has, perhaps surprisingly, come to occupy a contested place in debates on the use of language in late Republican Italy, since Lazzeroni argued (most strongly at Lazzeroni 1991: 181) that the Paelignian register employed in this text was deliberately chosen in order to convey anti-Roman sentiment. Lazzeroni pointed out that the words in this inscription differed from the 'normal' Paelignian, and also from the usual Latin equivalents. Moreover, the composers of this epitaph selected instead the very same variants which are common in Oscan (and also in some cases in the Italic language spoken to the north,

---

[19] The inscription is published with photograph and bibliography at Crawford et al. (2011: Corfinium 6).

Umbrian). Hence, to take just two of the six features which Lazzeroni identifies, women's names in the first declension end in *-a* in Latin (as Livia, Iulia), and the ablative singular of the word for 'life', *aetas*, is *aetate*, while in Oscan and Umbrian first-declension nouns have a nominative in *-o* or *-u*, and the Oscan ending of the ablative singular of nouns in the same class as *aetas* is in *-úd*. According to this theory, either the composers of this inscription deliberately made their language look less Latin, or they attempted to revive a moribund Paelignian on the model of Oscan, rather than write in Latin. Note, however, that the Latin alphabet was still employed.

If this theory is right, this single Paelignian grave-marker would represent a singular example of language manipulation in order to present an anti-Roman sentiment. Unfortunately, enforced reliance on a single inscription means that we will always remain in some doubt about whether the linguistic choices have political significance, as Lazzeroni suggested. The actual text of the inscription, as far as we can tell, has nothing to do with Paelignian nationalism or local dependence on Rome or the Social War (we do not even know the date of the inscription beyond very rough indications). Rather, the epitaph has clear religious import: we know that the Paelignian word *sacaracirix* means 'priestess' (its Latin equivalent would be *sacratrix*, although this word is not attested), and the text refers to at least four gods and goddesses. We have seen in the last section how, in the case of both Etruscan and Gaulish, the sphere of religion was one of the domains in which local languages persisted in use for the longest time, so it may be better to understand this Paelignian text as marked by a special religious register rather than a political one.

In conclusion, in Italy during the Social War it is difficult to find any good evidence of vernacular languages spoken or written self-consciously as an alternative to Latin. This may well reflect the fact that the spread of Latin across much of Italy at the expense of local languages took place much earlier than in other regions of Roman conquest. Already in the second century BCE we find many examples of local communities or individuals who were not under Roman control switching to Latin. A famous example is Livy's mention of an event in 180 BCE: 'at the request of the citizens of Cumae, it was permitted that they could use Latin in public assemblies and that it was legal for auctioneers to auction in Latin' (Livy 40.43). Greek was probably the official language in Cumae at the time, but this does show Latin being adopted by one Italian town, this time in a commercial context. Inscriptional evidence also testifies to Latin as the language of Italian business in the second century BCE. A body of commemorative inscriptions and dedications from Delos and elsewhere in the Aegean were set up by groups who styled themselves as *negotiatores* 'businessmen' and *Italici* 'Italians'. The names of these traders are usually recorded on the inscriptions, and they reveal that they were not Romans, although they could write in Latin (they also set up inscriptions in Greek or with near-parallel Latin and Greek versions). Adams (2002 and 2003a: 640–86) argued that the *negotiatores*, although using Latin, carefully cultivated a non-Roman identity, which was also marked by their choice of Greek in their inscriptions. Latin must therefore have been the *lingua franca* for these traders, despite their desire to mark themselves as separate from the Romans. The early spread of Latin in Italy perhaps also explains the disappearance of the vernacular languages from the epigraphic record early in the Roman Empire. In contrast to the situation in provinces such as Gaul, Spain or North Africa, Latin seems to have ousted all other varieties from Italy (except Greek) by the end of the first century CE.[20]

Bilingual inscriptions as markers of identity

We have already mentioned the presence of bilingualism across the ancient world, and how bilingualism can allow an individual or a society to have an identity spanning two separate groups. We have theorized that much of the bilingualism that existed in the ancient world went unrecorded. In this section, we shall instead concentrate on some examples where individuals did choose to make a conscious, public record of their bilingual status. Leaving aside documents which employ Greek and Latin side by side (which will be discussed in the next section), only a small proportion of surviving texts from the ancient world encode the same, or nearly the same, message written in more than one language. The upshot of this is that it is difficult to make any generalizations about surviving bilingual (and trilingual) texts, but each text is usually the outcome of a particular situation, or reflects a unique linguistic environment at a specific time and place. In this section, therefore, I shall examine two bilingual, and one trilingual, texts in some detail, to see what they can, and what they cannot, tell us about the communities or individuals who commissioned and composed them.

The first example is from the city of Amathus in south-western Cyprus, and features Greek, written in an Ionic variety of the Greek alphabet (apparently in the Attic or 'Great Attic' dialect, although the text does

---

[20] Adams (2007: 189–202) documents how Latin could be referred to as *sermo Italus* 'the Italian language' by the end of the first century CE.

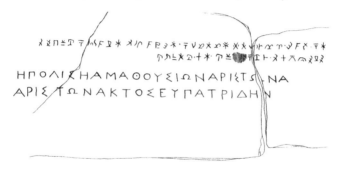

Fig. 3.1 Bilingual inscription from Amathus, Cyprus, third century BCE.
Reproduced from Masson (2007: 244).

not contain sufficient diagnostic features for us to be sure) and the language
known as 'Eteocypriot' (see chapter 1) written in Cypriot syllabic script.[21]
The same script is used to write the Cypriot dialect of Greek in other
parts of the island, which means we can transliterate the Eteocypriot part
of the inscription. However, since we have only a very small corpus of
Eteocypriot, with only a couple of bilingual texts, and Eteocypriot has
not yet been convincingly linked to any other known language, it is not
possible to translate this section, or even identify what part of speech most
of the words are (fortunately, word-dividers allow us to identify where
one word ends and the other begins). The inscription is dated to the third
century BCE (it must be later than the departure of the last king of
Amathus, in 312/311 BCE). Note that the Eteocypriot is written in a syllabic
script, so every sign of the script is here transliterated by a syllable (of the
type consonant + vowel or just vowel). The Eteocypriot portion is written
from right to left on the stone; the Greek from left to right.

> Eteocypriot: a-na ma-to-ri u-mi-e-s[a]-i mu-ku-la-i la-sa-na a-ri-si-to-no-se
> a-ra-to-wa-na-ka-so-ko-o-se
> ke-ra-ke-re-tu-lo-se ta-ka-na-[? ?]-so-ti alo– ka-i-li-po-ti
> Greek: Η ΠΟΛΙΣ Η ΑΜΑΘΟΥΣΙΩΝ ΑΡΙΣΤΩΝΑ
> ΑΡΙΣΤΩΝΑΚΤΟΣ ΕΥΠΑΤΡΙΔΗΝ
> (*hē pólis hē Amathousíōn Arístōna Aristónaktos eupatrídēn*)
> Translation (Greek). 'The city of the Amathusians (honour) Arístōn the son
> of Aristónax, the nobleman.'

---

[21] *ICS* 196, see also Masson (2007: 243–4) for an illustration. This inscription is also discussed at length
by Steele (2013: 167–72).

The Eteocypriot text has precedence over the Greek. In transcription it appears much longer than the Greek, with twice the number of words, but in the inscription itself it is compressed since the syllabary requires only one sign per syllable, and although the first line of the Eteocypriot extends across a wider space than the lines of Greek, the syllabic signs are smaller than the Greek letters. The Greek text contains a widespread honorific formula, with the omission of the verb and the name of the honorand in the accusative. It has proved difficult to match most of the Eteocypriot words to any Greek equivalents, except for the name formula: *A-ri-si-to-no-se* corresponds to *Arístōn*, and *A-ra-to-wa-na-ka-so-ko-o-se* to the genitive *Aristṓnaktos* (the sequence *-o-ko-* in this name recurs in other Eteocypriot inscriptions, and may be a patronymic suffix, indicating the father's name). Arístōn and Aristṓnax are both Greek names: Arístōn is formed directly from the adjective *áristos* 'best', and Aristṓnax from a compound of *áristos* with the word for 'king', *ánax*, or, in earlier Greek *wánax*. The Eteocypriot version of the first name appears to be a straightforward borrowing of the Greek, but the same cannot be said for the second name. *A-ra-to-* corresponds with three of the consonants of *Aristo-*, but drops the sequence *-is-*; *wa-na-ka-so-* (which may be the syllabic way of writing /wanaks-/) corresponds to the older Greek word, *wánax*, not the version without *w-* which lies behind the Ionic form *Aristṓnax* (with contraction of *o-a* to *ō* in the penultimate syllable). By this date, even the Greek dialect spoken in Cyprus has lost the *w-* at the beginning of the word for 'king', so this name seems to be an older form, perhaps surviving in Eteocypriot as a much earlier borrowing of the Greek name (and with *Arato-* for *Aristo-* possibly representing an original native pronunciation).

Even though we cannot understand the Eteocypriot well, we can work out enough to learn something about the place of language in forming a distinctive civic identity both for the Amathusians and for the individual who is honoured. Amathus is the only city on Cyprus to set up official decrees in Eteocypriot, continuing to do so into the third century BCE. However, by the time of this decree, they selected the Ionic script and, probably, the Attic dialect to create a parallel version in order to reach a wider audience. It is significant that they did not choose to write Cypriot Greek, the indigenous dialect variety which was still in use in other city-states on the island at this time; Amathus is marked out as being at once idiosyncratic, and more outward looking and open to wider Greek cultural influences, than the other Cypriot communities. The individual honoured similarly is revealed to have local allegiances as well as wider Greek connections through the onomastic formulae of the text. In the Greek version he bears a name that would be recognized across the Greek world, and his father's name, although uncommon, is found elsewhere both in Cyprus and in the rest of Greece.[22] Kingship survived in Cyprus until the end of the fourth century, and here it might have been advantageous to have a name that could be understood to mean 'whose king is best', though elsewhere in Greece monarchy was not so persistent or popular. The Eteocypriot version of his father's name further indicates that this may have been a local family, albeit one with remote Greek forebears.

Our second multilingual text is one of the rare examples of an inscription bearing three different languages. Although it is related in St John's Gospel (19:19–20) that the inscription on the cross was written in three languages, Aramaic (*Hebraistí*),[23] Latin and Greek, there is no surviving trilingual inscription from Palestine (although we do have other evidence for trilingual documentation, Eck 2009, see also Cotton et al. 2010–12 (*CII/P*) inscription 15). The stele erected by Cornelius Gallus when prefect of Egypt in 29 BCE employing hieroglyphic Egyptian, Greek and Latin also has no direct parallels.[24] Trilingual inscriptions from the Roman west are practically unknown. The exception is a second-century BCE text from near Cagliari on Sardinia in three languages (all of which are well understood): Latin, Greek and Punic. Unlike the other trilinguals we have mentioned, this records the dedication of a votive bronze altar to the god Asclepius Merre (or Eshmun Merre in the Punic) by a private individual. Even more remarkably, the dedicator is a slave, named in the Latin and Greek texts as Cleon and '*klyn* in the Punic (*CIL* I² 2226 = *IG* XIV 608 = *KAI* 66).[25]

> Cleon · salari(orum) · soc(iorum) · s(eruus) · Aescolapio · Merre · donum · dedit · lubens
> merito · merente. *Vacat* [26] Ἀσκληπιῶι Μήρρη ἀνάθεμα βωμὸν ἔστη-
> σε Κλέων ὁ ἐπὶ τῶν ἁλῶν κατὰ πρόσταγμα.
> L'DN L'ŠMN M'RḤ MZBḤ NḤŠT MŠQL LṬRM M'T 100 'ŠNDR
> 'KLYN ŠḤSGM 'Š BMMLḤT ŠM['
> Q]L' RPY' BŠT SPṬM ḤMLKT W' BD'ŠMN BN ḤMLK

---

[22] There are fourteen examples of the name Aristónax in the *LGPN* database, eight of them from Cyprus.
[23] See Chapter 6 for the meaning of this term, and for the language situation in Judaea/Palestine.
[24] See Hoffmann et al. (2009) for Gallus' stele.
[25] See Zucca (1996: 1463–5) for recent publication and discussion of this text with a photograph.
[26] The Latin word *vacat* indicates that there is a large space left in the inscription.

Fig. 3.2 Trilingual dedication made by Cleon, second century BCE.

LATIN: Cleon, the s(lave) of the comp(any) of salt-farm(ers), freely gave (this altar) as a gift to Asclepius Merre, who was deserving of thanks.

GREEK: (transliteration: *Asklēpiôi Mérrē anáthema bômon éstēse Kléōn ho epì tôn halôn katà próstagma*)
Kleon, who is in charge of the salt, set up this altar as a dedication to Asclepius Merre, according to command.

PUNIC: To Lord Ešmun Merre. Cleon, (the slave) of the concession which is in the salt, dedicated this altar of bronze of weight of 100 pounds. He heard his voice, and he cured him. In the year of the Suffets Himilkot and Abdešmun, son(s) of ḤMLK.[27]

(the translation of the Punic follows *SEG* 50.1030
and Amadasi Guzzo 1990: 83)

There is no surviving epigraphical or other evidence for the aboriginal language (or languages) of Sardinia, although Phoenician is attested on the island from the ninth century BCE and becomes the primary written medium until the Roman conquest in the third century BCE. Even after the Roman conquest, Punic (as the later stages of Phoenician in the western Mediterranean are known) continues to be employed particularly in the former Carthaginian settlements. In Cleon's dedication, the text in each of the three languages follows the appropriate conventions and formulae of the different epigraphical traditions. Thus the Latin text contains recognized abbreviations such as *s.* for *seruus* 'slave', and the Punic text has the formula 'he heard his voice' common to texts recording healing. As is usual in Latin or Greek texts with Punic parallel versions, the name of the divinity honoured is 'translated' into Punic, and here Asclepius is equated with the god of healing Eshmun. The other title of the god, Merre, which occurs in all three languages, is however not known from any other text,

---

[27] In the Punic script vowels are not regularly written in, and so when a name is not known from elsewhere, or could be read in two different ways, it is normal to leave just the consonants as in this case.

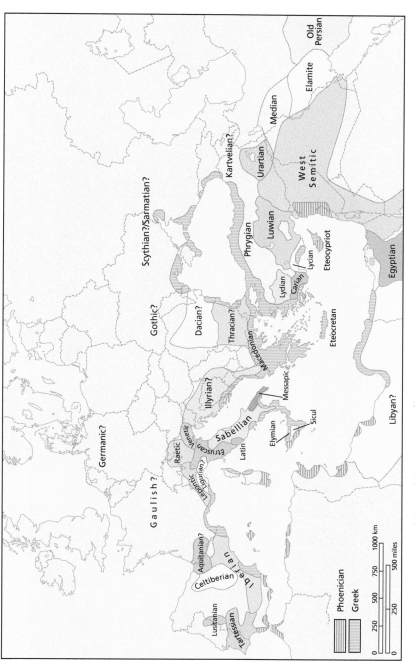

Map 1.1 Tentative map of languages around the Mediterranean basin in *c.* 500 BCE.

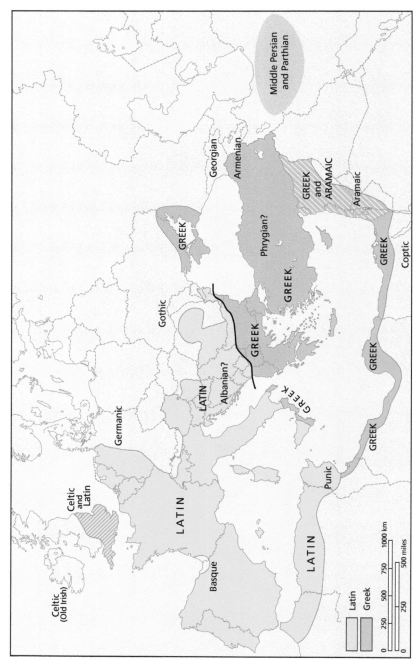

Map 1.2 Tentative map of languages around the Mediterranean basin in *c.* 400 CE.

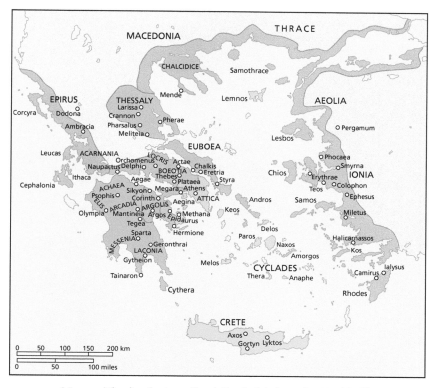

Map 2.1 The distribution of local Greek alphabets after Kirchhoff.

Map 2.2 Greek dialects in the Classical period.

and it may be that this is a divine name in a local Sardinian cult. Two factors suggest that the object was made in a Carthaginian or Punic milieu: the weight of the object is given only in the Punic text; and the date is recorded by naming the two men who were Suffets (Carthaginian religious officials) for the year. The default language of the cult centre would then most likely have been Punic.

The name Cleon is Greek, as were the names of many of the slaves in Italy after the Roman conquest of Greece, and it is tempting to see the presence of Greek on this dedication as a marker of Cleon's original identity. However, the Greek text is shorter than the other two, and it contains the curious tag *katà próstagma* 'according to command', which seems at odds with the statement in the Latin text that the offering was made 'freely' (*libens*). It may well be that the command is that given by Asclepius on curing him, but even so Cleon's failure to elucidate this reveals that his competence in all three languages is not as masterful as it appears at first sight. In the absence of a sufficient quantity of epigraphic information about Sardinia in the second century BCE, the social meanings of the three languages in context are not apparent. It is likely that southern Sardinia was undergoing a similar linguistic trajectory to that observed in Panormus (Palermo) in Sicily in the final centuries before the Common Era, with an epigraphic and written culture formerly dominated by Punic in the process of being replaced by Latin and Greek (Tribulato 2011, 2012: 316); the Sicilians are even termed *trilingues* 'trilingual' by Apuleius (*Met.* 11.5.22). But even in ancient societies where three languages were in common use, trilingual inscriptions are rare, and Cleon's decision to leave his dedication in three languages reveals his determination to make his name known, and display his own achievements, despite his servile status.

Our third multilingual example is a second-century BCE gravestone found in Todi, in Umbria, Italy (*RIG* II.1 E-5, *CIL* I² 2103, discussed in Adams 2003a: 187–8). It marks a memorial set up by a Gaul called Coisis, son of Drutos, for his brother Ategnatos. The inscription is unusually written on both sides of a slab-shaped stele, with virtually the same inscription in Latin and Gaulish repeated on each face. The Latin and Gaulish texts are written in two different scripts, the Latin alphabet for Latin, and the Etruscan alphabet for the Gaulish. Gauls are known to have settled in the Po valley from the fourth century BCE, but even so these brothers are a long way from home. No other Gaulish inscription is known so far south, and it is very unlikely that there was anything approaching a Gaulish community in Todi at this date.

Side A

LATIN: (two lines lost)
           / . . . . . . coi]sis / Drutei f.
           frater / eius / minimus locau/it et statuit
GAULISH: ateknati trut/ikni karnitu / artuaš koisis t/rutiknos

Side B

LATIN: (lines lost) / . . . c]oisis Druti f./ frater / eius / [m]inimus locau(it)
           [st]atuitqu<e>
GAULISH: [at]eknati truti[k]ni /[kar]nitu / lokan ko[i]sis / [tr]utiknos [

Translation (of both Latin and Gaulish): 'Coisis, son of Drutos, younger
brother, placed and set this up for (his older brother) Ategnatos'

Unlike the other texts discussed so far, here the message conveyed in the
two different languages is almost exactly the same (as far as we can be
confident in our translation of the Gaulish). Latin uses two virtually
synonymous verbs *locauit* 'placed' and *statuit* 'set up', where Gaulish
appears to have a verbal phrase, on one side *karnitu artuaš* and on the
other *karnitu lokan*. The Gaulish verb *karnitu* is known to have the
meaning 'set up' from Gaulish inscriptions in France, but no generally
accepted explanation has been offered for what *artuaš* and *lokan* (which
seem to be nouns) might refer to. Perhaps one of these words indicated
some physical aspect of the burial or memorial that changed after the
first version was inscribed, and Coisis was concerned enough about
the discrepancy to reinscribe the stone with the appropriate word on the
other side.

The name formulae of the two brothers are adapted into the onomastic
systems of the two different languages. In Gaulish inscriptions, a person
is generally identified through the combination of two names, the first
denoting the individual and the second, which takes the form of an
adjective, indicating the father. In this case, the patronymic adjective is
formed by the addition of a suffix *-iknos*, so *Trutiknos* means 'son of
Drutos'. Note that in the script used for Gaulish in Italy (which is
essentially the Etruscan alphabet) the same letter may indicate either *t* or
d, but we know Drutos should be pronounced with a D from the Latin
version of the name. In the Latin text, Coisis has adopted the Latin
convention of denoting the father's name through the abbreviation *f.* for
filius 'son of'. Despite Coisis' adoption of this Latin formula, his identity as
an outsider is still without doubt, since he does not hold a *gens* (or family)
name, as most of the peoples of central Italy did, including the Umbrians
and Etruscans as well as the Romans. The Gaulish text is clearly that of the

'insider', revealing the local identity which was important to Coisis and his brother; indeed, if we are right to suggest that the whole text was re-engraved because either the word *artuaš* or *lokan* was incorrect, Coisis went to considerable extra expense in order to make sure the Gaulish was accurate. Inscriptions from the third and second centuries BCE have been found at Todi written both in the Umbrian language and in Etruscan; the Gaulish bilingual is the only surviving text from the nearby area written in Latin. The choice of Latin for the leading text on the stele is significant, and the motivation seems to be similar to that for the selection of Ionic Greek as the language for 'outsiders' on the Amathus bilingual discussed above. We gave indications in the previous section for thinking that Latin was something approaching the *lingua franca* of central Italy in the mid-Republican period, so it is therefore the appropriate vehicle for Coisis to reach the widest possible audience for his memorial.

Although these three examples all date from within 200 years of each other, and are alike in that they appear to represent in each case roughly the same message in two or more different languages, they also reveal three very different multilingual situations. In the case of Amathus, the bilingual society of the city was on show, both in the display of two languages, and in the family history of Ariston, which appears to have had both Greek and Eteocypriot elements. We saw at the beginning of Chapter 2 another example of a state capable of erecting multilingual inscriptions: the Achaemenid dynasty in Persia, as recorded in the Behistun inscription of Darius, and we shall meet with further official bilingual texts in our discussion of Greek and Latin bilingualism in the next section. However, in general around the ancient world, the erection of bilingual inscriptions is the exception rather than the norm. Rulers or officials striving to legitimate or advertise new regimes or new power structures sometimes erected large public inscriptions written in different languages, as Darius at Behistun, or the Punic and Libyan inscriptions on the mausoleum of Massinissa at Dougga in Numidia (now Tunisia),[28] or the third-century CE monumental inscription of the Sasanian king Shāpūr I at Naqš-i Rustām in Iran (written in Middle Persian, Parthian and Greek).[29] Augustus' *Res Gestae* and Diocletian's Price Edict, both of which were displayed in Latin and Greek in various different locations in the eastern part of the Empire, may also fit into this category. But relatively few cities or states continued with a consistent system of parallel decrees in two or more languages over a long period of time: the cities of Palmyra and

[28] *KAI* 101 = *RIL* 2, dated to 139/8 BCE. [29] See Rubin (2002).

Dura-Europos were unusual in the Roman Empire for their continuous use of Palmyrene Aramaic versions alongside Greek, and sometimes Latin, in their epigraphy.[30] Lepcis Magna and other towns in Roman North Africa seem to have abandoned the public display of Punic in the middle of the first century CE;[31] and although hieroglyphs were maintained for imperial inscriptions in Egypt until the end of Empire, they usually do not stand in parallel with Greek or Latin texts. We shall see further below that most of the Latin and Greek bilingual inscriptions from the eastern Empire did not present exact parallel versions alongside one another.

In the latter two of our examples of bilingual texts discussed above, the texts are left by individuals rather than larger groups or communities. Cleon seems to have selected three languages in order to maximize the number of potential readers who would know of his munificence, whereas the Gaulish monument is the clear creation of incomers who felt it important to leave a record of their names in their own language. Few multilingual individuals in the ancient world would have had the competence or opportunity to display their command of two different languages in writing – for many languages there was probably no written version in any case. Often individuals preferred to blend in through their selection of the dominant language of the society. Even so, sometimes it is possible that a local identity is revealed through imperfect command of the written code, either through unintentional 'leaks' from a first language, or through the presence of a local variety of the dominant language, reflecting the outcome of a community discarding their native language in favour of the new one. Material of this type is sometimes called 'quasi-bilingual', but it would be more accurate to say that these are 'documents reflecting a bilingual situation', or ones that show bilingual phenomena.

The investigation of texts displaying bilingual phenomena involves the careful assessment of what is regular and what is 'unusual' for a variety that is no longer spoken. Furthermore, if one aspect of the language of a text or group of texts is out of step with the rest of the written corpus, this may be a regional or idiosyncratic development that need not necessarily be attributed to the influence of an underlying or 'substrate' language. The scholarly literature on language history is littered with over-enthusiastic explanations for a range of linguistic features ascribed to the action of a presumed substrate language: for example, non-Classical features of the Latin of the graffiti at Pompeii have sometimes been seen as the result of

---

[30] Kaizer (2009) gives a synopsis of the language use at Dura-Europos; see also Chapter 6 below.
[31] Wilson (2012).

Oscan speech habits, and the nasalized vowels of French as the outcome of Latin in Celtic mouths.[32] However, in some cases language and cultural factors combine to reveal a marked local identity. An example is provided by a late Republican funerary monument from Perugia (*CIL* XI 1960). The inscription is only three words long, chiselled along the lid of the chest that contained the ashes of the dead woman, who is also immortalized by an Etruscan-style reclining statue of a woman. The Latin text of the inscription just gives the woman's name:

Thania Caesinia Volumni
    Thania Caesinia daughter / wife of Volumnius

The grammar of the text is in accordance with Latin rules, but the naming conventions of Etruscan were slightly different from those of the Romans, and this text follows Etruscan practice in the survival of the praenomen *Thania*, easily recognizable as a non-Latin name owing to the initial consonant cluster *th-*, which does not occur in native Latin vocabulary. Roman women (unlike men) rarely show praenomina on their epitaphs, but in Etruscan society both sexes used first names, and Etruscan women often retained these even when they no longer had the competence to write in Etruscan script. The second non-Roman feature of the inscription is the lack of any indication of Thania's relationship to Volumnius, whether 'daughter', 'wife' or possibly 'freedwoman', which would normally be present in a Latin name formula (usually in abbreviated form, such as *f.* for *filia* 'daughter'). These departures from the standard Roman formulae, and the traditional Etruscan format for the object on which the text is written, are not uncommon in former Etruscan-speaking areas at the end of the Republic, revealing the attempt to maintain a distinct local identity, despite using Latin.

Latin and Greek bilingualism

We know far more about Latin and Greek bilingualism than any other language contact situation in the ancient world, and we have a far greater amount of bilingual texts and documents than for any other pair of languages. There is sufficient surviving bilingual material to enable us to track in detail the language habits of individual speakers adept in Latin and

---

[32] See Eska (1987), and Adams (2003a: 119) for discussion (and dismissal) of Oscan influence on the Latin of Pompeii, and Mees (2003) for a survey of potential Celtic substrates in French and other Romance languages.

Greek. In the letters and writings of Cicero we have the example of a fluent bilingual, able to discuss the most appropriate translation of a Greek word, and swap bilingual jokes and puns with his correspondents. In the archive of papyrus letters written by and to Claudius Terentianus, a Roman soldier stationed in Egypt in the first century CE, we find the same person writing to his father in both Latin and Greek, with an equally easy conversational style (*P.Mich.* VIII 467–72).[33] The range of surviving bilingual texts in Greek and Latin affords a much broader view of language use than for other languages. Translations range from those of high art, including the very first Latin literature, Livius Andronicus' translation of the *Odyssey*, to the barely competent beginner's translation of parts of Babrius' fables (*P.Amh.* II. 26, discussed at Adams 2003a: 725–41). Educational texts, both in papyri and handed down in manuscript tradition, contain parallel versions of word-lists and conversations and scenarios of everyday life (Dickey 2012). Countless inscriptions and graffiti record everything from religious revelations to brothel boasts.

Records of bilingualism between Latin and Greek and other languages are often restricted to the short period between the first contact between the languages, and the fading of the indigenous language from the inscriptional record. But Latin and Greek continued to be spoken and written alongside each other. The meanings conveyed by speaking or writing in Latin or Greek, or in both, were consequently quite different from what we have assumed about other languages, particularly in the period after the first century CE. The interplay of language and identity is often highly sophisticated. Many members of the Roman elite were equally comfortable with Latin and Greek;[34] we have already discussed the orator Favorinus, for whom it was possible to acquire Greekness through mastery of Greek rhetoric and culture, while retaining his Roman identity. The emperor Claudius' quip that Latin and Greek were 'both our languages' (Suetonius *Claudius* 42 *utroque sermone nostro*) would become a commonplace in the Roman Empire, when the phrase 'in both languages' (*utraque lingua*) was usually understood to refer to Latin and Greek.

However, Greek was not always viewed as on a par with Latin by the Romans, nor was it so readily accepted as their own. It will be helpful to sketch out the stages by which a mostly monoglot early Republic evolved

---

[33] The Latin and Greek letters are re-edited and published together by Strassi (2008), see also Trapp (2003: text 5) for discussion of one of the letters of Claudius. Adams (1977) discusses the language of the Latin letters and Adams (2003a: 590–5) the motivations for language choice.

[34] Although in some parts of the Western Empire, such as Africa, Greek seems to have been less prevalent; see the synopsis of Ameling (2012: 87–8).

into a bilingual Empire, before looking at the domains of the different languages in the Empire in more detail. From the first contact with Greek settlers and traders along the west coast of Italy, the Romans learnt Greek words for new material goods and technological advances. Some of these words, which became incorporated into the Latin language, can be shown by dialect features to be very old: for example, the Latin words for 'olive', *oliua*, and 'oil', *oleum*, were taken from the Greek words *elaíwā* and *élaiwon* at a period when the sound /w/ must still have been pronounced in the Greek source (the sound had dropped out of the Attic dialect of Greek by the earliest records, but was retained in West Greek dialects), and early enough to undergo the various changes in vowels which led to the Classical Latin forms. Names of some of the gods and heroes of Greece were also transferred to Rome at an early stage in history, including Apollo, Proserpina, Ulysses, Hercules and others, sometimes via an intermediary of another language such as Etruscan (Poccetti 2012). Other items reflect Greek influence on the social institutions of the Romans, such as the legal term *poena* 'punishment, retribution' taken from Greek *poinā́*. Romans had therefore been aware of Greek culture for centuries before Livius Andronicus translated the Odyssey in 241 BCE.

Livius was not only the instigator of Latin literary culture, he was also reportedly a Greek-speaking freedman from Lucania (his name corroborates this, with *Liuius* the gentilicium (i.e. family name) of his patron, and *Andronicus* the Latinized form of the Greek name *Andrónīkos*). The two poles of high literary culture and servile status continued to be important elements in the Roman encounter with Greek throughout the Republic. There was massive influx of Greek-speaking slaves into the western Mediterranean in the last centuries BCE (including, perhaps, the trilingual Cleon, whose offering to Asclepius was discussed above) following the Roman conquests in Greek-speaking lands to the east. In the comedies of Plautus, slaves are sometimes represented switching into Greek, to a greater degree than other characters (Adams 2003a: 351), and at least one of the freedmen depicted in Petronius' *Satyrica* (Hermeros) is represented as using Greek alongside Latin. Furthermore, of the slave-names recorded in Roman epigraphy, the majority (67 per cent) are of Greek origin (Solin 1996), although two of the most common of these, Hermes and Eros, function in Greece itself only as the names of gods, not men. The traffic from Greece and the Greek colonies of Sicily and southern Italy into Rome was not limited to slaves and high art. Sailors, traders, merchants, artisans and soldiers all left their mark on the Latin language between the fifth and first centuries BCE, as Romans adopted Greek terms for boats and seafaring, fish, animals, luxury goods, coinage, furniture, siege craft and weapons (Kahle 1918). Many of these terms can be seen to be borrowings from the spoken rather than the written language, as for example the names of the exotic animals *elephantus* 'elephant', taken from the Greek genitive case *eléphantos* (not the nominative *eléphās*) or *panthēra* 'panther' from the Greek accusative case *pánthēra* (not the nominative *pánthēr*). In Plautus' comedies many Greek words seem to have become naturalized citizens in Latin, but some, such as *trapezita* 'banker', *machaera* 'sword' or *clypeus* 'shield' are still recognized as resident aliens, and give a Greek flavour or signal a specifically Greek context beside the natives *argentarius* 'banker', *gladius* 'sword' and *scutum* 'shield' (Shipp 1954).

Many Romans of the late Republic may have linked spoken Greek with the speech of slaves, merchants and mercenaries, rather than with literary texts and high culture, and this no doubt partly explains apparent linguistic prejudices against Greek. There was an assumption that tribes vanquished in war should speak the language of their conquerors, and the conquerors need not stoop to address the conquered in their own tongue. Consequently some Romans clearly thought that the military supremacy of Rome should be matched by linguistic chauvinism: Sallust reports the general Marius in his speech on assuming the command in Rome (in 107 BCE) as saying that he had never studied Greek literature, since he saw no benefit in a study that had not helped the slaves who taught it (Sallust *Iug.* 89.32, see Adams 2003a: 12–13 on Marius's acquaintance with Greek). A similar attitude towards Greek is seen in the story that the praetor Scaevola and his official train in Athens insulted the Roman hellenophile Albucius by greeting him in Greek, not Latin (Lucilius 88–94, writing in the second century BCE, cited by Cicero *De finibus* 1.9 and discussed by Adams 2003a: 353–4). The bite of the insult may have been the accepted practice that Roman magistrates spoke only Latin on official business, and did not even address Greeks in Greek (Valerius Maximus 2.2.2); Cicero himself was criticized for giving a speech in the senate in Syracuse, a Greek colony in Sicily, in Greek (*In Verrem* 2.4.147, see further Rochette 2011 on this policy). The quasi-official address to Albucius in Greek stripped him of his Roman identity, and made him out to be of lower status than free Greek citizens.

Romans in the Republic who were too prone to interlard Greek vocabulary into their conversation may have met with ridicule, if this is the import of a fragmentary passage of Lucilius (frag. 15): 'Then we said *clinopodes* and *lychni* grandly instead of bed-feet and lanterns' (in the original the word here translated 'grandly' is also given in Greek *semnôs*).

The meaning of the passage is unclear, but it is likely that Lucilius is poking fun at the tendency among upper-class Romans to choose highfalutin Greek terms in preference to the basic Latin words; the Greek terms cited are largely avoided in later Latin literature (see Chahoud 2004 for fuller discussion of this passage). Even literary figures may have been censured for inappropriate use of Greek. Vergil's short poem *Catalepton* 7 refers to 'rules' of what can and cannot be said, and jokingly plays on the question whether a linguistic mistake is worse than a supposed moral transgression (note, however, that we are dependent on conjecture for the text given below, where the Greek word is rendered by a French word in the translation):

> In all honesty, dear Varus, I shall say this: 'I'm done for if that *amour* hasn't ruined me.' But the rules forbid me to speak this way, so of course I won't say that, but I shall say 'That boy has ruined me.'[35]

This purist literary attitude towards Greek vocabulary is also reflected in the general absence of Greek borrowings from Cicero's published forensic oratory or speeches to the Senate, although he is happy to use Greek freely in his correspondence. Thus, even when, as in the *Pro Murena* (section 61 and following), Cicero expounds Greek philosophical doctrines, he avoids Greek terms (including *philosophus* 'philosopher' and its derivatives). Similarly, Augustus avoids Greek words in the *Res Gestae*, though they occur in his surviving private letters.

This attitude towards Greek seems to have shifted by the time of the Empire. In terms of literary figures, generals and orators, Rome could now claim to match Greece. Indeed, Plutarch's *Parallel Lives*, written at the end of the first and beginning of the second century CE, did just that, offering Roman equivalents to Greek heroes, military leaders and statesmen. In literary culture, Latin speakers no longer had to be content with 'bad Greek books in worse Latin versions' referred to by Cicero (*De finibus* 1.8); Cicero's own translations and philosophical works had promulgated a new Latin vocabulary based on Greek philosophical and technical terms. Cicero (*De diuinatione* 1.21.43) reports that the first Roman historian, Q. Fabius Pictor (third century BCE), wrote the history of Rome in Greek, but a Latin version may have appeared during his own lifetime (Cornell 2013: 169); by the end of the Republic Cato, Livy, Caesar, Sallust and others had established the genre of historical writing in Latin. The

---

[35] See Oosterhuis (2013). I am very grateful to Dave Oosterhuis for sending me a copy of his paper before publication.

Augustan poets self-consciously strove to clothe their Greek models in Roman dress, as Horace openly acknowledged his debt to Archilochus and Alcaeus, Greek poets of the Archaic age (*Epistles* 1.19), and Propertius to the Hellenistic poet Callimachus (*Odes* 3.1). Vergil's debt to Greek poetry is also immediately apparent, and the rapid spread of the *Aeneid* as a text used in learning to read and write around the empire (see Clackson 2011a: 241–2) showed that he was quickly judged the Roman Homer, and came to occupy the same place in the Latin curriculum that Homer held in the Greek. By the first century CE, Romans no longer felt the cultural cringe.

In day-to-day life, and in administration, the roles of Greek and Latin in the Empire also approached parity, although here the situation differed between east and west. In the east, Greek remained the normal language of administration and the everyday language of business and commerce. In the terms of High and Low languages, which we introduced earlier in this chapter (p. 72), Greek filled the High position, whereas vernacular idioms, such as Aramaic in Syria and Palestine, spoken Egyptian in Egypt and various different tongues in Asia Minor, occupied the Low position. But Latin was also a High language, although not so widespread in the inscriptional record, and probably not well understood by the mass of the populace. In particular, Latin conveyed the nuances of imperial authority and power. Court proceedings recorded on papyri in Egypt show the interplay between the two languages. For example, *P.Oxy.* 9.1201, a mid third-century CE papyrus from Oxyrhynchus, records a petition to the Prefect of Egypt from Aurelius Heudaemon regarding his inheritance. The petition is given first formally in Latin, then a Greek section explains the basis of the petition. The single Latin sentence 'by edict I have read the petition' records the prefect's formal declaration, and then the entire petition is translated into Greek at the end (Adams 2003a: 566). As a Roman magistrate, the prefect makes his official pronouncement in Latin, although the working language of the court, which would have been understood by everyone, was Greek.

Epigraphy from the east can also reveal the balance between Latin and Greek, and their differing functions. For example, a bilingual inscription in bronze letters was set up by two freed slaves, Mazaeus and Mithridates, in the first century CE in Ephesus, on an impressive three-arched gateway (*ILS* 8897, discussed at Burrell 2009: 72–4, Eck 2009: 25). The Latin text, written above the two outer arches of the gate, is both much longer and carefully spaced so that one archway is occupied by the names and titles of Augustus and his wife, and the other by those of Marcus Agrippa and his wife (and Augustus's daughter) Iulia.

> Mazaeus and Mithridates [set this up] for their patrons: Augustus, son of the deified Caesar, Pontifex Maximus, twelve times consul, twenty times with the tribunician power, and for Livia, the wife of Caesar Augustus, and for Marcus, son of Lucius Agrippa, three times consul, imperator, six times with the tribunician power, and for Iulia, daughter of Caesar Augustus.

The two-line Greek text is inscribed over the central arch, which stands back from the outer two arches:

> Mazaeus and Mithridates set this up for their patrons and the people.

The Greek text consequently omits the full names and titles of the freedmen's imperial patrons, Augustus, Livia, Marcus Agrippa and Iulia. But the Greek line, under which the bulk of the traffic would have passed, includes the fact that the gate was a gift to the people of the city (many of whom would have been ignorant of Latin script let alone the epigraphical abbreviations) and was thus not just a celebration of imperial power. Mazaeus and Mithridates bear names which have clear Persian connections, although we do not know whether this necessarily reflects competence in any language other than Latin and Greek. In their bilingual inscription they have shown their powerful connections with the Roman hierarchy, but also their connection with the people of their city.

Not all inscriptions in Greek in the east were designed to be read by the inhabitants. Tourists and pilgrims to Egypt, for example, left records of their visits in pharaonic tombs or on statues, notably on the Colossus of Memnon. Some Romans left bilingual graffiti, both in Latin and in Greek, others in Greek alone. These Greek inscriptions can be displays of literary culture and erudition intended for a very limited audience: for example, the poems of Iulia Balbilla, written in the Aeolic dialect on the legs of the Colossus (see p. 59 above), which belong to a milieu of competing courtiers around the emperor Hadrian, and in a language comprehensible only to the most learned locals (see Brennan 1998). Romans could also choose to write in Greek for the purposes of display in the west. In Britain and Gaul, for example, we find epitaphs either wholly in Greek or in both Latin and Greek.[36] Bilingual grave-markers will sometimes give the bare facts of the deceased life in Latin, but follow with an epigram in Greek. Texts with Greek in them often show association with specific linguistic domains that were the province of Greek speakers – art, theatre and particularly medicine – or they may combine two of these domains. As

---

[36] Decourt (2004) gathers all the inscriptions containing Greek from France; for discussion of this corpus see Mullen (2013).

an example, consider a Greek votive inscription left by the doctor
Antiochos, who was serving in the Roman fort at Chester, which contains
rare poetic vocabulary and an extended hexameter verse form (unknown
outside Britain), set up in honour of Asclepius, Hygieia and Panakeia
(Clackson and Meißner 2000). Antiochos' use of Greek is unsurprising
for someone practising medicine; Pliny (*NH* 29.17) recounts how speaking
Greek is one of the essential requirements for people to trust a doctor. Latin
versions of Greek medical texts did eventually come to be made in the
later Empire, and some medical works in Latin do survive from the first
century CE, such as that of the Roman encyclopaedist Celsus, and the
freedman and physician to Claudius Scribonius Largus, but it would be
difficult to gain medical competence in the Republic and early Empire
without first knowing the Greek language. But Antiochos further adver-
tised his Greekness by his command of highly poetic, literary language and
recondite metre in the text of his dedication. The language is certainly
unlike anything Antiochos could have uttered in everyday speech, even to
a fellow doctor, and he doubtless was able to communicate at some level
with the Roman soldiers in Latin. But his selection of a literary form of
Greek advertises his professional expertise and his allegiance to a wider
Greek cultural world.

Modern and ancient identities

In the closing chapter of a volume on multilingualism and cultural identities in the ancient Near East, Sheldon Pollock launches an attack on the
alleged connections between language and identity: '[f]or many scholars
this term [identity] has lost all explanatory salience' (Pollock 2006: 289).
Pollock points out that identity has become a catch-all term which
ranges widely in its applications from ethnicity to a more transient sense
of connectedness or belonging, and that there is little sense in applying
modern western concepts of ethnic identities to pre-modern societies. The
concept of simple ethnic identities, and the hypothesized link between a
single ethnic identity and language, are certainly as flawed for the ancient
Mediterranean as for the ancient Near East. However, it is not true to
say of the Greek and Roman worlds that language choice was typically
regulated by a particular genre of discourse rather than identity. As the
examples of bi- and tri-lingual speakers and texts discussed in this chapter
have shown, one of the motivations for language choice in the ancient
world was the presentation of allegiance to particular groups, communities,
or even professions or cultural modes of existence. Although in many cases

we do not know enough about the specifics to write the full story behind the language choice of individuals such as Cleon, the slave of the salt mines in Sardinia, or Coisis, the Gaulish speaker in Todi, or Antiochos, the doctor of Chester, we can show that their use of language was part of their self-identification and self-definition.

CHAPTER 4

Language variation

Introduction

Variation is an inherent property of human language. Biological and physical factors mean that it is very difficult for two people to reproduce exactly the same pronunciation of a particular word, or even for a single person to utter the same sounds when speaking at a different volume, or when sleepy, breathless, or intoxicated. Human language has inbuilt mechanisms to overcome this variation in the sound of utterances, but it has taken decades to develop sophisticated voice-recognition software, and automated speech-to-text devices are still unable to match humans in the ability to correlate spoken language with particular words, as is very clear to anyone who has ever struggled to make their words understood on an automated telephone line, or watched a television news broadcast with live captioning. Linguistic variation also encompasses choice of individual vocabulary items and word-endings, or selection of different syntactic rules. A vast amount of modern linguistic research in the last sixty years has greatly increased our understanding of variation in speech, and its relationship to social status and language change.

However, as the examples of voice-recognition software or live captioning show, in modern societies written language exhibits a far more restricted range of variation than speech. This is especially true for the phonology (the sounds of language), where the almost infinite variety of noises that a human can produce is mapped onto a much smaller number of distinct letter-forms or signs. But it is also the case for other areas of language; even though less formal written styles are nowadays found in text messages, tweets or emails, most educated people avoid writing down vocabulary items and sentence structures that they may utter in everyday conversation. In modern western cultures where nearly all of the population is literate, most written texts are not direct transcriptions of speech, but are framed within the norms and styles inculcated by education and the models provided by books, newspapers, articles, essays and blogs. The greater part of the variation encountered in everyday speech goes unrecorded in writing, whereas variation in written documents, such as different spellings or punctuation, or choice between 'which' or 'that' as a relative pronoun, need not correlate with anything in the spoken language.

The mismatch between speech and writing clearly causes problems for the researcher of ancient linguistic variation. When investigating linguistic variation in ancient societies, we have only the written record to work from, with occasional, usually unscientific, observations about the speech habits of individuals or different groups. Literacy was much lower in the ancient world than in modern developed states, and generally the written documents of any length left to us are those composed by or for a predominantly male elite. Rates of literacy varied over time and place, but scholars have generally accepted Harris's estimates (1989: 114, 259) that in Attica during the Classical period 5–10 per cent of the adult male population were literate, and in Italy during the late Republic/High Empire male literacy was 'well below the 20–30% range'; the rates for women were certainly much lower.[1] Many shorter texts are formulaic, including graffiti and scratched records of ownership on ceramic vessels, and longer texts are often bounded by literary models and conventions. Furthermore, for most of the languages spoken in the ancient world, we do not have enough information about the language, or a large enough body of surviving evidence, to begin talking about variation. For this reason, in the rest of this chapter, I shall confine the discussion to variation in Greek and Latin, although there are a growing number of studies on variation in some of the other ancient languages discussed in this book.[2] For Greek and Latin, we have not only a wide variety of different types of text, but also some literary works that represent the different voices of individuals, while others contain discussions about the correct use of language or anecdotes about the foibles of particular speakers, where variation in speech is recorded, commented on and evaluated.

Studying linguistic variation

Across a community which uses the same language, linguists sometimes separate out three different axes on which variation may occur: diatopic,

---

[1] There is an enormous scholarly literature on ancient literacy, but important collections of papers include Beard et al. (eds) (1991), Bowman and Woolf (eds) (1994), and Johnson and Parker (eds) (2009).

[2] See van Heems (2011a) on previous studies of variation in languages of ancient Italy, and (2011b) on possible traces of social variation in Etruscan.

diastratic and diachronic. We have already met with diatopic variation, the ways in which language varies across space, in earlier chapters. The diastratic axis encompasses variation across sets of speakers who differ in, for example, social class, age or sex; diachronic refers to the changes observed in a language over time. Until the 1960s, traditional dialectology, which in part derives from the Greek grammarians' recognition of literary dialects, tended to concentrate on diatopic variation only, and was also prone to view dialects as fixed entities which could be identified by a list of features that differed from the standard language. But pioneering work by William Labov in the United States and Peter Trudgill in the United Kingdom, amongst others, revealed the extent of diastratic variation as well, and showed how the majority of speakers were able to adapt their language to different speech situations, employing at one time a higher frequency of standard speech forms, at another more non-standard features.

Of course, it had long been recognized that there are different registers for speech appropriate for different occasions. A doctor might address her six-year-old child with different vocabulary and sentence structure than she would a patient in her surgery, and she might employ another register again when talking to colleagues; her child has tummy-ache, the patient stomach-ache and the fellow doctor colitis. However, words such as 'tummy-ache' or 'colitis' are still part of the lexicon of standard English, which encompasses a range of registers from nursery vocabulary to technical languages. A word from the wrong register might be confusing or jarring to her audience, or it might be intended to amuse or provoke. A technical term such as 'colitis' may reveal the professional qualifications or interests of the person who utters it, but on its own it does not tell the audience anything about the speaker's social background or class. Register-variation is also found in ancient texts, and sometimes explicitly recognized, for example at Cicero *De finibus* 3.4:[3]

> Geometry, Music, Grammar also have an idiom of their own. Even the manuals of Rhetoric, which belong entirely to the practical sphere and to the life of the world, nevertheless employ for purposes of instruction a sort of private and peculiar phraseology. (translation by H. Rackham, Loeb Classical Library)

In the discussion of sexual and obscene vocabulary in Chapter 5, we shall return to the question of register-variation in ancient languages, and meet

---

[3] See also Langslow (2000), López Eire and Ramos Guerreira (eds) (2004), Willi (2010), Fögen (2011) on register-variation and technical languages in the ancient world.

some of the problems in attempting to determine whether individual lexical items are specific to a certain register.

However, the sort of variation that Labov and other sociolinguists have observed in modern languages is different in degree and scope from register-variation. The single most important observation to come out of Labov's work is that a single speaker need not have a consistent pronunciation of a particular variable, or select the same word, word-ending or syntactic structure on each occasion. We can exemplify this by the phenomenon of *r*-dropping, that is to say, not pronouncing *r* when it follows a vowel (and does not precede another vowel), which is prevalent in many varieties of British English, including in the prestige standard accent known as Received Pronunciation. Speakers who drop *r* after a vowel (sometimes called *non-rhotic* speakers) pronounce the automobile brand-name *Ka* exactly the same as the vocabulary item *car* before a word beginning with a consonant or before a pause, and in their speech *lore* and *law* are also homophonous in the same environment; when the next word begins with a vowel, the final *r* of *car* and *lore* are both pronounced. In American English, speakers of the standard variety retain *r* after vowels whatever the following sound is, but its loss is a feature of African-American Vernacular English and some regional varieties, such as that spoken in the cities of New York and Boston. The fact that loss of *r* is generally stigmatized in American English but not in British English is incidentally sufficient in itself to show that the social meanings given to speech variables are independent of the variables themselves; there is nothing inherently lazy or deviant in particular non-standard variants, but they may be characterized as such by other speakers.

The retention or loss of post-vocalic *r* was one of five speech variables which William Labov studied in his ground-breaking 1964 Columbia University dissertation on linguistic variation in New York City (Labov 1966, 2006). Labov showed that in New York speakers did not divide neatly into *r*-sayers and *r*-droppers, but that nearly all speakers sometimes pronounced the sound after vowels, sometimes not. Labov used a wide variety of techniques to elicit speech from a broad spectrum of informants. The most famous study, repeated in most handbooks (and published separately in Labov 1972), took only a day and a half during an eighteen-month survey: Labov visited different department stores and requested to be directed to items he knew were situated on the fourth floor, in order to hear whether his informant replied with an audible *r* in *fourth* and *floor*. Labov also conducted extensive individual interviews, which required informants to answer questions on their speech and their attitudes to recordings of other speakers, as well as perform tasks such as reading written passages, word-lists and pairs of words such as *dock/dark* and *god/ guard* (for New York speakers who drop *r* these words are homophonous). During interviews Labov also elicited more natural conversational styles by asking questions requiring more personal responses, for example whether the interviewee had ever been in mortal danger. In order to tap into informants who refused to participate in the interviews, Labov and an assistant made telephone calls, pretending to check up on television reception (these were the days before research proposals were submitted before ethics committees), and listening to see whether respondents pronounced the *r* in 'Channel Four' or 'Thirteen'. Labov further made tape-recordings of conversations overheard in diners and on the street, guessing the age and social class of the speakers he heard and noting their clothes and appearance.

Labov's findings show conclusively that speakers are inconsistent in their speech. For each speaker in a particular context, Labov arrived at a score for the variables by allocating 1 to the standard pronunciation (in the *r*-variation case, the maintenance of *r*), and 0 to the non-standard (loss of *r*), and then averaging out the occurrences as a percentile: if speakers pronounced *r* in exactly half of the cases where it occurs in standard English, they have a score of 50 per cent. No speaker in the survey has a consistent 100 per cent or 0 per cent score across all possible contexts, and some respondents ranged from a score of 0 per cent in the most casual conversational style, where they always dropped *r*, to 100 per cent in reading word-lists, with figures in between for the more formal conversation or reading passages. Even within a single speech event an individual's frequency of *r*-pronunciation may vary. For example, Labov cites the following case:

> A professor of sociology, born and raised in New York City, began a lecture with an (r) index of 50% to 60%; as he proceeded, and warmed to his subject, the index dropped precipitously, as low as 5%; then as he began to make his final points, the (r) index began to rise again, although it never quite reached its initial value. (Labov 2006: 37, slightly adapted)

Overall, however, all speakers tended to use more non-standard forms in less formal contexts. For all speakers, social class correlated with variation. Most clearly, working-class speakers deviate the most from the standard in all different speech styles. Upper middle-class speakers deviate least from the standard in casual speech (unsurprisingly, since the standard is itself largely based on the diction of those with some social standing). Through his inclusion of questions on attitudes towards language in his survey, Labov was also able to show that speakers tended to misreport their own speech styles, and that many middle-class speakers, particularly women, were disparaging about the New York dialect, and admitted having attempted to change their speech in favour of the standard variety. These results help to explain a particularly striking finding: lower middle-class speakers showed the greatest range of variation, with all speakers consistently pronouncing *r* in the reading exercises, while many of them did not use post-vocalic *r* at all in their most casual style of speech.

Subsequent research on language variation in a range of different communities has further demonstrated the clear correlation between linguistic variation and the class, age and sex of the speaker. Speakers, in particular male speakers, tend to deviate more from the standard in conversation with peer groups than when they read out written passages or in a formal environment, and male speakers may over-report their deviation from the standard (Chambers and Trudgill 1998: 85). Even though speakers may be aware that they use a non-standard pronunciation or word or syntactic structure, most of the time the choice between the standard and non-standard form is made subconsciously. Furthermore, speakers who become aware of non-standard forms in their speech, either through interaction with members of different social groups, or through correction by school-teachers or other authority figures, may attempt to correct their 'faults' (either deliberately or without realizing it). In these circumstances, it is not unusual to find overcompensations, which are termed *hypercorrections*. Thus, for example, if people become aware that words that they pronounce without an initial *h* have an initial *h* in the standard language, they may start adding *h* to words that never had *h* while continuing to drop the sound in other words where the standard has it. This is the origin of Eliza Doolittle's *hever* in the line from *My Fair Lady* 'In 'ertford, 'ereford and 'ampshire, 'urricanes 'ardly hever 'appen'. Sometimes hypercorrections themselves even become embedded in the standard language; most British speakers of English pronounce the phrase *law and order* the same as *lore and order*, that is with a linking *r* before the initial vowel of *and*, and this originates as an overextension of the pattern with words which originally ended in *r*. In any particular language, it is often possible to identify where hypercorrections have taken place, particularly if we know something about the history and origin of the language. Historical examples of hypercorrections may be an indication that there has been a period of social differentiation of the language in question, and that one variant has been stigmatized or another favoured or inculcated in schools.

Language variation is now understood to be closely linked to the process of language change; indeed, change can be viewed as variation along a diachronic axis. One of the most straightforward demonstrations of this is to consider a language such as English, which is spoken by millions of people with a huge geographical spread. Some of the features which are found as diastratic variants for speakers of English in some areas are insignificant in other parts of the world, because nearly all speakers have adopted the innovative alternant. Thus the deletion of r after a vowel, which Labov investigated in his department store survey with the phrase *fourth floor*, is still a variable for many New York speakers of English. But it is no longer a living variable for most middle-class speakers from England, who will never pronounce the r in *fourth*, and only pronounce the final r in floor when the next word begins with a vowel. At an earlier stage in the history of British English loss of post-vocalic r was a diastratic variant, but in time, the innovative variant won out across the majority of the population.

It is possible to map the loss of post-vocalic r across all the global varieties of English over time, thus demonstrating some of the long-term outcomes of variations.[4] British colonization of Australia, South Africa and New Zealand took place in the nineteenth century, at a time when some British speakers of English varied their pronunciation between rhotic and non-rhotic styles. Recordings of New Zealand speakers of English made in the nineteenth century reveal variation in r-dropping, with post-vocalic r still present in men's speech in some words (but absent from the speech of the six women of whom recordings survive). In present-day speech from Australia, South Africa and England, r-dropping is the norm, indicating that the variation present in the language of the first colonials has developed in the same way in these English dialects as it has in standard British English. The bulk of the United States was colonized by English speakers before the beginnings of r-dropping, usually dated to the eighteenth century, and the preservation of r in all positions in American standard English reflects the rhotic speech of seventeenth-century settlers. However, the variation found in speakers in New York (as in other northeastern American cities such as Boston) may reflect the influence of later migrants and incomers into the ports of the East Coast from London. This variation has been a living feature of the dialect for around 200 years, and is still alive. Repeats of Labov's department store survey in New York made in 1986 (Labov 1994: 86–94) and 2009 (Mather 2012) showed the

---

[4] See Trudgill (2010) for the following account.

maintenance of the *r*-variable, with a contrast between the speech of sales assistants in the high-class stores and the non-standard usage found among the workers in their downmarket competitors. In British English, as we have seen, the standard language lacks post-vocalic *r* except before vowels, but dialects such as the Norwich dialect and Scottish and Irish varieties remain completely rhotic. Variation may therefore lead to a change in the language, but it need not do so, and variation may persist in the same society or in the same community for generations. Furthermore, change may affect migrant communities at different rates or in different ways than it does in their original homeland, while the social meanings of variation vary from place to place.

So far we have considered linguistic variation just in terms of spoken language, but in the modern world, writing can have a marked effect on the way in which speakers view variation. For example, the survival of initial *h* and post-vocalic *r* in some varieties of English may be partly due to the fact that their presence can be inferred from the written form, so anyone who can read knows where to place the sound. In the case of initial *h* a few tell-tale signs such as the British English pronunciation of *herb* (where the *h* reflects the influence of French and Latin spellings, and is alien to the inherited English word), or the creeping tendency to pronounce the letter name *haitch* rather than *aitch* (possibly since the letter name is not normally spelt out), reveal something of the history of the sound.

Tracking linguistic variation in the ancient world

The study of ancient language variation is hampered by our lack of access to spoken language. All our evidence for the ancient world is written, whereas modern linguistic research on variation focuses on speech. Getting behind the written record to uncover actual spoken variation is a perennial challenge for researchers into ancient language use. Two of the principal obstacles to research into ancient language variation are our lack of suitable records for individual speakers, and problems with the writing system itself. I shall briefly set out these in this section, before later addressing ways in which researchers have attempted to surmount them.

First, the problem of tracking the language use of individual speakers. It is true that some individuals have left us quantities of text, either surviving directly on papyri, wooden tablets or other media, or maintained through the manuscript tradition, which appear to be amenable to study in variation. Perhaps the best example of a public figure for whom we possess a considerable surviving corpus of work in different genres is Cicero. Furthermore, Cicero both commented on his own habits of linguistic usage, and was the object of the observations of others, some of which survive in later grammarians. Cicero himself acknowledged his own variation in style in different works in a letter to Paetus:

> But tell me now, how do you find me as a letter writer? Don't I deal with you in colloquial style (*plebeio sermone*)? The fact is that one's style has to vary. A letter is one thing, a court of law or a public meeting quite another. Even for the courts we don't have just one style. In pleading civil cases, unimportant ones, we put on no frills, whereas cases involving status or reputation naturally get something more elaborate. As for letters, we weave them out of the language of everyday. (Cicero *Ad fam.* 9.21.1; translation D. R. Shackleton Bailey, Loeb Classical Library)

Cicero's introduction of the phrase translated here as 'colloquial style' has aroused much interest. The Latin expression *sermo plebeius*, which can also be translated as 'plebeian language', or 'the language of common folk',[5] seems to indicate a diastratic variety of Latin. But this is probably to read too much into the remark, which must be understood in the context of the playful style of the letter as a whole, which proceeds to discuss the history of various patrician and plebeian families (see Müller 2001: 85–8). It is true, however, that there are differences between Cicero's epistolary style and his prose works and speeches. Some vocabulary items occur more frequently in the letters, such as *bellus* 'fine, pretty', while others have slightly different meanings and usages, such as *bucca* which means 'cheek' or 'jaw' in Cicero's literary prose, but is used in the letters in a proverbial expression corresponding to 'say whatever comes into one's head'; in both of these cases the words or meanings survive into modern languages derived from Latin, for example Italian *bello* 'pretty' and *bocca* 'mouth'. But Cicero's coinages in his letters are representative rather of a more intimate register of educated language than the language of the urban plebs, and they do not always necessarily correspond with the forms that survive in the spoken Latin which gives rise to the later Romance languages. His use of *bellus* (a diminutive of *bonus* 'good, pretty') is part of a wider predilection for diminutive forms of adjectives such as *integellus* 'safe' (beside Classical Latin *integer*), *longulus* 'long' (beside *longus*) and even *barbatulus* 'a bit bearded' (beside *barbatus*) (see Leumann 1977: 308); all of these forms drop out of the later spoken language.

---

[5] Thus W. Glynn Williams, in an earlier Loeb Classical Library translation.

Furthermore, the language of Cicero's letters varies according to his correspondent, and also at different periods of his life. With his close friend Atticus and other educated males he sometimes switches to insert a word or phrase in Greek (Swain 2002, Adams 2003a: 308–47). As we saw in Chapter 3 (p. 91), Cicero avoids Greek in his published orations. However, it is impossible to make a clear-cut division between a conversational style where switching into Greek is permitted, and a more formal style where it is not, since the collection of Cicero's jokes recorded by Macrobius (*Saturnalia* 2.3) includes those made in the Senate which include Greek words. Cicero also avoids Greek when writing letters to other correspondents, including his wife (who may not have known Greek), and stops using Greek altogether for several months after the death of his daughter (Adams 2003a: 344). Other factors show similarities between Cicero's epistolary style and his oratory: in a recent study of hyperbaton (i.e. deviation from an expected word order), Powell has shown that Cicero's letters and oratory use similar techniques in order to focus on particular words in the sentence (Powell 2010). Powell underlines the orality of ancient letters (we know that Cicero's were dictated) and speeches, and highlights the difficulties of contrasting different Latin genres (rhetorical and epistolary) in terms of formal and informal registers. Letters had their own conventions in the ancient world, and were not necessarily any more colloquial than law-court speeches.[6]

In the process of committing Cicero's dictated text to a written form, all of the variation in pronunciation was necessarily ironed out, as were probably other non-standard features either in the first transcription or possibly at later stages in the manuscript tradition. In tracking ancient variation we might at first appear to be on surer ground when surveying material that has not been passed down through the manuscript tradition, but where we can check the original spellings surviving on the original media. There is always the problem, of course, of the amount of surviving text generated by a specific individual: scarcely more than a score of letters or documents can be associated with any particular individual, despite the survival of private and public archives on papyri from the deserts of Egypt and the Near East, or on wax tablets from sites around the Bay of Naples buried under the Vesuvian eruption, or on wooden tablets in Vindolanda and other waterlogged sites from the Roman Empire. Where we do have more than a single document emanating from the same person,

---

[6] See Dickey (2002: 213–20) for discussion of one Latin epistolary convention which does not seem to reflect colloquial language of the day, the use of *mi* 'my' with vocatives.

there is a further problem in detecting whether scribes were used, or whether the text is an autograph. Divergences of spelling may be significant, but it is difficult to be sure when one writer shows various aberrant spellings whether this really reflects his or her spoken practice, or simply written incompetence. A case in point is the sixth-century BCE Athenian black-figure vase painter Sophilos, who has left four vase paintings inscribed with his signature and a further two which can be confidently attributed to him (as well as further fragments), and who has the habit of writing the names besides mythological figures depicted on the vases, leaving just under fifty inscribed records of personal names. The language of Sophilos has been discussed recently both by Kilmer and Develin (2001) and by Hawkins (2012), and both studies claim that it is possible to attribute specific speech habits to Sophilos, reflected by unusual spellings such as *Patroqlus* (i.e. ΠΑΤΡΟϘΛΥΣ) for the genitive of the name Patrokleos, which would be expected to be spelt *Patrokleous* at this date. However, with such a small corpus it is doubtful whether meaningful conclusions can be drawn, particularly in the absence of a larger collection of Archaic Attic vase inscriptions against which we can judge Sophilos' idiosyncrasies. Sometimes deviant spellings can signify underlying peculiarities of diction, but sometimes they are just mistakes. In order to reach significant conclusions from documentary evidence of this type, it is necessary to have a more substantial collection of documents of a contemporary date and of similar types, or from a single speech community as reflected in a documentary archive. For example, a study by Evans (2012) of the third-century collection of Greek papyri known as the Zenon archive, comprising nearly 2,000 papyri from the Egyptian Fayyum, has shown that it is possible in some instances to detect whether a particular individual's language stands out from that of the rest of the archive, or in what contexts an individual's speech varies.

Clearly, the study of surviving original documentary text can never hope to attain anything like the results Labov could achieve in his New York survey, owing to the reliance on writing rather than speech. For modern languages, the standard variety usually has a fixed written orthography maintained by spell-checkers and dictionaries; when a non-standard spelling is found in a written text, it may reflect the spoken form, or confusion arising from imperfect education or the vagaries of the spelling system. Ancient languages had no standard orthography, despite the standard spelling for Greek and Latin employed by editions of classical texts and modern dictionaries such as the *Greek–English Lexicon* of Liddell and Scott or the *Oxford Latin Dictionary*. Scribal schools, or stone-cutters' workshops, undoubtedly had preferred spellings and conventions, but these could not be checked against any central authoritative source. Consequently, ancient papyrus or epigraphical texts often vary considerably in their spelling, both within the same document and among those of comparable age and provenance. The historical sociolinguist is constantly faced with the difficulty of interpreting this variation. We have already seen in Chapter 2 an example from Linear B texts, where small discrepancies in spelling are taken by some scholars as evidence of an actual sound change in progress, but by others as the result of scribes struggling with learned written forms which no longer correspond with what they actually say. Linear B shows far fewer alternate spellings than are found in later texts written in the Greek alphabet, but even here we are not sure what to make of the variation.

Furthermore, variation in spelling in ancient texts need not correlate with any variation in speech, but may rather reflect different orthographic practices. For example, in both Greek and Latin compound words may be formed by combining a verbal stem with elements which function as prepositions when they stand as independent words: hence *syn* 'with' and the stem *makh-* 'fight' can be combined to give the Greek noun *symmákhos* 'ally' and derivatives, and Latin *con-* 'with' combines with the stem *leg-* 'select' to form the nouns *collega* 'colleague' and *collegium* 'college'. In both languages these words can be written with an *n* or *m*, so in Greek inscriptions both *symmakh-* and *synmakh-* are found (the first spelling the norm in Classical times, with the unassimilated spelling becoming more frequent in the Roman period, Threatte 1980: 611–12). In Latin both *conlega* and *collegium* are found at different places on the copy of the *Res Gestae Divi Augusti* erected at Ancyra in Turkey, and similar variation is widely attested elsewhere, in both inscriptions and manuscript traditions.[7] However, we can be fairly certain that the spellings in both cases with *n* do not reflect the pronunciation of either word at any time in the history of Greek and Latin, since speakers of both languages would have automatically assimilated the *n* to the following consonant. The process can be compared to the way native speakers of English automatically pronounce the word *input* as *imput*, except in careful speech or special conditions. The fluctuation in writing in these examples shows that speakers are observing a convention whereby in compound words each element of the compound is spelt as it would be if it stood as a free-standing word. In the same way, alternation between the spellings *extra* and *exstra* in the Latin word for 'without' is insignificant for speech.

---

[7] See further Clackson (2011a: 246).

Other variations in spelling may be due to the ways in which words were written down or transcribed. Take for example the Greek verb *anéthēka* 'I dedicated' (or the third person form *anéthēken* 'he/she dedicated'). This occurs in around a dozen inscriptions written without the long *ē* vowel: *anethka* (i.e. ΑΝΕΘΚΑ rather than ΑΝΕΘΗΚΑ or ΑΝΕΘΕΚΑ). Although in many languages medial vowels do drop out in speech, in Greek this sort of change is unusual, and the spelling *anethka* can be better explained as a result of a mistake that many different Greek stone-cutters or scribes seem to have made as they spelt out the word, as cleverly explained by Rudolf Wachter (1991). Wachter suggested that, just as children usually learn to spell in syllables, so Greeks with limited literacy may have spelt out their words syllable by syllable, uttering the sound, and then carving the corresponding letter. Wachter showed that where vowels were dropped after consonants in this way, they generally correspond to the first syllable of the letter name; in the case of *anethka*, the letter Θ was known by the name *thēta*, with a long *e* in the first syllable. The writer of the word *anéthēka* might therefore understand Θ on its own to stand for the syllable – just as in modern SMS text messaging the sign 2 can stand for the first syllable of the word, as in *2day* 'today'. Investigating language variation in ancient societies is consequently frequently a balancing act between working out what is going on in speech, and what is going on in the writing system.

Representing language variation in literary texts: Greek comedy in the fifth century BCE

Variation in the language of individuals is not the only way in which we can approach the quest for unearthing differences in ancient spoken languages. Literary texts also frequently represent speech events and speech communities, and their evidence is vital for gaining an understanding of the range and types of different speech in the ancient world. Literature can also give access to some of the meanings of language alternations. Many ancient texts show varying registers of language, and ancient authors may employ different styles associated with individual characters, types of discourse, or types of metre (see the use of different dialect types in stichic verses and lyric passages in Greek tragedy discussed on p. 52). The Homeric epics employ a wide range of linguistic variables, some of them from different dialectal backgrounds, or reflecting more archaic stages of the language, retained or even extended in the long course of the oral transmission of the poems in order to give the bards a stock of words and phrases with equivalent function and meaning but different metrical values. However, among the abundance of linguistic variation in Homer, it is possible to detect some patterns of usage: for example, there is a higher preponderance of archaic linguistic forms in recurring scenes, such as preparing food, launching a boat, or making a sacrifice and battle narratives. One such archaic feature is the sound *w-*, which is often referred to as *digamma* from the shape of the ancient letter used to represent it, Ϝ, which looked to the Greeks like a combination of two gammas (Γ), one on top of the other. A number of Greek words were originally pronounced with a *w*, such as *érgon*, earlier *wergon*, meaning 'work' and indeed a distant cousin to the English word *work*. As the Greek language changed, and this sound dropped out of speech, it had knock-on effects on the way the bards composed the verses in metre. The more traditional scenes, and descriptions of warfare, show a higher proportion of words which have to be scanned as if they still have their original *w*, but in speeches made by characters and passages of drawn-out comparison, known as similes, there are more occasions when the sound does not count for the metre (Shipp 1972). Furthermore, it is also possible to isolate distinct patterns among the speech of individuals in the *Iliad* and *Odyssey*. A classic paper by Friedrich and Redfield (1978) reveals that Achilles has idiosyncrasies in his speeches that can be quantified and shown to distinguish him from other characters.[8] Linguistic variation of this sort may enhance the appreciation of Homer's artistry and characterization, or be significant for understanding the layers of composition within the oral epics, but it is not revealing about the everyday linguistic behaviour of any individual or community in the ancient world (except insofar as revealing that individuals may have had characteristic speech habits). The language of Homer is an entirely artificial literary idiom, which has no direct correspondence with any spoken Greek dialect of a single speech community, and variation in the Homeric epics does not correlate with speech variation in the society in which they were created.

From Athenian comic drama, however, we may gain a better idea of the place of language in society. In the words of Willi (2002b: 149): 'Greek comedy is not just a literary genre. It is also a vast set of sociocultural attitudes encoded in language.' Surviving comedies and comic fragments from fifth-century Athens, principally the corpus of works by Aristophanes, show characters speaking in a range of different styles, including different

---

[8] Achilles predominantly favours some particles or particle combinations (such as *nũn dé* 'but as it is'); he employs vocatives in a different way from other speakers; and he has a predilection for certain specific rhetorical moves.

Greek dialects (see Chapter 2). Although characters may not always be consistent in their language or linguistic choices, there does appear to be a correlation between linguistic features and representatives of certain well-defined groups, such as women, foreigners, or speakers of different dialects. Characters also sometimes undergo changes of costume, or disguises: for example, the kinsman in Aristophanes' *Thesmophoriazusae* is dressed up as a woman, while women disguise themselves as men in the *Ecclesiazusae* (note that the actors on the Athenian stage would all have been male, with the result that a man would have been playing a woman pretending to be a man). When characters in Aristophanes' plays cross-dress, they also attempt to fit in by using the words and expressions of the opposite sex, and they are represented as being corrected when they do so. For example, in the following passage the female protagonist Praxagora corrects a woman who is practising to take the part of a man in the Assembly (*Ecclesiazusae* 156–60).

WOMAN: I don't agree, by the two goddesses.
PRAXAGORA: By the two? Wretch, have you lost your mind?
WOMAN: What? I haven't asked for a drink?
PRAXAGORA: No, by Zeus, but you swore by the two goddesses although you're meant to be a man. Everything else you said was excellent.
WOMAN: OK. 'By Apollo.'

Praxagora recognizes that her oath 'by the two goddesses', i.e. by Demeter and her daughter Persephone, is an exclusively female trait, after which the speaker uses the exclusively male oath sworn by the god Apollo.

     We shall explore the evidence for linguistic differences between men and women in ancient societies further in Chapter 5. But the representation of gendered differences of speech and their recognition by characters within Aristophanes' plays do reveal that comedy could represent some diastratic variation, as well as the diatopic variation seen in the dialectal representation of non-Attic characters. However, in Aristophanes' comedies linguistic characterization is generally not continuous; that is to say, most characters on stage are not represented as speaking a single consistent variety, but switch between a range of different registers, including parodic representations of the speech of other literary or technical genres (Dover 1976, Willi 2002a: 29). Even in the case of the representation of female speech, Willi (2003: 196) observes that there is a greater proportion of distinctively female idioms in the opening scenes of the three plays which involve women as protagonists or major characters. Once the setting for feminine language has been established, the characters no longer show so many specific female markers; furthermore, the speech of some female characters, such as Lysistrata herself, generally does not show a preponderance of characteristically feminine features. The only characters who consistently use a distinctive linguistic idiom are either Athenian celebrities with some sort of speech impediment, or minor characters who do not occupy the stage for more than a scene or two, such as the dialect speakers in *Lysistrata* and *Acharnians*, or the Scythian Archer in the *Thesmophoriazusae*, who is represented as speaking a broken Greek without knowing the correct verbal or nominal endings (and also unable to pronounce some of the sounds of Greek).

As an example of the difficulty of tracking social variation in Aristophanes' plays, let us have a look at one particular linguistic variable. We have already noted in Chapter 2 that in an inscription recording a treaty between Athens and Chalcis in 446 BCE, the official parts of the treaty and those clauses added by individuals differ in the presence or absence of final -*i* in the dative plural ending of the first and second declension. In the Ionic dialect, and in earlier Attic dialect (the form which is used in official inscriptions until *c.* 420 BCE), the dative plural endings were *ēsi* (or -*āsi*) and -*oisi*, as in the phrase *kalêsi parthénoisi* 'for the fine girls', but after that time the official inscriptions tend to have -*ais* and -*ois* (as *kalaîs parthénois*). Aristophanes (and the tragedians) represent characters using both the endings -*aisi* and -*ais* (but not the inscriptional forms -*ēsi* or -*āsi*), and -*oisi* and -*ois*. Méndez Dosuna (2004: 179) counted up the occurrence of both the -*ois*/-*oisi* and the -*ais*/ -*aisi* endings in the speech of various characters in Aristophanes' play *The Clouds*. His figures are given in Table 4.1.

Strepsiades is the rustic and conservative hero of the play, and Pheidippides his more urbane and 'modern' son. Strepsiades uses a greater

Table 4.1 *Dative plural endings in Aristophanes* Clouds, *according to speaker*

	-*ois*	-*ais*	%	-*oisi*	-*aisi*	%
Pheidippides	9 (11)		100			0
Strepsiades	22 (35)	9 (11)	67.39	14	1	32.61
Socrates	3 (5)	5 (9)	57.14	4	2	42.86
Just Argument	5 (13)	2 (3)	50	6	1	50
Unjust Argument	4 (4)	0 (1)	40	4	2	60

Note: Figures in brackets represent total occurrences, including those in positions where final -*ois* occurs before a vowel, so may possibly represent -*ois*', i.e. -*oisi* with the regular loss of final -*i* before a following vowel.

proportion of the *-oisi* and *-aisi* variants (32.6 per cent), whereas
Pheidippides does not use any at all, and thus the evidence would appear
to support the view that the *-oisi* and *-aisi* endings were associated (by
the playwright and perhaps the audience) with the speech of older, more
traditional members of the public. However, in the *Clouds*, Socrates
represents the hyper-modern sophisticated intellectual, and he uses an
even greater number of *-oisi* and *-aisi* forms, and in the contest between
the Just and the Unjust argument, the Unjust represents the modern to the
Just's traditionalist position, so here the correlation between linguistic
form and character breaks down. Since official inscriptions are frequently
the most prone to preserve old-fashioned spellings and probably retain
archaic forms much later than speech, it has been suggested that the forms
-oisi and *-aisi* (and certainly *-ēsi* and *-āsi*) were not heard in spoken Attic,
and reflect only literary forms (Willi 2003: 241–2). Here the variation
represented by Aristophanes probably does not correspond to any real-
life variation in the streets and marketplaces of Athens.

The lack of consistent linguistic characterization in Aristophanes' plays
has generally meant that scholars have been unwilling to draw conclusions
about social variation (other than that involving women and foreigners)
from the linguistic variation in his plays, and, in his 2003 analysis of
variation in Aristophanes, Willi largely concentrated on the ways the
comedies represent different registers of spoken Greek. In representations
and parodies of religious and technical languages (such as the languages of
law, science and literary criticism), there are clear preferences for certain
sentence structures and vocabulary items, and means of forming new
words. For example, the suffix *-sis* is used in Greek to derive new abstract
nouns. Although it is already present in the language of Homer, fifth-
century prose writers start to employ the suffix to create new technical
terms in medicine, legalese and other areas loosely associated with the
itinerant fee-charging teachers of philosophy, rhetoric and science known
as 'Sophists'. Certain characters in Aristophanes, for example Socrates in
the *Clouds*, use the suffix freely to form words with a scientific or rhetorical
ring to them, such as *diálexis* 'discourse' (*Clouds* 317) and *perílexis* 'circum-
locution' (*Clouds* 318);[9] these two words are only attested here in Classical
Greek (Willi 2003: 134). Aristophanes may have picked Socrates to represent the typical Sophist, unfairly since Socrates didn't charge money for
his teaching. It could be for this reason that Aristophanes appears to have

---

[9] Two other *-sis* nouns also occur in *Clouds* line 318: *kroûsis* 'tapping' or 'chicanery', and *katálēpsis*
'seizing'.

missed out of his representation a feature that is characteristic of Socrates'
speech in Xenophon's portrayal in the *Memorabilia* (which also is found
in the representation of Socrates in Plato's dialogues, although there also
shared by other characters), i.e. the overuse of particularly affectionate
terms to address his interlocutors, of the type translated in English as 'my
good fellow' or 'my dear sir' (Dickey 1996: 119–27).

Aristophanes and other Greek comedians thus tell us a lot about how
Athenian free men saw outsiders: whether barbarians, Greeks of other
city-states, slaves or women; and they also show an awareness of register-
variation among elite males; but they give surprisingly little away about
social variation in the speech of Athenian men themselves. This may be
due to the fact that, as Willi has argued (2002b: 121–5), comedy attempts to
represent the language of the Athenians as a whole, and is not interested
in a socially divisive portrayal of the *polis*. However, comedy is not unaware
of linguistic divisions between social groups in the city, and we should not
be tempted to think that democracy necessarily flattened the variations,
since a famous fragment of Aristophanes separates out three different social
levels (and also, incidentally, shows how social values overlap with other
markers, such as gender, free status and country as opposed to town):
'Having the middle-of-the-road speech of the city, neither the more refined
effeminate variety, nor the more slavish country one' (Aristophanes Fr. 706
(*PCG*). We can perhaps make some guesses about what the markers of the
'refined effeminate' variety of speech to which Aristophanes refers are; this
will be examined in more detail in Chapter 5. But markers of the 'slavish
country' sociolect largely escape us. Despite the huge amount of literary
and inscriptional material surviving from Athens in the fifth century, the
lack of explicit statements about the language of the poor, and their low
participation in the epigraphic record of the city,[10] mean that our attempts
to find out about their speech rest on a very small amount of hard and fast
evidence, and a lot of guesswork and hypothesis. Thus, for example, Colvin
(2004) has argued from an inscribed potsherd with the verb 'I ostracize'
written *ostrakídō* (rather than the regular *ostrakízō*) that the Athenian
underclass would have used the sound -*d*- in words which our transmitted
texts spell with the letter Z, and which is usually thought to have represented a pronunciation /zd/ (Allen 1987: 56). But the supporting evidence,
although suggestive, is too scanty to be conclusive.

---

[10] Missiou (2011) argues for a higher rate of functional literacy among Athenian males than is usually
assumed; see the skeptical review of Jim (2011).

Representing language variation in literary texts: Rome, comedy and the novel

We are fortunate to have a much greater amount of surviving comedy written in Latin than in Greek, even though most of the Roman comic material is translated or adapted from Greek originals. The dramas and fragments of Roman comedy show that the genre also exhibited a great deal of variation, and some specific variables can be linked to the language of identifiable social groups, including women, old men and slaves.[11] However, the bulk of Roman comic writing comes from a period when we have very little other surviving Latin literature or inscriptional material: the twenty-one surviving comedies of Plautus were written before 180 BCE, and the six comedies of Terence before 160 BCE; the first complete prose work to survive is Cato's work *On Agriculture*, which also dates to about 160 BCE. Hence we lack the sort of background information that enables us to make some of the more refined decisions on comic usage and its relation to spoken Attic in the fifth century. Work on Roman comedy has consequently so far failed to find conclusive markers of social variation.[12]

A more rewarding literary account of social variation in the Latin language is found in the longest surviving portion of the *Satyrica*, a novel written in the first century CE by Petronius. The *Cena Trimalchionis*, as this section has come to be called, describes in extravagant detail a dinner party hosted by the wealthy freedman Trimalchio, where bad taste and excess culminate in the staging of a mock funeral for the former slave. Petronius represents the conversations at dinner, including a number of speeches by Trimalchio, his wife, and a band of fellow freedmen. In vocabulary, sentence structure, and word-endings, the speeches of the freedmen differ markedly from those of other characters in the novel and from the surrounding prose narrative. What is more, the characters themselves are aware of their linguistic foibles. This is most evident in a section of a long speech by Echion, identified as a collector of rags, who addresses Agamemnon, a pedantic teacher of rhetoric, who has been silent up to this point in the dinner, as follows:

> 'uideris mihi, Agamemnon, dicere: "Quid iste argutat molestus?" quia tu, qui potes loquere, non loquis. non es nostrae fasciae, et ideo pauperorum uerba derides. scimus te prae litteras fatuum esse. quid ergo est?'

---

[11] For the language of women see Chapter 5, pp. 124–34; for old men in comedy, see Clackson (2011b: 512–13); and for the language of slaves Clackson (2011b: 514–15).

[12] See Adams (2013: 537) for criticisms of the search for 'colloquial' features in the language of Terence in Karakasis (2005: 21–43).

'Agamemnon, you look like you are saying "What is this bore going on about?" Because you, who can speak, don't speak. You are not one of our gang, and so you laugh at the words of us 'umble folk. We know that you are mad for learning. What's it all about then?' (Petronius 46)

Agamemnon is presented as 'able to talk', meaning that he can speak correct or standard Classical Latin, but he holds back from the conversation, and instead laughs at the language of the freedmen, who belong to a different social group. It is certainly true that the narrator of this section is poking fun at the language of the freedmen, since the introductions and conclusions to their speeches include statements such as 'Such sweet conversation . . . ' (39); 'the dinner table sparkled with conversation' (47); 'Trimalchio, charmed by his fellow freedman's eloquence' (59). It is also true that the freedmen's speeches contain infringements of statements of grammarians (and most literary usage) in vocabulary and syntax; moreover, some of these departures from the norms are mirrored in subliterary documents and graffiti. Indeed, the language of the freedmen's speeches is so far removed from Classical Latin that when the *Cena Trimalchionis* was published in 1664, on the basis of a single manuscript, many scholars thought that it was a later forgery or pastiche, and passages were thought to reveal an original French or Italian version, imperfectly translated into Latin (Grafton 1990).

The non-standard features of the freedmen's language can be illustrated by consideration of some features of Echion's speech, of which the first sentences were given above. First, the word *pauperorum* is assigned to a different declension class than is normal in Classical Latin (it should be *pauperum* 'of the poor'), and we know that the grammarians censured this switch of declension (Palladius *GL* 4. 83–4, Appendix Probi). Second, in the expression *prae litteras* 'for learning', the preposition *prae* is followed by an accusative, whereas in Classical Latin it takes the ablative case; graffiti from Pompeii show other Latin speakers making the same mistake. Later in his speech Echion goes on to include a number of non-standard ways of expressing the future tense: *habituri sumus* for *habebimus* 'we shall have', *daturus est* for *dabit* 'he will give' and *persuadeam* in place of *persuadebo* 'I shall persuade'. The first two forms make use of a periphrasis of the verb *esse* 'to be' with a future participle, while the third employs the subjunctive mood in place of the future. Similar forms are also found in the papyrus letters of Claudius Terentianus writing at the beginning of the first century CE (Adams 1977: 49, see above p. 88 for Claudius Terentianus). Finally, Echion, like other freedmen, sometimes confuses the gender of nouns, making masculine nouns neuter (and vice versa), and turning Greek neuter

nouns (such as *stigma* 'brand') into Latin feminine nouns (hence the
accusative *stigmam*); these sorts of changes are also found in inscriptions
and other low-level Latin writings (Adams 2013: 419–26).

Petronius' representation of the freedmen's language undoubtedly contains pastiche, and incorporates some traditional comic parodies of the
speech of the lower class, freedmen and slaves (including second-language
speakers of Latin). The description of the dinner party includes portrayals
of nouveau-riche and uneducated excess: hundred-year-old wine is served,
a boar is stuffed with live birds which are then caught by fowlers, an
ungutted pig turns out to be full of sausages, Trimalchio allows a slave
boy to ride on his back, and the feast ends with an elaborate mock funeral.
The representation of language may once have been considered to be
equally over the top, but now seems more genuine given the growing
number of parallels from other subliterary material from around the
Empire at a similar date (see Adams 2003b for a collection). Furthermore,
the remarkable survival from Murecine near Pompeii of wax tablets, still
legible despite their carbonization by the eruption of Vesuvius, can show
something of how a real freedman from the Bay of Naples spoke Latin.
One of these tablets, dated to 15 September 39 CE, records a loan agreement
made by a grain merchant and former slave called Gaius Nouius Eunus. The
words he writes are standard formulaic legalese, but Gaius Nouius Eunus'
spelling shows that he is not pronouncing Latin the way that an educated
Roman would have done: he consistently spells Latin *Caesaris* 'of Caesar'
Cessaris, and he writes *quator* for the number *quattuor* 'four'.[13]

The parallels to the freedmen's linguistic foibles mean that Petronius
does seem to have been modelling his characters' language in part on real
speech. He is therefore an unparalleled source for language variation in
Latin, offering the clearest indication from the ancient world of the speech
of the sub-elite. What is more, the *Satyrica* helps to shed some light on
the social meanings of linguistic variation, and it is significant that it
represents individual speakers, some of them with distinct idiolects,[14]
changing register between conversational and literary or rhetorical styles.
Given that we know that there were considerable differences between the
education, wealth and social standing of freedmen in Roman society, it is
tempting to try to draw connections between the characters in Petronius

---

[13] See further Adams (1990) and Clackson and Horrocks (2007: 238–41) on Gaius Nouius Eunus'
Latin.
[14] An idiolect is the term for an individual's particular speech, i.e. a 'dialect' of one person. See Boyce
(1991) for an analysis of the language of different speakers in the *Satyrica* (with the corrections of
Adams 2003b).

and their language. Thus Echion, who, as we have seen, has a high level of departures from the norm in his speeches, is a dealer in rags and mistrustful of the benefits of education; he has property in the country, but this he only describes as *casulae* 'little huts' (46.2). On the other hand, the freed-man Hermeros, who is the speaker most likely to employ Greek phrases and exclamations in the novel, boasts of having to provide for a household of twenty people (57.6). On the basis of a fictional work it is, however, difficult to draw any strong conclusions from these correlations. While Petronius' novel does present a remarkable window onto language varia-tion in first-century CE Italy, it is far removed from a study of the type Labov made on spoken English in New York.

However, Petronius' vivid picture both of the language of freedmen and of the reaction to them from the educated guests at the dinner party does tie in with other anecdotal evidence about attitudes towards the language of the lower classes in Rome. Various other testimonia from Rome in the late Republican and Imperial ages also show a link between certain speech 'errors' and social status. Perhaps the most famous literary example is provided by Catullus' comments on the unfortunate Arrius in poem 84:

> **Chommoda** *dicebat, si quando* **commoda** *uellet*
> *dicere, et* **insidias** *Arrius* **hinsidias***,*
> *et tum mirifice sperabat se esse locutum*
> *cum quantum poterat dixerat* **hinsidias***.*
> *credo, sic mater, sic liber auunculus eius,*
> *sic maternus auus dixerat atque auia.*

> Arrius said 'hadvantages', when he wished to say 'advantages', and, when he wants to say 'ambush', he says 'hambush', and he hoped that he was speak-ing remarkably well, when he had said 'hambush' as loudly as he could. In the same way, I believe, his mother, his free uncle, his maternal grandfather and grandmother used to speak.

Arrius has the same tendency that we saw in Eliza Doolittle, both speakers of a dialect with *h*-dropping, but with hypercorrect *h* added in the wrong places. Arrius combines this with a second, slightly different hypercorrec-tion, aspirating the initial *c* in the word *commoda* 'advantages', perhaps through influence from Greek, or a desire to imitate it (and thereby sound educated or 'posh'), since Greek had distinct aspirated consonants *kh, ph* and *th* alongside *k, p* and *t*. Catullus joins this slur on Arrius' speech with a comment about the servile origins of his mother's side of the family. Cicero also comments on the hypercorrect addition of *h* to consonants in his rhetorical treatise *Orator* (160), which is set in 91 BCE (although written four decades later), and reveals that some of the standard Latin pronunciations were in origin hypercorrections:

> quin ego ipse, cum scirem ita maiores locutos ut nusquam nisi in uocali aspiratione uterentur, loquebar sic ut pulcros, Cetegos, triumpos, Cartaginem dicerem; aliquando, idque sero, conuicio aurium cum extorta mihi ueritas esset, usum loquendi populo concessi, scientiam mihi reseruaui.

> Indeed, I myself, since I knew that our ancestors did not employ the aspirate anywhere except with a vowel [i.e. before an initial vowel or between two vowels] I used to say *pulcer* ['beautiful', for later *pulcher*], *Cetegus* [a Roman cognomen, for later *Cethegus*], *triumpus* ['triumph', for later *triumphus*] and *Cartago* ['Carthage', for later *Carthago*], but after some time – a long time in fact – the true pronunciation was wrested from me by the protest of my ears, and I gave way to the people in the way of speech, and kept my learning to myself.

Note further that hypercorrect *h* is condemned as *rusticus* (here meaning the opposite of *urbanus* 'cultured', 'refined') by the scholar Nigidius Figulus, a contemporary of Cicero and Catullus (cited by Gellius 13.6.3, see also Adams 2007: 174). These three different sources reveal an anxiety about speaking in the correct fashion in the late Republic, and the differing pulls towards the pronunciations which were sanctioned by previous usage and hypercorrect forms which had gained popularity. Hypercorrect forms which could be shown to be in error owing to their formation (such as *hinsidia* and *chommodus*, which could be recognized as compounds involving *in* 'in' and *con-* 'with') were avoided in later written Latin. But where there was no such direction, or no Greek origin possible for the word (as is the case with *Cethegus, triumphus* and *Carthago*), the hypercorrect form won out, as it also did for the word for 'shoulder' *humerus*, which can be shown, from modern etymological research (it is cognate with Greek *ômos* 'shoulder'), to have a hypercorrect initial *h*.

Language variation and language change

Ancient depictions of members of society other than the elite consequently go some way towards the recognition that different levels of language were employed by different social classes. As we have seen, ancient authors such as Cicero also acknowledge that their language may vary according to different stylistic registers. However, although it is known that there was variation across an ancient speech community, and furthermore that this variation sometimes correlated with social status, it is much less certain whether a particular word, pronunciation or grammatical form is a significant social variable at any particular place and point in time. The care with which the inscriptional record of the Athenian treaty with Chalcis appears to differentiate dative plurals with or without final *-i* does not seem to be mirrored in the comedians' depictions of characters, so we are left uncertain about the social significance, if any, of this variation. Or, to take another example, although Petronius has two characters (Echion and Trimalchio) substitute the accusative for the ablative case after the preposition *prae*, a solecism mirrored in the Pompeian inscriptions, we do not know how widespread this construction was, or at what levels of society it occurred.

The Renaissance critics of the first edition of Petronius' description of the language of the freedmen, who imagined Italian or French constructions underlying non-Classical usages, unwittingly realized that many of the substandard elements, in terms of Classical Latin, of the speeches were the very same features that won out over time in the spoken language. As we saw earlier, modern accounts of language variation show that a feature which is originally associated with a specific social group may be adopted by all the speakers in a community, hence linking social variation with linguistic change. In the history of English, numerous changes over the past thousand years are thought to be 'changes from below', i.e. features of lower-class speech which eventually become incorporated into the language. Many scholars have in consequence uncritically accepted a similar model for change in Greek and Latin. Hence the search for social variation in Latin and Greek often becomes entwined with the study of language change, and sometimes the two are lumped together. For example, the language of the sub-elite in the Roman world, which is commonly termed 'Vulgar Latin', is thus closely linked to later stages of Latin, both in handbooks and in scholarly discourse. Note for example, that there is an ongoing regular series of conferences devoted to 'Vulgar and Late Latin'. These assumptions lead to the view that if there is unexpectedly early evidence for a sound change or another linguistic development, this must reveal a social dialect.

Examples of this sort of thinking are not difficult to find. Aristophanes represents the Scythian Archer in the *Thesmophoriazusae* as speaking a kind of debased 'foreigners' Greek'. He cannot decline nouns or conjugate verbs according to Attic rules, and is unable to pronounce Greek 'aspirated' consonants *ph, th* and *kh* (represented by the Greek letters φ, θ and χ). The Scythian also mangles the vowels of Attic Greek, not differentiating

between the two long vowels represented by the Attic spellings *i* and *ei*
(which sound respectively like French *i* and *é*); thus he says *péri* where
an Athenian would say *phérei* 'he carries' and *akoloúti* for *akoloúthei* 'he
follows'. There is abundant evidence from the third century BCE that many
speakers merged the vowels represented by the spellings *ei* and *i* (Modern
Greek speakers pronounce both the same). Confusion between the sounds
represented by *ei* and *i* is evident already from the fifth century BCE in
inscriptions and some vocabulary items, such as *hīmátion* 'cloak', the
diminutive of an archaic and poetic word for 'garment' *heîma* (Hawkins
2012: 152–4). This led Brixhe (1988) to suggest that the Scythian had picked
up his Greek from the lowest social classes of Athens, and that he spoke
not just with a non-Greek accent, but also the uneducated Attic of the
underclass. Willi argued (2003: 202–3) against taking Brixhe's conclusions
as certain, however, since the inability to distinguish these vowels may
reflect the Scythian's native language, rather than the source of his Greek
knowledge. We can add to this: the assumption that the later pronunciation is necessarily linked to any sub-elite variant is also unproven.

In Latin too, the association of what has been called 'Vulgar Latin' with
the language of the underclass has recently been robustly countered by
Adams (2013). He notes that some of the features that are covered by the
catch-all term 'Vulgar Latin' can also be found recorded at various times as
features of the speech of members of the Roman elite, and moreover turn
up in the works of 'good writers'. For example, the dropping of initial *h*
is mentioned explicitly in a sermon by Augustine (*Serm.* 1.18.29). Adams
argues that Augustine implies that the pronunciation of the aspirate is
pedantic and overly reliant on trying to reproduce the speech of a former
era; for the Christian, saving souls is more important. Adams also notes
that a dictation error by Cerialis, the commanding officer at the Roman
Fort at Vindolanda on Hadrian's Wall in the early second century CE,
shows that he did not pronounce the initial *h-*. Moreover, loss of *h* in words
such as *uehemens* 'violent' or *nihil* 'nothing' is nowhere seen as a substandard variation. Romans were keen that the orthography with initial *h-* was
maintained in writing, but we cannot jump to the conclusion that it was
only members of the servile class who dropped it in speech. Most likely,
speakers of all classes during the Empire dropped *h-* on occasion.

Adams (2013) further emphasizes the finding from modern linguistics
that all speakers in a community may upgrade or play down their con-
formity to the standard at different times. He reminds us that 'Vulgar
Latin' should be taken as a label for language which does not follow the
precepts of grammarians, rather than the language of an undifferentiated

sub-elite or social group. Vergil and Cicero themselves did not follow the precepts of the grammarians (as commentators such as Servius were at pains to explain to readers of the *Aeneid* and *Georgics*). As Quintilian states (*Inst.* 1.6.27), 'speaking grammatically is not the same as speaking Latin'.[15] Furthermore, some of the changes in Latin over time seem to reflect change from above as well as from below. That is to say, some features found in the Romance languages derived from spoken Latin reflect usages found in Roman elite writers and even the grammarians themselves. One such feature is the construction of the future through the combination of an infinitive and the verb meaning 'have' (of the type *amare habeo*, the ultimate source of the French future *j'aimerai* 'I will love' and Italian *amerò* 'I will love'), which is almost only found with this meaning in Latin technical or grammatical works (Adams 2013: 657–8). 'Change from above' was also clearly operational at some times in the history of Greek; we have already seen in Chapter 2 (p. 54) how some features of literary Attic won out in the *koinḗ*, such as the use of *ss* rather than the more widespread Athenian variant *tt*. Indeed, at different times the choice of a lexical item such as *thálassa* or *thálatta* to refer to the 'sea' could have very different meanings. In fifth-century BCE Athens *thálassa* was the more elevated literary form, while in the second century CE the Atticist form *thálatta* had acquired greater cultural pretensions.

A survey such as this can only touch on some of the considerable body of research into linguistic variation in the ancient world. Variation is widespread both in ancient literary works and in surviving documentary and epigraphical texts. Sometimes variation in the written record has no straightforward correlation with variation in ancient speech. We have already noted that the variation found in Homeric Greek (which papyrus 'school texts' from Egypt indicate was as overwhelming for the ancient learner as it is for the modern student) is an artificial effect created by the long oral history of the epic. Variation in spelling in ancient texts is sometimes taken to be indicative of speech differences, but may simply reflect variation in orthographic traditions, or a speech habit which is widespread but for which the spelling has become fixed at a certain date. Thus, in the late Republic the Latin spellings *ei* and *i* could both be used to spell the same sound, but the choice between them was dictated by considerations other than spelling, for which the satirist Lucilius attempted to give rules (see Colson 1921). In later centuries *ae* stood for a vowel

---

[15] On Quintilian as a grammarian, see Ax (2011: 2–17).

which was no longer pronounced as a combination of two vowels (i.e. a diphthong) by any but the most pedantic speakers, but which continues to be represented by its ancient spelling in the orthography of the educated (Clackson 2011b: 516–17). The challenge for the historical sociolinguist is twofold. First, to work out which variations in our texts correlated to real variations in speech; and second, to try to understand whether ancient communities interpreted these speech differences as indicative of social background or status.

CHAPTER 5

Language, gender, sexuality

Introduction

Dio Chrysostom delivered his first speech to the inhabitants of the city of Tarsus in Asia Minor sometime between 105 and 115 CE (Salmeri 2000: 78 n. 126). The speech is a curious work, since the orator spends most of his time criticizing the people for habitually 'snorting', making an unpleasant sound with their noses that makes the visitor want to block his ears.[1] In order to hammer home his objection to this noise, Dio compares what would happen if the men spoke with female voices:

> Well then, supposing certain people should as a community be so afflicted that all the males got female voices and that no male, whether young or old, could say anything man-fashion, would that not seem a grievous experience and harder to bear, I'll warrant, than any pestilence, and as a result would they not send to the sanctuary of the god and try by many gifts to propitiate the divine power? And yet to speak with female voice is to speak with human voice, and nobody would be vexed at hearing a woman speak. (Dio Chrysostom *Oration* 33.38, trans. H. Lamar Crosby)

Dio suggests that for men to speak like women would be considered an affliction worse than the plague, and one that would cause an immediate public call for divine intervention. His invocation of the calamity of men's loss of a distinctively male speech pattern underscores the importance of looking at the link between gender and language. Gender intersects with all the aspects of language discussed in this book so far: the language choices made by bilinguals, the utterance of non-standard linguistic variants, even the progression of language change. The study of gendered speech further cuts across divisions of time, place and social structures, and scholars have observed cross-cultural similarities in the ways in which male and female

---

[1] See Salmeri (2000: 83–4) for references to speculation about what Dio might have meant by this 'snorting'.

speakers choose to differentiate themselves through language. Modern studies have consistently shown the importance of gender in addressing questions of language use: the sex of the speaker and the sex of the addressee are major factors in determining what speakers say and how they say it in every society in the modern world, and it is unlikely that the ancient world was any different.[2]

Gender differences in speech

Although there is no doubt that women and men spoke differently in the ancient world, scholars have had difficulty in elucidating exactly how those differences played out in actual speech. This partly reflects the fact that most of our surviving evidence from the ancient world is written by men for men. Very few works by female poets and prose writers survive from the ancient world (see the collection by Plant 2004). In the last two centuries surviving fragments of and references to the Greek poetesses Sappho, Corinna, Erinna and Nossis in the manuscript tradition have been supplemented by papyrus finds, and three other Greek female versifiers are attested among the inscriptions left on the legs of the Colossus of Memnon (Iulia Balbilla, Damo and Cecilia Trebulla, see Cirio (2011) for texts and commentary). The Latin evidence is even more scarce: from the early years of the Empire, there are six elegiac epigrams in the Tibullan corpus under the name of Sulpicia, and two surviving verses attributed to another Sulpicia, a contemporary of the epigrammatist Martial. The Christian martyrdom account from North Africa at the beginning of the third century CE, entitled the *Martyrdom of SS Perpetua and Felicitas*, includes a first-person account attributed to Perpetua, which has been dubbed 'the first preserved autobiographical account written by an ancient woman'.[3] From the fourth century CE, the evidence is bulked out by a more substantial prose account of a pilgrimage to the Holy Land by a woman known either as Egeria or Aetheria, and an epic poem about the life of Christ ascribed to Faltonia Betitia Proba, which is composed by cobbling together lines of Vergil with the addition of some biblical names. Other texts attributed to female authors, such as the Pythagorean philosopher Theano, are likely to be later confections rather than genuine survivals.

---

[2] Much has been written since the influential studies of Labov (1966; 2006) and Trudgill (1974) on social variation which drew attention to gender as an important sociolinguistic variable. See Eckert and McConnell-Ginet (2013) for a recent re-edition of a standard handbook.

[3] Bremmer and Formisano (2012: 1); see also Heffernan (2012) for a recent commentary on the text. It is not certain, however, that the narrative is not a confection in Perpetua's name.

Indeed, there is debate over whether the poems attributed to Erinna are really the work of a sixth-century woman, and not the fictive persona of a male poet (West 1977). There is a greater amount of surviving subliterary material written or commissioned by women (see the collection of epistolary material from Egypt gathered by Bagnall and Cribiore 2006), but the usefulness of much of this is constrained by the formulaic nature of correspondence or of commemorative mortuary inscriptions.

For all of the female writers in the ancient world, it is difficult, perhaps impossible, to isolate what is specific to the poet herself and what, if anything, can be ascribed to her gender. In the absence of substantial corpora of text written at the same date and in the same place by individuals of both sexes, any attempt to identify which linguistic features are peculiar to either women or men are doomed, if not to complete failure, certainly to only very partial success. We have seen in Chapter 4 that literary representations of speech can be helpful in assessing ancient linguistic variation, but here again, caution about what can be gleaned from the surviving textual record is necessary. The ancient convention of representing inserted direct speech in narrative in the same register as the surrounding text (see p. 46 above) means that we are unlikely to gain much insight into how women actually spoke from passages such as the speech of Diotima, reported by Socrates in Plato's *Symposium*. We have a better chance of gaining ancient (male) ideas of the characteristics of female speech from depictions of women in comedy, and in the testimonia of ancient commentators, grammarians and others.

In Chapter 4 (p. 110) we saw already that Aristophanes was able to play with concepts of linguistic variation between the sexes, and based some of his comedy on the switching of gender roles and speech when characters transition between male and female identities. The example given there plays on the existence of oaths which were exclusive to either sex, a gender-based language trait common to both Latin and Greek and doubtless other languages of the ancient world, reflecting the fact that the cultic practices of men and women were different. Aristophanes also plays with the expectations the audience has of male and female characters in other areas of discourse. For example, in the cross-dressing scene in the *Thesmophoriazusae* (lines 253–4), where Euripides' kinsman adopts female clothes (borrowed from the poet Agathon) in order to infiltrate a woman-only festival, linguistic codes are transgressed the moment the gendered garments are put on:

EURIPIDES: This pretty dress here, try it on first.
KINSMAN: By Aphrodite, it has a nice smell of weenie.
                   (translation by J. Henderson, Loeb Classical Library)

The oath 'by Aphrodite' is used elsewhere in Aristophanes only by female characters, and marks out the gendered nature of the kinsman's speech. This may be further reinforced by the word translated 'weenie', *posthíon*, which is a diminutive form of the vulgar word for penis, *pósthē* (just as the translation term is a diminutive of *wiener* 'sausage'). The kinsman uses the same word *posthíon* later in his speech in the next scene to the women at the festival when in disguise (515), but otherwise the term is attested only once in the Aristophanic comedies, in the semi-barbarous language of the Scythian Archer later in the same play.[4] Commentators usually understand the diminutive form *posthíon* to be a slighting or affectionate reference to the manhood of the notoriously effeminate poet Agathon, who lends the dress (e.g. Austin and Olsen 2004: 136–7), but the joke surely lies in the incongruity of the obscenity coming from a woman's mouth. The selection of the diminutive may even be a vain attempt to feminize the vulgarity, in line with ancient observations, and the comic practice, that women favoured words with the ancient equivalents to English *-let, -ling* or *-kins* (Gilleland 1980: 181, Bain 1984).

In her novels, Jane Austen never attempts to reproduce the language of men talking amongst themselves when there is no woman present, but ancient male writers were not so fastidious about imagining how the other sex spoke. Aristophanes, Menander and the Roman comedians are happy to set scenes where women are the only characters on stage, and other ancient sources on female speech are ready to pronounce on the habits of women speakers when no man is present. Thus, in a much-cited passage in discussions of gendered language in the ancient world, Cicero has Crassus, a character in his dialogue *De oratore* (3.12.45–7), state that his mother-in-law Laelia has retained a pure and unspoilt diction owing to the fact that she has not conversed with many other people in her life. Crassus' statement about Laelia reflects a more widespread prejudice (not limited to the ancient world), that silence was the best state for women: compare, for example, the proverbial phrase 'silence confers credit on women' (Sophocles *Ajax* 293). The representations of women in literature are accordingly prone to reflect what male authors thought was appropriate or befitting for their female characters.

The difficulty of separating what men thought women said and what women actually said runs through all the evidence from the ancient world. Take, for example, the case of the personal addresses with *anime (mi)* '(my)

---

[4] See Chapter 4, p. 119–20 above for the language of this character.

mind, soul' or *anima* (*mea*) '(my) soul, life' in Latin.[5] The ancient commentator Donatus (writing on Terence *An.* 685) observed that *anime mi* was a suitable blandishment in the mouth of a woman, and this phrase is more frequent in the speeches of female characters than those of male characters in Roman comedy (as noted by Adams 1984: 71 and Dickey 2002: 158). But does this reflect reality? In the Latin writing tablets excavated from the fort of Vindolanda on Hadrian's Wall, there are only two cases of the address *anima mea* 'my soul', both occurring in the three surviving letters by Claudia Severa, wife of Aelius Brocchus. The documentary evidence might therefore seem to confirm the view of how women spoke found in Donatus. However, the phrase *anima mea* 'my soul' is also found in the published correspondence of well-known male authors, including Cicero's letters to his wife and son, and the missives from the emperor Marcus Aurelius to Fronto. Like most other words and phrases in Latin and Greek, the address 'my soul' is thus not exclusive to either one or other sex, but exists in the language of both. In order to confirm that it really is a marker of female speech, we need to be sure that it is more prevalent in the language of women, or, in other words, that it is a 'sex-preferential' feature. The evidence we currently possess does not yet allow us to make that decision. The phrase occurs among the Vindolanda tablets only in letters composed by a woman, but the bulk of the correspondence from the site deals with military or camp matters, such as requests for provisions or the loan of castrating shears, and does not contain the same level of intimacy and affection that is found in, for example, Claudia Severa's invitation to her friend Sulpicia Lepidina to her birthday party. Until we have a more representative corpus of everyday letters written by both women and men, we can't be certain that in the same circumstances women would employ a particular phrase any more than men.

Such limited evidence has not held back modern scholars from attempting to describe female language. The description of Sulpicia's Latin by the nineteenth-century philosopher and poet Otto Friedrich Gruppe gives a vivid instance of the sexism found in older discussions of gendered speech, which linked language to wider conceptions of women's capabilities (this pattern is also found in ancient writers, for example Plutarch, who stated that speech naturally reflected the (inferior) character and disposition of women (*Moralia* 142d)):

> On close inspection the critic will readily recognise here a *feminine Latin*, impervious to analysis by rigorous linguistic method, but which finds

---

[5] The following discussion is based on Dickey (2002: 157–9) and Clackson (2011b: 510–11).

natural, simple expressions for everyday ideas without conscious and artistic elaboration of style, and in which the sense is augmented and assisted by free *constructio ad sensum*. (Gruppe 1838: 49, cited and translated by Lowe 1988: 194)

Commentators from the twentieth century identified 'feminine syntax' in passages spoken by women in the Homeric epics.[6] No one actually defined what feminine syntax was, but its characteristics included perceived illogicality, missing clauses and the tendency to lose the thread of the sentence. In his monumental work on Greek particles, Denniston (1934: lxxiii) proposed, on the basis of a tiny sample of ancient textual evidence, that Greek women would have been more prone to fill their speech with particles (words which could be used to emphasize, contrast or highlight), 'just as women of today are fond of underlining words in their letters'.

In more recent years, research into gender differences in the ancient world has refocused attention on women's language. Ground-breaking in this regard have been the studies by Adams (1984) and Bain (1984) on Latin comedy and Menander respectively, even though they mainly dealt with male representations of women's speech. Both studies show that ancient observations about feminine preference for diminutive forms, or particular vocabulary items, were borne out in the comedies. Furthermore, these investigations unearthed sex-preferential linguistic phenomena which had escaped the notice of ancient commentators. For example, Adams demonstrated that women in Roman comedy tend to use a greater predominance of 'polite' forms, using modifiers equivalent to 'please' with requests more frequently than male characters, and preferring *amabo* 'I will like' (= 'please') to the masculine *quaeso* 'I ask' or 'I demand'. This pattern is mirrored by Willi's (2003) finding that female characters in Greek comedy favoured 'polite' forms and discourse strategies. Since Adams (1984) and Bain (1984), many researchers have sought to unearth further cases of words or speech styles which either are exclusive to women, or which are more frequent in representations of female speech than that of males.[7]

Modern sociolinguistic work has also fed into the debate. Once again, Labov's work on the stratification of speech in New York City (1966, 2006), discussed in Chapter 4, and his subsequent studies, have led the way in the modern understanding of gender differentiation in language.

---

[6] Gildersleeve (1907: 209) on Hera's speech at *Iliad* 14.331–6, Stanford (1947–8) on *Odyssey* 4.681, 6.262, 19.351 and 23.174–6, see also Mossman (2001: 376).

[7] See Fögen (2004, 2010) for summaries of this work, and Kruschwitz (2012a) for a reconsideration in terms of social network theory and power dynamics.

Labov observed that a greater proportion of lower middle-class and working-class women than men modified their utterances towards the standard language (i.e. the socially more prestigious variety) in formal settings, or when reading out passages, or when asked to repeat something by the researcher. Moreover, for the pronunciation of some variables (such as differing vowel qualities), women showed a greater range between their most formal style and their conversational style. They were thus sometimes, in their least formal styles, the leaders in innovatory changes in the non-standard dialect (what Labov and others have called 'change from below'). A third result was also significant: in assessing their own speech, and in self-criticism, women showed a greater linguistic insecurity than men. Labov summarizes his findings (2006: 197) as follows: '[w]e observe the tendency of women to favor prestige forms; their extreme shift in formal styles; and most importantly, their leading position in change from below.'

Labov's findings can help us understand a paradox in the ancient evidence concerning female speech. Crassus' observation (in Cicero's *De oratore*, cited above) that his mother-in-law has kept her language unchanged appears to chime with Socrates' statement that women best preserve the archaic form of speech (Plato *Cratylus* (418c)). However, closer inspection of the context reveals that the Platonic passage is more complex. In the dialogue *Cratylus*, which addresses the question of whether words have their meaning by convention or not, Socrates gives a number of etymologies for Greek words to show that sound and sense are intrinsically related. In support of some of these etymologies, he refers to forms used by women. Socrates claims that Greeks of an earlier time, and women of his day, tend to substitute the sound *i* for *ē* and *d* for *z*, so that they say *himérā* in place of *hēmérā* 'day' and *duogón* in place of *zugón* 'yoke'.[8] However, neither Plato nor Socrates had access to the historical development of Greek, and the discipline of comparative and historical linguistics is able to show that these pronunciations are not in fact old-fashioned, but innovations in respect of the standard dialect of Athens. Scholars have disagreed about how to explain the apparent contradiction that women were thought to speak in an archaic manner while the cited examples of female speech are recent creations. Sommerstein (1995) was of the opinion that the variant pronunciations of Athenian women were low prestige forms, borrowed from the neighbouring Boeotian dialect and established

---

[8] In each instance, the form cited by Socrates is used in support of an etymology he gives for the word; in the case of *duogón* the extra *o* helps Socrates to connect the Greek word for 'two', *duó*.

in the speech of the Athenian underclass.[9] Willi (2003: 160–2) took the
same forms to be evidence that Athenian women were, in fact, employing
the more socially prestigious linguistic innovations of their day, in line with
Labov's first finding, that women in modern urban settings tend to favour
more socially prestigious language. While it is problematic to place much
weight on the pronunciations attributed to women by Plato, which are not
supported by any direct evidence, and it may not be appropriate to push
the modern parallels too far, it is possible to align the interpretation of the
female speakers of Attic closer to Labov's research. Some ancient women
may have favoured prestige language in formal surroundings (we shall see
further evidence for this later in this chapter), and this may have been
perceived by contemporaries to be archaic diction. But, as in New York,
some women may also have led the way in language change by using the
most extreme forms of substandard language at other times and in other
contexts. In Plato's *Cratylus*, the two phenomena have just been telescoped
into a single statement.

The dynamics of female dialectal choices in the urban setting of ancient
Athens may not have been typical for speakers at all times in the ancient
world, any more than the speech patterns of New York City can be
generalized across the modern world. Nevertheless, Labov's findings that
women tend to be at the forefront of language change have been repeated
in studies focused not just on contemporary urban environments but also
on rural western Europe, where women have been shown to be the
innovators in adopting linguistic varieties that are associated with education and commerce, in contrast with rural males, who continue to use
dialectal forms.[10] Indeed, dialect specialists know that their best informants
for obscure regional words are what are known as *NORMs*: non-mobile
older rural males. In other situations around the world, however, particularly in cases involving the imposition of a state or colonial language on
indigenous populations, women have been the preservers of traditional
modes of speech and idioms (Langslow 2002: 28). Among Romani speakers
in northern Greece, for example, it is often women who are most adept at
the archaic and conservative varieties of the language, while men use codes
which mix Romani and Greek (see Matras 2002: 245–6 and Sechidou 2005
on Finikas Romani spoken in Thessaloniki). Indigenous languages typically survive longer in the domain of the household, while the new or

---

[9] I have already discussed the use of *d* for *z* on a potsherd with the verb *ostrakídō* 'I ostracize' on p. 113.
[10] The classic study is by Gal (1978, 1979) on the Austrian village of Oberwart; see also Eckert and
McConnell-Ginet (2013: 240–3) for further examples.

dominant language prevails outside the home, in the market, the factory, the law court and the town hall.

There are clear ancient analogues with the modern processes of colonialism in the expansion of Greek and Latin around the shores of the Mediterranean from the Hellenistic period through to late antiquity. As in the colonial case, in many areas of the ancient world local languages coexisted alongside Greek and Latin, the dominant languages of the army, imperial officials and merchants. In most cases we have little access to the language spoken in the domestic sphere, but there is one ancient community where the cumulative evidence can begin to give us an idea of gender and language use. As already mentioned, the largest surviving sample of texts written by women comes from papyrus letters composed in Egypt between 300 BCE and 800 CE (collected and published by Bagnall and Cribiore 2006). After the fourth century CE, the Coptic language, the last phase of ancient Egyptian, first spreads beyond strictly monastic settings and begins to feature in the correspondence of individuals alongside Greek (which was the principal medium for epistolary texts since the Hellenistic period). Writers now have the option to compose letters in Coptic as well as in Greek, which was not possible before. Most day-to-day correspondence at this period was of course written by scribes, rather than by the person in whose name the letter is sent, but it appears that during the late antique period there was a widespread availability of scribes proficient in either language. The correlations between language choice and gender in the Egyptian epistolary material after 400 CE are striking: Bagnall and Cribiore (2006: 19) note that women 'simply disappear as writers of letters in Greek after the fourth century'. Men also write in Coptic during this period, so the situation is more complex than a gender split of men using Greek and women using Coptic, but women's choice of Coptic over Greek when they are the authors of a letter is surely significant (Cribiore 2001: 78).

A more detailed account of the complete corpus of surviving epistolary material from an individual community in fourth-century Egypt can help put the language choices of women into context, through consideration of their correspondents. The village of Kellis is one of a string of ancient settlements situated along the Dakleh Oasis, over 700 km to the southwest of Cairo in the middle of the Egyptian western desert. Excavations since 1978, particularly those undertaken in the 1990s by a team from Monash University, have yielded a large number of papyri from the settlement, including literary works and account books, as well as texts written in Coptic, Syriac and Greek associated with the Manichaean religion. Not all of the surviving texts from Kellis, reckoned to number

Table 5.1 *Published letters from Kellis sorted by gender and language*

	From women, addressed to men, women or uncertain	From men, addressed to women	From men, addressed to men	Fragmentary – addressee and author uncertain	Total
Coptic	5	13	12	5	35
Greek	0	2	26	4	32

over 2,000 in total, have yet been edited, but several dozen letters are now published. What makes these papyri particularly noteworthy is the early date: none of them is later than 392 CE, which means that the Coptic letters are some of the earliest examples in existence. In Clackson (2012b) I gave the language of each letter according to its author and addressee in a table reproduced in Table 5.1.

The numbers in this sample are not large, but the conclusion is the same as that reached by Bagnall and Cribiore, and further shows men's preference for using Coptic in correspondence intended for a female audience. These findings must be used with some caution: Bagnall has recently discussed (Bagnall 2011: 75–94) the context of the Kellis documents, and has shown that, even though some letters mix Greek and Coptic in the same document, it is not fully evident that all members of the community were bilingual (although he also notes that no woman writes in Greek). Most of the Coptic texts come from a particular area of the settlement, and there is no example of a letter written in Coptic with either an addressee or an author who does not have either an Egyptian name, or a specifically Christian name if it is Greek. There are thus additional factors to a pure gender split at work here. Analysis of other self-contained archives from Egypt tells a similar story: for example, in one bilingual collection of letters and contracts involving a boatman Patermouthis and his wife Kako from Syene (modern Aswan) in the sixth century, business deals which involve Kako on her own are written in Coptic, and the others in Greek. In a Greek sales contract from the same archive (*P.Münch.* I 13.71), two women with Egyptian names sign, having declared that the text 'has been read to us and translated into Egyptian' (Fournet 2009: 445).

Was women's preference for the local language over the language of the administration and the 'public sphere' limited to late antique Egypt or did it also hold true at earlier periods? As we have seen, in Egypt at earlier periods letters to and from women are written in Greek. Yet it could be that the use of scribes to write letters, and the invisibility of interpreters in the ancient record (as discussed in Chapter 1), hide more complex linguistic situations. Telling in this respect is a second-century CE private letter of unknown provenance (but certainly from Egypt) sent by Ptolemaios to his mother Zosime and her sister Rhodus, in which the errant son attempts to exculpate himself from various accusations of bad behaviour (*SB* 18 13867, cited in Bagnall 1993: 234 and discussed in Rowlandson 2004: 159). The letter is written in Greek, but opens with the plea 'By Sarapis! You, whoever you are, who are reading the letter, make a small effort and translate to the women what is written in this letter and tell them.'[11] This sentence implies that Ptolemaios would normally have used a spoken Egyptian variety at home when conversing with the female members of his family, who were ignorant of how to read, write or even speak Greek. Without this short statement, the only one of its type from thousands of papyrus documents, we would have no reason to believe that the late antique gender difference in language in Egypt also prevailed there at earlier periods.

In other parts of the Roman Empire, we have nothing like the amount of documentation that survives from Egypt, and different patterns of marriage and settlement make it difficult to generalize the split between men speaking Greek or Latin, and women an indigenous language, which we might be tempted to deduce from the evidence of the papyri. Claudia Severa, for example, and her correspondent Sulpicia Lepidina, wife of the prefect at Vindolanda on Hadrian's Wall at the end of first century CE, probably accompanied their husbands to Britain, and were not locals who adopted Roman customs (Bowman 1994: 57); it is unlikely that they spoke to each other in anything other than Latin, as the correspondence between them suggests. But other soldiers in Britain did marry local women, such as the Palmyrene Barates, who left a memorial in South Shields for his freedwoman and wife Regina, identified as of the tribe of the Catuvellauni, from southeastern England (*RIB* I 1056).[12] Although Barates commemorates Regina's death with an impressive monument in which she is represented in Palmyrene style (and inscriptions both in Latin and Palmyrene Aramaic), her native language never had an established written form, and she remains silent.

In Gaul, however, where there was some native tradition of epigraphy in Gaulish, there are some indications that Gaulish was particularly associated with the domestic domain. The best supporting evidence for the hypothesis that women retained the native language longer than men comes from

[11] The translation here is taken from the *APIS* project, available online at www.papyri.info.
[12] For detailed discussion of this monument see Mullen (2012: 1–5), 32–5.

a collection of small decorated spindle-whorls from eastern France from the third and fourth centuries CE. A dozen or so of these spindle-whorls include short inscriptions, some in Gaulish, some in Latin, others in a mixture of the two. The texts take the form of flirtatious or suggestive statements, mostly as if made by a male lover, but sometimes with the woman's voice. Ones in Latin read: 'greetings, young girl'; 'hello, goodbye, you are beautiful'; 'hello lady, I am thirsty'. The ones in Gaulish or part-Gaulish are sometimes more direct: 'pretty girl, give me some beer'; 'I am a good girl, and pretty'; 'pretty girl, drink some wine'; 'my girl, take my little . . . [meaning obscure]'; 'can I play horsey?'[13] These spindle-whorls are usually interpreted as love tokens given by young men to their girlfriends, and the choice of language may be due to the more intimate nature of the gift, or more likely because this idiom is one that is more prevalent among women. Some evidence from literary texts also lends support to the assumption that Gaulish remained spoken for longer among the women of the region, or was particularly favoured for domestic and intimate scenes. For example, in the late Latin *Life of the Saint Symphorianus*, his mother is described as 'saying in familiar Gaulish: "Son, son, Symphorianus, think of your God!"'[14] Although the language of her utterance certainly has Latin elements, it also contains words that can be taken to be Gaulish or are the result of the convergence of Latin with Gaulish.

Anecdotal, literary and epigraphic evidence from other places around the Mediterranean during the late Republic and the Roman Empire can also be interpreted in the light of women being the last speakers of the native languages, as men switched to the imperial languages. Recall the discussion of the Paelignian texts in Chapter 3, most of which were epitaphs of women's graves (women who were also religious functionaries). Or the statement recorded in the *Historia Augusta, Life of Septimius Severus* (15.7) that the emperor was so embarrassed by his sister's bad Latin that he had to send her back to Africa (cited by Adams 2003a: 237, and see further Clackson 2012b: 55).

Male speech

Although the crass statements about illogicality and lack of artistry made by Gruppe and other earlier scholars are generally avoided today, most

---

[13] Translations follow Lambert (2003: 125–8); the spindle-whorls inscribed with Gaulish or part-Gaulish are published at *RIG* II.2 L-III to L-121.

[14] The Latin text is *nate, nate Synforiane, †mentobeto to diuo†*, cited and discussed by Adams (2003a: 198; 2007: 302). The daggers surrounding the last three words indicate that the text does not make sense in Latin, and that editors have been unable to agree on any alternative reading.

modern studies fall into the same paradigm as these attempts, in that they view the language of women as the category which is in need of an explanation, whereas the male speech style is understood as the unmarked norm against which female speech is in some way marked as 'deviant' or different. Given the nature of our surviving texts, mostly written by and for men, this concentration on the easily identifiable and largely self-contained body of evidence for women's language is understandable. However, the picture afforded by this perspective may be misleading. In some societies (including perhaps ancient Sumer), women and men use different linguistic varieties, sometimes with alternative pronunciations, grammar and vocabulary (Langslow 2002: 27–8), but among the Greeks and Romans the interplay between gender roles and language was not so clear-cut. Gendered speech may not have been encoded in the same way among different social groups, but it is likely that, as in modern societies, the key to the distinction between male and female language was the scale and degree of variation in different speech circumstances. Indeed, in some respects, it makes better sense to view male speech as more 'deviant' than female speech. In modern studies, men are the speakers who are reported as consistently using non-standard forms, or retaining dialect pronunciations, even in formal or semi-formal environments, and men are sometimes afforded linguistic licences unavailable to women, either in using prestige forms which are the result of educational attainments, or in using taboo or obscene language.

In the ancient world we can also observe the male predominance in some areas of stylized or stigmatized language. Papyrus texts, teaching manuals and other sources make clear the extent to which schoolboys in the Roman period were drilled in grammar and in the literary classics, with attention given to poets such as Homer and other authors whose language would not have been readily understandable without instruction. The expense of a literary education meant that, although women may have undergone some training in basic literacy, only those from the very richest families were given a full education comparable to that of males (Cribiore 2001: 75, Ameling 2012: 84–9). There were some women who were proficient in the worlds of literature, rhetoric and philosophy, such as the poets mentioned at the beginning of this chapter and the late fourth-/early fifth-century CE philosopher and mathematician Hypatia of Alexandria. But these are very much the exceptions, and the fact that we know them all by name is testimony to the exceptional nature of their achievement. The ability to control and manipulate Greek and Latin literary codes was, consequently, mostly the preserve of educated males – some of whom were not yet adults,

such as Quintus Sulpicius Maximus, eleven years old when he died in
94 CE, whose tombstone in Rome preserves his prize-winning Greek verse
composition (Carroll 2006: 157, Coleman forthcoming). Women who
attempted to enter this male domain might be the subject of criticism, as
Juvenal berates the wife who reads the *Art of Grammar* and corrects her
husband's speech (*Satires* 6. 451–6, discussed by Kruschwitz 2012a: 219).
Dedications or epitaphs with poetic texts or allusions to the classics, such as
the doctor Antiochos' verses in Chester (discussed in Chapter 3, p. 94), are
evidence for men's display of their learning. Sometimes funerary markers
further highlight the masculine context by presenting an imagined conversation between the dead speaker and a male passer-by or viewer; even
where the deceased was a woman, the epitaph imagines a male gaze (see
Kruschwitz 2012a for examples). It may be significant that two of the very
few women whose attempts at a similar epigraphic display of learning
survive, the courtier Iulia Balbilla and Damo,[15] selected a literary dialect
that was associated with the poetess Sappho.

Educated Latin-speaking men in the Roman Empire had a further code
afforded to them by education, from which their wives and daughters were
largely excluded: Greek. The letters and other writings of Cicero and other
elite males in the Roman world, and surviving representations of and
anecdotes about their speech, show that cultivated men were able to switch
into Greek or employ Greek words and phrases in their Latin conversation,
reflecting their shared bilingual education. Cicero does not, however,
generally insert Greek words into his letters to his wife. In the words of
Swain, Greek is the language of 'advanced male solidarity' (Swain 2002:
164). In Roman comedies slaves, their masters and other characters may
switch into Greek, but women generally do not (Karakasis 2005: 89). This
is not to say that no woman in Rome was conversant with Greek. Greek
was typically the language on the lips of prostitutes (many of whom may
have been Greek), and Greek phrases were considered titillating in a young
lover (Adams 2003a: 360–1). Juvenal's satire against women includes a
section which reviles women who speak Greek, particularly at inappropriate moments:

> After all, what is more nauseating than the fact that no woman thinks she's
> beautiful unless she's turned herself from a Tuscan into a Greeklette, from a
> woman of Sulmo into a pure Cecropian woman? Everything is in Greek.
> They express their fears and pour out their anger, their joys, their worries,
> and all the secrets of their souls in this language. What else is there? They get

---

[15] See Brennan (1998: 227–31) for speculation about the identity of Damo and for her poem.

laid in Greek. And though you may allow that in young girls, do you still use Greek when your eighty-sixth year is knocking on the door? This language is not decent for an old woman. Whenever that sexy 'Mia vita, mio spirito' [in the original a Greek phrase] pops out, you are still using in public words that should be spoken only beneath the blanket. Is there any crotch that's not in fact aroused by such a seductive and naughty phrase? It has fingers of its own. (Juvenal 6. 185–97, translated by S. Morton Braund, Loeb Classical Library)

Juvenal's satire is clearly over the top, and there were clear domains in which women could speak Greek in public without any sexual motivation. For example, in the later Empire Greek was associated with Christianity in the western Empire (see Chapter 6): the martyr Perpetua speaks Greek with her bishop and her priest (*Martyrdom of SS Perpetua and Felicitas* 14). Juvenal's tirade does make clear, however, that a woman, particularly one seen as no longer sexually desirable, speaking Greek outside the bedroom could leave herself open to mockery or abuse. In concentrating on the seductive aspects of the language, with the same power to arouse and provoke as fingers, Juvenal implicitly links Greek with what we might call obscene language, and this is clearly another axis on which it is possible to draw gender-based distinctions, as we shall see in the next section.

Obscenity

Obscene and offensive language is a highly elastic category, and one that has very different topographies across societies. Even among speakers of the same language taboo vocabulary may vary greatly depending on region or religion; profanities, such as the French Canadian *ostie de tabarnak* 'host of the tabernacle', may arouse shock in one listener but bemusement in another. In modern languages we are used to an easy slippage between curses and swearwords based on religious belief, terms for body parts, sexual acts or excreta (e.g. 'fucking hell!', 'holy shit!'). But in Latin and Greek, apart from reports of the utterance of obscenities in rituals of Demeter and Persephone such as the Eleusinian Mysteries and the Thesmophoria (Diodorus Siculus 5.4.7), it is easier to separate out religious vocabulary from words for sexual acts and bodily functions. At times of extreme emotion, pain or stress, Greeks and Romans were more likely to use a religious oath where modern speakers might use an obscenity, although the conventions of our written texts leave us in some doubt as to what exactly Cicero would have said if he stubbed his toe (Kruschwitz 2012b makes a strong case for supposing the meaningless interjection *attat* in Roman comedy is a cover term for expressions which could not be committed to paper). In what follows I shall concentrate on obscenities that denote male or female genitalia, sexual practices, or vocabulary associated with urination and defecation.

The first task in discussing ancient obscene language is to identify which words counted as obscene. In this case, the translation problem is particularly acute, since much obscene language in modern English has a wide range of transferred meanings and functions, so it can be very misleading to render an ancient word by what appears to be its modern equivalent. Of course, it is also necessary first to elucidate what the modern equivalent is, and for some of the ancient sexual vocabulary this itself can be problematic. We shall illustrate these problems with discussion of two Greek verbs *bīnéō* and *laikázō*, although it would be possible to give further examples (see further Bain 1991 on these two words and others). These are glossed in the ninth edition (1940) of the *Greek–English Lexicon* (*LSJ*), which carried over the definitions given in earlier Victorian editions, as follows:

BĪNÉŌ: *inire, coire*; of illicit intercourse
LAIKÁZŌ: *wench . . .* II *deceive*

For *bīnéō* the editors clearly considered that the Latin equivalents would be less outrageous than an English term, and would keep snooping schoolboys at bay. The meaning of *bīnéō* was clear, but that given to *laikázō* made little sense in the contexts in which it occurred. The correct meaning of *laikázō*, already recognized by Housman in a famous paper on Latin obscenity, a topic considered so filthy that it was composed entirely in Latin (Housman 1931), was demonstrated briefly by Shipp (1977: 1–2) and at length by Jocelyn (1980); the revised supplement of the Greek–English Lexicon of 1996 (Glare 1996) corrects the English equivalent to *practise fellatio on*. But knowing what acts these verbs describe does not tell us how obscene they were considered at the time, or whether they have the transferred uses of English equivalents, even though some scholars have attempted to draw direct parallels. Thus Henderson (1975: 151) states that *bīnéō* 'seems to have had the same force and flexibility in Greek as *fuck* does in English'. Certainly the word is used as the direct term for the sexual act (for example at Aristophanes *Lysistrata* 934), and it is declared a Greek obscenity by Cicero in a letter to Paetus, which is one of our best sources for the ancient views on what words are taboo (*Ad fam.* 9.22.3). But *bīnéō* does not get used in the many exclamatory, derogatory, or expressive ways that the English equivalent does. Moreover, it is also used in public notices forbidding fornication in temples (*LSAG* 42.5 from Olympia), and the ancient lexico-grapher Hesychius records it in the laws of Solon. The word *laikázō* on the other hand has transferred usages which are foreign to English *fellate*, and, together with its derivatives, it occurs in insults and exclamations in a way that more closely mirrors the English *f*-word. Indeed, *laikázō* is even used in Latin in a sense close to the English 'fuck off' by one of the freedmen in Petronius' *Satyrica*, who claims that he can say it to the cold when he has been warmed by some mulled wine (Petronius *Sat.* 41). In general, Greek and Roman speakers are very restrained in comparison with many modern languages in their application of obscenities in insults, intensifiers and in general evaluative senses. Latin speakers could call someone *uerpe* 'cock', but terms relating to crime and punishment such as *fur* 'thief', *scelerate* 'guilty' or *furcifer* 'gallows-bird' can be as strong and are more common in our sources (Dickey 2002: 163–85). In Greek comedy, there are no exam-ples of words for body parts applied directly to an individual, and insults based on religion, such as *miāré* 'polluted', would probably have sounded more extreme than *eurúprōkte* 'wide-arsed', which implies frequent sub-jection to sodomy (Dover 2002).

The discussion of the words *bīnéō* and *laikázō* reveals a further impor-tant difference between ancient and modern obscenity. In English, much of the taboo vocabulary is paired with higher-register terms that are not in themselves obscene. Thus English legislative or medical texts can use terms such as 'fornication' or 'sexual intercourse' without ambiguity or offence. In early Greek epic and other high-register poetry, more general terms are used to refer to intercourse, such as the word *mígnūmi* 'I mix' (which later gets taken up by medical writers in the same sense), but there is no parallel for the English system of a high-register word next to the obscenity. The absence of pairs of 'respectable' and 'dirty' words with synonymous mean-ing helps explain why *bīnéō* turns up in early Greek laws. Later on, however, in literary Greek and in Latin, transferred senses of the words originally meaning 'mix' (Greek *mígnūmi*), 'come together' (Latin *coeo*) or 'sleep with' (Greek *koimáō*, compounds of *klínō*, Latin *dormio cum* or *iaceo cum*) do become generalized (see Adams 1982). Greek medical texts also generally avoid obscenity, using euphemisms instead; for example, 'with-draw' (*hupokhōréō*) and other expressions stand in for the coarse term *khézō* 'shit'. Occasionally a few derivatives of obscene words make their way into the literature, such as a plant named 'cowshit' (*khésis boôn*, or *cesisboum* in Latin transliteration), which the Roman doctor Cassius Felix recommends as one of the ingredients of a cure for rabies (Bain 1999: 275). Some words which originate as polite alternatives sometimes themselves become taboo, providing examples of what has been called the 'Allan–Burridge law of semantic change': 'Bad connotations drive out good', i.e. euphemistic replacements of obscenities come to take over the primary meanings (Allan and Burridge 2006). Cicero's comments on the Latin word *penis* in his letter to Paetus are an example of exactly this development. For Cicero the word *penis*, originally a euphemism, had itself become a mild obscenity:

> The ancients called a tail a 'penis' – hence 'penicillus' ['paint-brush'] from the similarity. But nowadays 'penis' is an obscene word. And yet Piso Frugi in his *Annals* complains of young men being 'devoted to the penis'; but because many others did the same, it became no less an obscene word than the one you have employed. (Cicero *ad Fam.* 9.22.3 translation by D. R. Shackleton Bailey, Loeb Classical Library)

Although *penis* is here 'an obscene word', it is clearly not in the same league as *mentula*, the term which he alludes to in this passage ('the [word] you have employed'); he further teases the reader later in the letter by asking why the Romans do not form diminutives from the words for 'mint' and 'pavement' (these would be *mentula* and *pauimentula*).

In recent decades studies on Latin and Greek obscene language (particularly Adams 1982 and Henderson 1975) have clarified many of the meanings of obscene terms, and elucidated some of their functions. Obscenities were not tolerated in the mouths of women, except in special arenas such as festivals and marriages, where ritual utterance of obscenities was sanctioned by practice, or, as we have seen, in amatory contexts, where lascivious talk may have heightened the erotic thrill (Adams 1982: 216–17). In Attic comedy there is direct evidence for the disapproval of women's use of obscenity in male company; in the words of Sommerstein (1995) 'while men are quite uninhibited about using these words in the presence of women, women never normally utter them in the presence of men.' When women do use this vocabulary in front of men, they may be directly reprimanded, as at Aristophanes *Lysistrata* 440–2: when an old woman threatens that the magistrate's enforcer will 'shit himself' if he lays a hand on Lysistrata, the magistrate repeats the obscenity and exclaims 'see how she talks!' In Aristophanes' comedies men tend to employ scatological obscenities when speaking to one another without women present, while women generally avoid scatological terms (see below for women's use of sexual vocabulary), as for example in the scene involving Blepyrus, his neighbour and Chremes at *Ecclesiazusae* 311–82, where the male speakers parody tragic lines after Blepyrus has overshared the details of his relief from constipation (McClure 1999: 212–16, 246–8). Non-Greek speakers may reveal their ignorance about the normal codes in society by their overuse of profanities. Thus the speech of the Scythian Archer in the *Thesmophoriazusae*, whose imperfect command of Greek we have already noted (p. 119), makes excessive use of the adjective *miārós* 'polluted' (McClure 1999: 235), and the Persian Pseudartabas in Aristophanes' *Acharnians* cannot string a Greek sentence together but does know the insult *khaunópróktos* 'gape-arsed' (*Acharnians* 104). Obscenity may play a role in what has been called male 'flyting' styles, that is, the competitive exchange of insults. This can be a feature of sophisticated poetry, such as Catullus' celebrated address to Furius and Aurelius in poem 16 (*pedicabo ego uos et irrumabo* 'I will bugger you and fuck you in the mouth'), and is also found in the gutter conversations of the freedmen in Petronius' *Satyrica*. Obscenity and self-aggrandisement are also notable features of graffiti and other writing left by male authors at sites all over the ancient world, including the early Greek pederastic inscriptions on the rocks at Thera, such as 'Krimon fucked Amotion here' (*IG* XII, 538b, see further Dover 1978: 122–3), or the boasts scratched on the brothel walls of Pompeii, including 'I fucked many girls here' (*CIL* IV 2175).[16] Sometimes sexual language openly reinforced male aggression, as is the case with Greek and Latin inscribed slingshots, which carried messages such as 'I'm aiming for Octavius' arse', 'I'm aiming for Fulvia's clit', or (apparently) 'impregnate yourself on this' (Benedetti 2012: nos 31 and 32; Kelly 2012: 291–6). As in modern societies, obscenity clearly could be used to demarcate male speech and reinforce male solidarity.

In Aristophanes' comedies, women are sometimes represented uttering sexual obscenities amongst themselves, although there are also times where they employ euphemisms, or different terms from those used by men. For example, at *Ecclesiazusae* 920, *laikázō* is replaced in the speech of one woman by 'do the *L* like the Lesbians' (in fifth-century Athens, women from the island of Lesbos were more usually associated with fellatio than homosexuality, as another euphemism for *laikázō*, *lesbiázō*, makes clear). At *Lysistrata* 152, the heroine Lysistrata uses the otherwise unknown term *splekóō* for the activity men describe with the verb *binéō*, and Duhoux (2004: 135) takes this to be a specifically female term used in place of the male obscenity. But one example of a term is difficult to make sense of,

---

[16] See Levin-Richardson (2011) for examples of the brothel graffiti from Pompeii, and the connection with display of masculinity; her interpretations of the meaning of particular graffiti should, however, be used with caution.

particularly when that is uttered by the character Lysistrata herself, who in her willingness to discuss sexual matters is not typical of a female character (McClure 1999: 210). The kinsman in Aristophanes' *Thesmophoriazusae* is quickly exposed when he tries to speak before a group of women in female disguise (*Thesmophoriazusae* 466–519), not so much because of his utterance of directly obscene terms (although he does make use of the diminutive *posthíon* and some scatological terms), but through his transgressive discussion of sexual conduct in the open, including describing the sexual position he took with his lover and chewing garlic to cover up the smell of a night's debauch.

The comedies of Aristophanes constitute nearly all the extant evidence for women speaking obscene language amongst themselves in the ancient world, outside of ritual contexts, but there are a couple of hints in Latin sources about the language of midwives, wet-nurses and others (Adams 2005). A statement of Varro informs us that women would refer to the sexual parts of girls by the word *porcus*, literally 'pig' (*Rust.* 2.4.10). More promising is Mustio's Latin version of the *Gynaecia* by the Greek medical writer Soranus (the original was written at the beginning of the second century CE, the translation probably much later). In his preface, Mustio states that the work will include 'women's words' so that even uneducated midwives will be able to understand it. Mustio uses a range of vocabulary, from the primary obscenities *cunnus* 'cunt' and *landica* 'clitoris' to technical terms based on the Greek, though he sadly does not specify which words were considered particularly female. Adams (2005) does not identify any of the obscene terms as particularly associated with female speech, but speculates that the words *dida* 'breast' and *mamma* 'wet-nurse' may be two of the women's words that Mustio refers to. More striking, perhaps, is the word *titina* which Mustio claims is what the 'rustics' call a nipple-shaped baby's beaker. Adams explains this rare form, which otherwise occurs only in a few other medical works and late glossaries with the meaning 'nipple', as a diminutive of the word *titta* 'breast, nipple', a word which is nowhere attested in Latin, but is presumed to have existed by the widespread derived words in Romance languages, including Italian *tetta* and French *tette* (English *tit* appears not to be directly connected but *teat* is a borrowing from the French word). If this is correct, it darts a flicker of light into the otherwise unseen world of the nursery, babies and breast-feeding, and incidentally reminds us how much of the everyday spoken language of women (and men) from the ancient world we have lost.

CHAPTER 6

The languages of Christianity

Bible translators and cradle-snatchers

Sacred books and texts are central to many religious traditions. These may be based on a believed divine or mystical revelation to a single individual, as the Qur'an was transmitted to Muhammad or the Book of Mormon to Joseph Smith. Alternatively, the central texts of a religion may be a compendium of a variety of separate texts, perhaps associated with named authors or perhaps anonymous, which have been grouped together sometimes centuries after they were first written. The Zoroastrian sacred texts, known as the Avesta, provide one example of such a compendium, including both hymns thought to be composed by Zoroaster at some time earlier than 600 BCE and later hymns and accounts of myths and rituals, which may be as much as a thousand years later than Zoroaster himself. The Jewish faith makes use of the Hebrew Scriptures or Tanakh, known in Christian contexts as the Old Testament of the Bible, which include material ranging from the Torah (or Pentateuch), five books combining narrative and religious prescriptions, to works of prophecy and poetic texts. The Christian Bible incorporates the Hebrew Scriptures with a collection of texts, originally written in Greek, known as the New Testament, which include four different versions of the life of Jesus (known as the gospels), a narrative of what happened after Jesus (called the Acts of the Apostles), and a number of letters, many of them written by, or ascribed to, the apostle Paul. Religion can be a key factor in language change and language spread, as the impact of Arabic, the language of the Qur'an, on North Africa and the Near East shows. In this chapter, I will focus mainly on the effects of one religion in particular, Christianity.

Christianity changed the linguistic map. Early translations of the Bible provide the first written evidence for a diverse array of languages, and missionaries devised new alphabets that have remained in use until the present day. For example, the distinctive Armenian and Georgian alphabets were invented by Christian evangelists, as was the Cyrillic script used by Russians and other Slavic peoples. Bible translations provide linguists with a unique resource: not only do they show how the same material is expressed in several different languages, but in some cases they provide almost the only surviving record of a language now otherwise lost. One such case is Gothic, a Germanic language in the same family as English, German and Swedish, which is known almost entirely from a single splendid Bible written in silver letters on vellum, now housed in Uppsala (Munkhammar 2011); another is the language of the Caucasian Albanians (an ancient people completely unconnected with the Albanians of the Balkans), which was long thought lost, but recently recovered from parchments later reused by Georgian monks at Saint Catherine's Monastery in the Sinai peninsula (Gippert 2012). We know the names, and something of the lives, of some of the individuals who were instrumental in spreading the Christian message in languages other than Greek and Latin. Wulfila (Greek *Oulphilas*), the translator of the Bible into Gothic, was descended from a Christian Greek family which had lived in Cappadocia (now in central Turkey) but were kidnapped in 257 and came to live in Gothic-speaking areas of the Balkans. He was sent from there to Constantinople in 336, but returned to his homeland as 'Bishop of the Goths' land' in the 340s, dying in 383 (Schäferdiek 2004: 374–5). Wulfila preached in Latin, Greek and Gothic, and was the first to commit Gothic to writing. He devised a new script, based largely on the Greek alphabet, but adding some new letters to represent sounds unknown to the Greeks, such as *hw* (a sound still found in the Irish pronunciation of English words such as *which, when* and *whiskey*). We know about the fourth-century Armenian saint Mesrop Mashtots from the account of his life written by his pupil Koriwn (Winkler 1994). Koriwn records Mesrop's missionary endeavours among the Armenians and two neighbouring peoples of the Caucasus. According to Koriwn, Mesrop devised an alphabet in order to write down the Armenian language, after which a Bible translation in Armenian quickly followed. Having discovered his talent for script creation, Mesrop also invented distinctive new alphabets for the Georgians, and for the Caucasian Albanians, acts of generosity still frequently unacknowledged.

We do not know the names of the individuals whose efforts led to the creation of new scripts in other Christian traditions, nor can we be sure when the first attempts were made to translate the Christian message into languages, such as Latin and Aramaic, which already had a tradition of written literature. But we do have surviving evidence for a large array of separate translations of the Bible, made in the first centuries of the Christian era. The first Bible translations into Aramaic seem to have been made from the Hebrew Old Testament, probably in the second century CE, with versions of the New Testament following in the third or fourth. There was originally no single Aramaic translation, but there seem to have been a number of separate attempts and revisions. Most of these were made into Syriac, which is in essence a northern dialect of Aramaic associated with the town of Edessa (now modern Urfa in Turkey), but which came to be the main written medium for Christians in Syria and Palestine.[1] There is also a large surviving portion of the Bible rendered into another dialect of Aramaic, known as Christian Palestinian Aramaic, made some time before the fifth century (Metzger 1977, Williams 2013).

The Latin translation of the Bible still in common use, and known today as the Vulgate, was made by Jerome (*c.* 347–420) at the end of the fourth century; it replaced a number of earlier versions (sometimes called the *Vetus Latina* or Old Latin versions), which may have been made at any time in the preceding two hundred years. Augustine, writing in the late fourth century, gives an indication of the number and quality of the different versions:

> Translators of scripture from Hebrew into Greek can be easily counted, but not so translators into Latin, for in the early days of the faith any man who got hold of a Greek manuscript and fancied that he had some ability in the two languages went ahead and translated it. (Augustine, *De doctrina Christiana* 2.11.16, translation from Green 1995: 73)

In Egypt, the translation of the Bible seems to have taken place in a similarly piecemeal and *ad hoc* fashion. Here the local language is known by the name Coptic, in effect the last phase of Ancient Egyptian, written in the Greek script with the addition of seven letters derived from Demotic Egyptian (whose own script is the ultimate outcome of handwritten hieroglyphs). There is no surviving text of the Bible in Coptic dating to earlier than the mid-fourth century; but after that date, a number of different versions are found, made in several separate dialects (Metzger 1977: 99–141).

This flurry of translation activity by the early Christians did not go unnoticed in the early church. John Chrysostom, Archbishop of Constantinople (347–407), was one of the most prolific preachers of all time (see Kelly 1995 for his life and career). In one of his numerous

---

[1] On the meanings of the term 'Syriac' in ancient and modern texts, see Millar (2006: 383–4).

surviving sermons he claims that the Scythians, Thracians, Sarmatians, Mauretanians and Indians have translated the scriptures (*Serm.* 8.1, Migne *PG* 63, 501), and in another that the Syrians, Egyptians, Indians, Persians and Ethiopians 'and countless other peoples' have made versions in their own language (*Serm.* 2 *in John* 1.1. 2, Migne *PG* 59, 32). It is true that the Bible was translated into the native language of Ethiopia, certainly before the sixth century, and perhaps as early as the fourth (Isaac 2012: 113). Isolated fragments suggest that there were also Persian and Nubian versions made before the seventh century (Metzger 1977: 276 and 270), and perhaps even Arabic at around the same date (Griffith 2012: 124). However, at the time John Chrysostom was preaching, we have little firm evidence for any translations beyond the Coptic, Syriac, Gothic and Latin. John Chrysostom's claims thus seem to reflect aspirations rather than achievements, but they do show the apparent readiness of the early Christian church to embrace spreading the word in languages other than Greek. Indeed, the description of 'speaking in tongues' in Acts of the Apostles (2: 4–11, cited in Chapter 1, p. 29–30) can be seen to legitimize the practice of letting individuals of all nations hear the gospel 'in their own language'.

Other sources corroborate the readiness of early Christians both to acknowledge, and to make use of, local languages. The church historian Socrates (*Historia Ecclesiastica* 5.22, Migne *PG* 67, 648) states that the Arian bishop Selinas, whose mother was Phrygian and father a Goth, preached in both languages in Asia Minor in the early fifth century. At the same time, another bishop was using his knowledge of vernacular tongues to convert the locals: Saint Patrick, once a slave in Ireland, later missionary to the Irish. Patrick laments his lack of proficiency in Latin, which he states is not his first language (*Confessio*, ch. 13).[2] Indeed, Peter Brown takes Patrick's *Confession*, together with his *Letter to Coroticus*, to be the earliest surviving Latin literary text written by someone from outside the Roman Empire (Brown 2013: 131). The readiness of the Christians to recognize other spoken languages beyond the classical idioms is further seen in the tendency to compile lists of the seventy-two languages spoken in the world, a number drawn from the Genesis account of the fall of the Tower of Babel (Genesis 10–11). These lists of languages and peoples first appear in the third century, and draw from both biblical and classical accounts. The best-known version of this linguistic checklist occurs in the seventh-century Isidore of Seville's *Etymologiae* (9.1–9.2). Isidore privileges

---

[2] See Charles-Edwards (2000: 231–3) for discussion of Patrick's Latin style, and demonstration that it is more artful than Patrick claims.

Hebrew, Greek and Latin as the three 'sacred idioms', but earlier examples of the list significantly do not mark off the classical languages from others, and Greek and Latin are sandwiched between diverse tongues such as Thracian and Macedonian, or Ligurian and Etruscan (Borst 1959: 931–52). This might suggest that the Christians originally were more open-minded than their pagan predecessors as regards the place of Greek and Latin among the world's languages, and avoided the Greeks' and Romans' earlier lack of interest in foreign tongues.

A similar apparent tolerance of linguistic diversity is found in the works of the Latin speaker Augustine (354–430), a native of North Africa. The Punic language, the offspring of spoken Phoenician brought to the region by the founders of Carthage, was still spoken in North Africa during his lifetime, and Augustine seems to have had some command of it, albeit imperfect (he reports himself confusing two Punic words at *De magistro* 13.44). Punic is a Semitic language, of the same family as Hebrew, and Augustine occasionally uses Punic to help explain a Hebrew word in the Bible (*Loc. in Hept.* I ad Gen. I: 24). In a sermon delivered in North Africa, he assumes that his audience are familiar with a Punic proverb (*Sermo* 167.3), and one letter records his search for a priest who knows Punic for an appointment to the bishopric of Fussala, a small town forty miles from Hippo, situated in what is now Algeria (*Epist.* 209.3). The contrast between Augustine's open attitude towards Punic and the pagan Roman ignorance and disdain of local vernaculars is most clearly seen in the exchange of letters, *c.* 390 CE, between Augustine and Maximus of Madaura, a grammarian who refers to himself as an old man, and who some have speculated was once Augustine's teacher.[3] Maximus teases Augustine for his adherence to a cult that worships a god in 'secret places' and whose martyrs have names 'hateful to gods and men'. Indeed, Maximus can bring himself to mention only one local name, Namphamo, and he does that with an exclamation of disgust. In reply, Augustine refuses to be drawn into Maximus' bantering tone. He notes that, as two Africans writing to each other in Africa, they should not be embarrassed by the native language of the country, whose 'cradle is still warm' – a memorable phrase, implying as it does that Latin speakers have snatched the Punic baby. Far from viewing it as a ridiculous foreign word, Augustine knows that Namphamo is an auspicious name, meaning 'with a good foot', a metaphor which he notes is sanctioned by usage in the classical poets.

---

[3] Kaster (1988: 311); the letters survive as Augustine *Epist.* 16 and 17, edited by Mastandrea (1985).

Just as Augustine champions the local language, Punic, against the sneers of the grammarian, so he also makes a case for the everyday language against the classical forms prescribed by the linguistic puritans of his day. Augustine looks back on his education as a lost period, when he was terrified to make a grammatical mistake, and when his teachers inculcated the grammatical rules made by men, but ignored the divine rules made by god. Speakers, he wrote in his *Confessions* (I 18.28–19.30), were more afraid to drop the *h* of *homo* 'human' than to say they hated somebody. Augustine accordingly appears to have a relaxed approach to the grammatical norms of his day, recommending that the preacher to the uneducated should use the neologism *ossum* 'bone' rather than the Classical Latin word *os*, since the latter could be confused in the speech of Africans with *ōs* 'mouth' (*De doctrina Christiana* 4.10.24).[4] Augustine's position here is in keeping with the paradigm of the gospels, in which Jesus' message is conveyed in simple, everyday language for an audience of the uneducated as well as for the rich.

It is tempting to view the evidence for the existence of a number of early versions of the Bible in light of the later history of the emergence of literacy and written vernaculars in Europe and the wider world. In Ireland, Anglo-Saxon Britain, Germany and among the Slavic-speaking peoples, missionaries and monks kick-started the tradition of writing in the language of the country, just as in the seventeenth century Protestant missionaries translated the Bible into tongues as diverse as Native American Algonquian and Turkish (Malcolm 2007). Even in the modern day, Christian missionaries are creating new written forms for languages that have previously existed only as spoken idioms. This may lead us to assume that, in the ancient world too, the translated words of Jesus injected new life into local languages. In reality, the effect of Christianity may have been entirely the opposite. Apart from the exceptional cases of Coptic and Syriac (which we shall discuss more fully below), within the Roman Empire there was no linguistic pluralism in Bible translations. The early versions discussed above were made in the Balkans, the Caucasus, Persia and the Nile valley south of the first cataract, all areas outside the bounds of imperial control. The Bible was never translated into Phrygian, Gaulish or Punic (although Augustine does suggest that some hymns were composed in Punic, *In Psalm.* 118.32.8). These three minority languages were still in spoken use within the Roman Empire during the third and fourth centuries, and all

---

[4] This statement is significant for the knowledge of regional varieties of Latin in the Empire, since it shows the merger of short and long vowels; see further Adams (2007: 261).

had a tradition of being written down; indeed, inscriptions survive for all three languages into the fourth century. Moreover, all three languages seem to die out by the sixth century at the latest. As Peter Brown (1968: 93) pointed out, despite the many references to Punic in the work of Augustine, in the 250 years following him there is not a single mention of the Punic language in texts or documents from North Africa. Christian evangelism in the Roman Empire may have been the real cause for the demise of these local languages: 'far from fostering native traditions, it widened the franchise of the Latin language' (Brown 1968: 92).

Augustine's openness and tolerance towards Punic may therefore not have been typical among educated Christians speaking and writing in Latin or Greek. Augustine's contemporary Jerome knew Hebrew well, and translated the Old Testament into Latin from Hebrew sources; he also claims to have used Arabic and Syriac as well in order to understand the Old Testament (*Praef. in Iob*, Migne *PL* 28, 1081) and is aware of linguistic differences among the Hebrew Scriptures (*Praef. in Daniel*, Migne *PL* 28, 1291–2). Jerome is at pains to stress that the poetic passages of the Old Testament are for Christians what Horace or Pindar or Sappho are for pagans (*Praef. in Iob*, Migne *PL* 28, 1081), but he understands that the foreign fare of Hebrew may not be to everyone's taste: country dwellers do not buy the exotic eastern goods balsam, pepper or date-palms, as he puts it (*Quaestiones Hebraicae in Genesim*, Praef., Migne *PL* 23, 938). Indeed, Jerome's linguistic tolerance seems to have been stretched by the non-classical languages. Writing early on in his life from northern Syria, in a region surrounded by Aramaic speakers, he complains that his only Latin conversation is in the letters sent to him by his friends, and that he will have to learn a barbarous half-language (Latin: *barbarus semisermo*) in order to have anyone to speak to (*Epist.* 7.2, Migne *PL* 22, 339).[5]

A similar paradox is observable with the Christian attitude to the Classical forms of Latin and Greek. As we saw, Augustine rebuked Maximus for his snobbery towards Punic names in Latin texts, and had harsh things to say to those who follow the precepts of grammarians. Jerome was also turned against the classics by divine injunction, as he famously recounts in a letter (*Epist.* 22.30, Migne *PL* 22, 416). While a young Christian, he continued to read Cicero and Plautus, thinking them

---

[5] Taylor (2002: 304) also finds linguistic intolerance in John Chrysostom (*De statuis ad populum Antiochum* 19.1, Migne *PG* 49, 188), translating his comments about Syriac speakers in Antioch with 'they seem a backward people to us in language'. But the Greek itself does not seem to carry this interpretation: λαὸς κατὰ μὲν τὴν γλῶτταν ἡμῖν ἐνηλλαγμένος 'they are a people at variance from us in language'.

better written than the crude language of the prophetic books of the Old
Testament (which he must then have been reading in one of the early
Latin translations). But he fell sick, and had a vision that he was being
judged in front of God, who asked whether he was a follower of Christ,
and then rejected his affirmative reply with the words 'You lie! You are a
Ciceronian, not a Christian'. After this, Jerome renounced reading the
works of pagan literature. John Chrysostom is fond of the trope that the
philosophers have been vanquished by the words of fishermen and tentmakers (e.g. *Serm.* 8.1, Migne *PG* 63, 501).[6] This rhetoric might lead us to
expect that Christianity marked the end for the earlier, prescriptive rules
of grammar, and we might look for a break from the earlier efforts of
Greek authors to write in the idiom of fifth-century BCE Athens, or of
Romans to use the style and vocabulary of the Augustan period of the
early first century CE. But although the new religion did lead to the
closure of ancient temples, it did not shut the grammar schools. Despite
the humility of their founding documents, and their protestations against
pagan learning, many of the church fathers showed themselves to be
steeped in the classical tradition, and were not afraid to display it.
Augustine, in his reply to Maximus of Madaura, cites Vergil and
Cicero to prove his point; Jerome name-checks Terence, Vergil, Cicero
and Quintilian, and directly quotes passages from Horace and the
Eclogues in the opening of his discussion of the correct interpretation of
Biblical Hebrew (*Quaestiones Hebraicae in Genesim*, Praef., Migne *PL* 23,
938). John Chrysostom does not use the language of fishermen or tentmakers himself, but prefers artificial Atticist forms such as *glôtta* 'tongue'
rather than the *koinē* form *glôssa*.[7] Jerome mounts a spirited defence of
the use of classical sources in a letter to a Roman rhetorician, Magnus,
giving the precedent of the apostle Paul (who cited the Greek poets
Callimachus, Menander and Aratus in his letters), as well as numerous
earlier Greek and Roman Christian authors (*Epist.* 70.2, Migne *PL* 22,
665). He draws a striking analogy between the use of classical sources and
the ancient Hebrew law of Deuteronomy (21) that allows Jews to take a
foreign concubine as long as she is shaved of all her hair, and her nails
clipped; so too Christians can take the classics to bed, as long as they strip
away the paganism.

---

[6] By 'fishermen' John refers to the original occupation of some of Christ's disciples and by 'tentmakers'
    to the apostle Paul, who continued to make tents during his ministry.
[7] For the contrast between Atticist (and Atticizing) Greek and *koinē* Greek, see pp. 54–8.

In the rest of this chapter, I shall address the question of whether Christianity led to a definitive break in the linguistic history of the ancient world. Why did Christianity apparently give birth to some new written forms of vernacular language, but lead to the smothering of others? Did the language of scripture bring about a change in the evolution of Greek and Latin, leading to their liberation from grammatical strictures, and the creation of new varieties of Patristic Greek and Christian Latin? Before addressing these issues, however, it will be helpful to explore the history of the language of the Greek New Testament, and examine the complex linguistic history of the ancient Near East.

What would Jesus say?

What language or languages could Jesus speak? The answer to this question is, perhaps surprisingly, far from straightforward. Part of the problem arises from the complexity of the language situation of ancient Judaea/Palestine (see Millar 1993: 351–66 and Casey 1998 for excellent surveys). The story in Acts of speaking in tongues, already cited in Chapter 1, gives one picture of the linguistic diversity of Jerusalem in the first century CE, although this relates to visitors to the city rather than its inhabitants. Inscriptional remains from Jerusalem are not extensive, owing to the successive destructions and rebuildings of the city in the last 3,000 years. However, these texts are now published in Cotton et al. (2010–12, hereafter referred to as *CIIP*), a corpus which, unusually, gathers ancient inscribed material no matter what language it was written in. The corpus, together with an ever-growing amount of documentary and religious material reclaimed from the Judaean desert, shows that there were four written languages in regular use in Judaea/Palestine in the first century CE. In first place comes Latin, not because of the number of remaining texts in Latin script (there are only two surviving from Jerusalem, *CIIP* 40 and 570, both single names on ossuaries), but because it was the language of imperial power. Other cities of the Roman Near East show Latin used as the language of display for both members of the imperial government, and leading citizens of the local community. It is likely that Jerusalem would have fitted into this pattern if more of the ancient fabric of the city had survived successive destructions. Indeed, the first-century CE Jewish historian Josephus' description of the Temple in Jerusalem before its destruction explicitly mentions signs in Greek and Latin forbidding entry for non-Jews (*Jewish War* 5.194). The second language of the imperial administration, Greek, was in more widespread use than Latin to record dedications and public works. In Jerusalem, the few remaining longer public texts from the Imperial period are written in Greek, including a memorial left by a Jew bearing the Greek name Theodotos, which records his family's contribution to the construction of the synagogue (*CII/P* 9). Furthermore, a large number of funerary inscriptions from Jerusalem are in Greek, and about a dozen pair Greek and Hebrew or Aramaic on the same stone.

The last two languages recorded in significant numbers in Jerusalem are Hebrew and Aramaic. Both Hebrew and Aramaic share a fundamentally similar grammatical system, and a large proportion of their vocabulary. However, the two languages differ in details: for example, Aramaic makes plurals with the ending -*n* rather than -*m*. Hebrew and Aramaic are part of the Semitic language family, whose other members include Phoenician, Ugaritic, Arabic and Akkadian.[8] Aramaic was originally limited to the region north of modern-day Israel/Palestine, but it came to be spoken over a much wider area in the first millennium BCE owing to its adoption as one of the administrative languages of the Persian Empire (see Chapter 2). By the beginning of the Christian era, Aramaic had spread south, and it would eventually overtake Hebrew as the spoken language of Judaea/Palestine. It is not altogether certain when Hebrew died out of everyday spoken use – most modern estimates put the date at 200 CE (Schniedewind 2006: 148). However, Hebrew remained a written language, even after that date retaining its status as a sacred tongue for Jews (and later for Christians); Modern Hebrew, spoken in the state of Israel, is the result of a deliberate revival of the language in the late nineteenth and twentieth centuries. From the third century BCE, Hebrew was written in the same script as Aramaic, and in short texts, such as grave-markers, it is often impossible to tell the two languages apart; to add to the confusion, both Classical and Semitic sources often make no distinction between them, and refer to Hebrew and Aramaic using the same terms (such as the Greek word *Hebraisti* 'in Hebrew' or the Greek expression meaning 'in the Hebrew language'). Hence, despite the survival of hundreds of Semitic funerary inscriptions from Jerusalem in the period between 100 BCE and 100 CE, it is not possible to give a clear indication of whether there were distinct Hebrew- and Aramaic-speaking groups in the city. Aramaic itself encompasses a wide range of different dialects, some of which were written in their own distinctive forms of the Aramaic script in the first centuries of

---

[8] Hebrew, Aramaic, Ugaritic and Arabic all belong to the West Semitic branch of the family (which also includes numerous other languages), and are subsumed under the label 'West Semitic' in Map 1.1.

the Christian era, including Palmyrene, Nabataean, Syriac and Samaritan. Other Aramaic dialects never achieved the same inscriptional or literary status, but we know of their existence through statements in sources such as the Talmud, which pokes fun at the incomprehensibility of the speech of Galileans (Taylor 2002: 303).

Although only a few, very short, bilingual inscriptions survive from Jerusalem, it is certain that many Jews in the area were bilingual in Greek and Aramaic, while most probably also had knowledge of Hebrew. The Hebrew Scriptures had been translated into Greek in the third or second century BCE; according to legend, the Greek version was made by seventy or seventy-two scholars, so it came to be known as the *Septuagint*, from the Latin for 'seventy'.[9] The Septuagint was intended for the Jewish population of Egypt, who were largely Greek-speaking, but also came to be used by Jews elsewhere, as shown by the inclusion of citations from it in various books of the New Testament. Greek was to become the usual language in which Jews in the Roman Empire left private inscriptions (see Noy 1993–5, Ameling 2009), and there are indications that it was also spoken by many of the Jews in Judaea (Millar 1993: 352). We have already mentioned the dedicatory inscription for a synagogue in Jerusalem by Theodotos, and documents from the Judaean desert from the late first and early second centuries CE show Jewish communities ready to use Greek alongside Aramaic in legal contracts, wills and letters. One revealing short letter dated to 135 CE (*P. Yadin* 2.52), taken from an archive of documents discovered in the 'Cave of Letters' situated on the modern border between Israel and Jordan, asks the recipient to send citrus fruits and staves for the celebration of Sukkot (the Feast of Tabernacles), and the author apologizes for writing in Greek, since he had not found anyone to write *Hebraistí*.[10] Levels of competency in Greek doubtless varied, however. The Roman military commander who seizes the apostle Paul during a riot in Jerusalem (Acts 21:37) is surprised he can speak Greek, although Paul's letters reveal that he is able to quote from the classics. The first-century CE historian of the Jews Josephus recounts his own difficulty in mastering Greek as a second language, and confesses he still speaks with an accent (*AJ* 20.263).

The language Jesus spoke must be situated somewhere in this multi-lingual society. In Mark's gospel, Jesus is represented preaching in Greek, but occasionally switching to Aramaic. At 5:41 he restores to life the

---

[9] See Wasserstein and Wasserstein (2006: 52–3) for the fluctuation between seventy and seventy-two translators in ancient accounts of the translation.

[10] See Cotton (2003: 143–8) for discussion of the various possibilities of what *Hebraistí* means in this letter.

daughter of Jairus, a leader of a synagogue near Lake Galilee, with the Aramaic phrase *talitha qum*, which the gospel glosses as 'child get up'. In the Garden of Gethsemene (Mark 14:36) he addresses God with the words '*Abbâ* father' (using both the Aramaic word for 'father', *abbâ*, and the Greek) and both the gospel of Mark and that of Matthew record that Jesus' final utterance on the cross is in Aramaic, not Greek (Mark 15:34, Matthew 27:46). But Jesus is represented talking in Greek elsewhere in the New Testament, and some of his interlocutors, such as the Greek woman (Mark 7:26–7) and Pontius Pilate (Mark 15:1–2), were most likely more at home in that language. The other gospels remain largely silent on Jesus' linguistic choices, though that has not stopped ancient and modern commentators from speculating. Mel Gibson's 2004 movie *The Passion of the Christ* presents a different view from that of Mark. Jesus is shown speaking mainly in Aramaic but on occasion in Latin, even mastering the Latin pluperfect subjunctive in his debate with Pontius Pilate (who addresses him in Aramaic). Jesus probably didn't speak Latin, and Pilate almost certainly had no Aramaic, but apart from that, modern scholars are generally more in agreement with Mel than Mark: Jesus' everyday language, and that of his early teaching, was Aramaic, and he was probably able to switch into Greek when occasion demanded (Casey 1998, with a review of the earlier scholarship, Horsley 2009). A telling indication of such intermeshing of Aramaic and Greek is Paul's conversion experience, as told in Acts 26:14. Paul grew up in a Jewish household in Tarsus, a largely Greek-speaking port on the southern coast of Anatolia. In his early life he was a steadfast persecutor of Christians, but he was stopped on the road to Damascus by a light brighter than the sun, and addressed by the voice of Jesus speaking *têi Hebraḯdi dialéktōi* 'in the Hebrew [or Aramaic] language'. The voice tells Paul that 'it is hard for you to kick against the pricks', using a Greek proverbial expression applied to pack animals, which appears in exactly the same words in one of Euripides' plays (*Bacchae* 795).

We do not know the processes by which the Aramaic teaching of Jesus became written down in Greek as the gospels. There were ancient suggestions that the gospels and other books of the New Testament were first composed in Aramaic, which can mostly be traced back to a fragment of a lost work by the second-century CE bishop Papias, who stated that a man called Matthew (who may or may not be the same as the gospel writer) originally collected Jesus' sayings in 'the Hebrew language'. Jerome and other church fathers were apparently aware of Hebrew/Aramaic gospels which have not survived (see Ehrman and Pleše 2011: 197–200). Translation from a written Aramaic version to Greek is not impossible;

after all, the historian Josephus admits that his history of the Jewish wars was translated from a written version 'in the language of the country' (*Jewish War* 1.3). However, all surviving Aramaic versions of the New Testament were translated from the Greek, and it is likely that the early Christian texts were originally written in Greek with the aim of appealing to gentiles as well as Jews, building on oral Aramaic traditions which were lost by the second century CE. Attempts to reconstruct the lost Aramaic archetype have been vitiated by over-enthusiastic searches for puns, rhymes and wordplay. For example, in Jesus' criticism of those who 'strain out a gnat'[11] but 'swallow a camel' (Matthew 23: 24), Black (1967: 175) saw an original jangle between the Aramaic words for 'gnat' (a type of small fly), written *qlm'* and pronounced *qalmā*, and for 'camel', written *gml'* and pronounced *gamlā*. On further investigation, most of the putative examples of Aramaic wordplay behind Jesus' words turn out not to work so well. The Aramaic word *qlm'* actually means 'louse', not 'gnat', and straining lice from wine was never common practice, while there was a belief that drink could be contaminated by gnats' eggs (Casey 2002: 77–8).

The language of the Greek New Testament itself varies between different authors. The gospel of Luke is written in a more classical style than the other three, and the letters of Paul include literary flourishes not found in the gospels. Some phrases in the gospels and Acts, such as the ubiquitous 'it came to pass (that)' (*egéneto* (*hôs*)) are taken from the earlier Greek translation of the Hebrew Scriptures, where they are closely based on Hebrew originals. Others may reflect the Aramaic scaffolding behind the gospels,[12] or continue features of the spoken Greek of the day, such as Matthew's use of a regularized *ês* 'you were' in place of Classical Greek *êstha* (Matthew 25:21). Further colloquial features include the incorporation of Latin words and expressions which were largely representative of Roman military and administrative life, such as *kentūríōn*, from Latin *centurio* 'centurion' or the phrase 'take care that' (Greek *dòs ergasían*, Latin *da operam*, Luke 12:58, see Blass et al. 2001: 4–5); the avoidance of the verbal mood called the optative (except in set phrases such as *mè génoito* 'may it not happen'); and the merger of senses of originally distinct prepositions, leading to *eis* (originally 'into') overlapping with *en* 'in'. Hence, where

---

[11] The King James Version has 'strain at a gnat', but later English translations generally have 'strain out', a closer translation of the Greek verb *diulízō*; the reference is to filtering wine to avoid consuming insects in it.

[12] A much-discussed example is the expression by which Jesus refers to himself, 'the son of man', for which an Aramaic origin has often been suggested; see further Casey (2007) with references to earlier work.

Mark's gospel has *ho eis tòn agrón* 'the man into the field' (Mark 13:16), Matthew (14:18) and Luke (17:31) 'write up' the phrase to *ho en (tôi) agrôi* 'the man in the field'.[13] It is not always easy to distinguish between apparent Semiticisms, which could be the result of translated Greek, and features that stem from the spoken language, although scholars have taken positions on both sides (see the synopses of the debate in George 2010 and Horrocks 2010: 147–52). It is clear, however, that these non-literary forms are avoided by writers with higher levels of exposure to the Greek literary canon and Greek education. Paul avoids Latinisms in his letters and is able to keep the prepositions meaning 'in' and 'into' apart. But he does not achieve the mastery of Greek style that is found in the contemporary historian Josephus, who uses the Greek optative in all its classical constructions with confidence, and prefers the Atticist forms with -*tt*- in words such as *glôtta* 'tongue' and *práttō* 'do' (whereas all books in the New Testament have *glôssa* and *prássō*).

Christian Greek and Christian Latin

The spread of Christianity around the Mediterranean was achieved principally using Greek texts, and preaching to populations who had a command of Greek. The Acts of the Apostles was probably composed at around 100 CE and thus many years after the actual missionary activities of the apostles, but it does bear testimony to a rapidly expanding network of Christians drawn from both Jews, inside and outside Judaea, and gentiles. Greek was probably the first language of Jews in much of the diaspora, including Tarsus, the hometown of the apostle Paul (see Noy 1993–5 and Ameling 2009). Knowledge of Greek was widespread in the multilingual Roman Empire, whereas even Jewish communities outside Judaea might have had minimal command of Aramaic. Although there is hardly any surviving epigraphic evidence for Christians before the third century from which to unearth the language of the first Christian communities, it is likely that they were predominantly Greek-speaking, even in the western half of the Roman Empire.[14] In the first two centuries CE, alongside oral traditions there was a proliferation of different Christian writings in Greek, only a selection of which made the cut into the New Testament, the final form of which was still a subject for debate in the third and fourth

---

[13] This example is taken from Browning (1983: 36); see Turner (1976: 58) for other examples where Luke adjusts Mark's language closer to the literary standard.
[14] Cooley (2012: 228–50) gives a survey of the emergence of Latin Christian epigraphy from the third century on.

centuries CE. Papyrus discoveries in the last 150 years have unearthed some of the variety of these works, now generally known as 'apocryphal gospels', which circulated in the early centuries of the Christian era (over forty texts are gathered in Ehrman and Pleše 2011). In both the New Testament as we have it, and in the apocryphal texts, there is a gradual fading of the Aramaic contributions to the story. In Paul's letters, the apostle Simon Peter is mentioned several times by his Aramaic name *Cephas* 'rock', but in the gospels he is known by the Greek name *Peter* 'rock' (John 1:42 is a noteworthy exception, since here the Aramaic name is given with its Greek translation); whereas the gospels of Matthew and Mark record Jesus' last words on the cross in Aramaic, Luke, John and the apocryphal gospel of Peter omit to mention them.

The mere fact that several versions of Jesus' life and ministry were in circulation, which differed between themselves on linguistic detail, meant that Christian preachers were always more interested in the meaning of scripture, rather than the words in which it was couched. In the words of the apostle Paul:

> And my speech and my preaching was not with enticing words of man's wisdom, but in demonstration of the Spirit and of power. (I Corinthians 2: 4, King James Version)

As we have already seen in the previous section, among the different gospels and early Christian writings themselves there were different levels of language, with Luke closer to the administrative standard Greek (the *koinē*) of his day. However, by the end of the second century, as Christian writers engaged in polemic with pagans, and set their sights on proselytizing to the better-educated classes, we can observe growing signs of defensiveness, if not embarrassment, about the language of scripture. Origen (born in Alexandria in Egypt at the end of the second century, died in Palestine *c.* 254) was one of the great scholars of the early church, who has the misfortune to be remembered more for his religiously motivated self-castration than his erudition. Although of a Christian family, he received an education in pagan Hellenic culture, which he put to good use in his voluminous works on Christian doctrine and commentaries on the Bible. A passage of his *Commentary on John*, now known only from its inclusion in a fourth-century anthology of his works (*Philocalia* 4), is an example of an early Christian text which defends the gospels against the charge of being written in bad Greek, including *solecisms* (Greek *soloikismoí*), the usual Greek term for grammatical features or expressions not acceptable in the educated written register. Origen's defence was to become a staple of later writers: the simplicity and humility of the language of the gospels is enough to contain divine truths, so no one could argue that believers are swayed by rhetoric or elegance of expression, rather than the power of the Christian message. To the regret of the historian of language, the later excerptors of the passage leave out the section where Origen goes into detail about the awkwardness of the gospel style.

Origen interpreted Paul's statement (Romans 1:14, King James Version) that he was a 'debtor both to the Greeks and to the Barbarians, both to the wise and to the unwise' to mean that Paul wanted to deliver the Christian message to wise Greeks and Romans, amongst others. In order for that message to get through to the educated classes, the church fathers realized that its vehicle needed an upgrade. As they grappled to overthrow or integrate classical learning, Greek writers increasingly adopted the linguistic prescriptions of the grammarians and those authors who recommended a return to the purity of Attic diction of the fifth century BCE. Thus authors such as Origen, Gregory of Nazianzus, John Chrysostom and others wrote, and apparently preached, in registers far removed from everyday language. The shift made by church fathers writing in Greek from the second century CE towards a more formal, Atticizing, language, away from the more colloquial and contemporary language of the gospels, may not seem to be in keeping with the commitment to intelligibility and accessibility for which the apostles argued.[15] But by promoting the Christian message in the language of the literary classics, and indeed incorporating the teachings of Jesus within the framework of Greek philosophy, the church fathers were actually trying to make themselves understood by the intellectual elite of the time. Moreover, the language of the Greek classics gave these church fathers prestige, and thereby ensured that later generations of scholars would continue to read and copy them.

A similar movement can be observed in the church in the western Roman Empire following the introduction of Christianity to predominantly Latin-speaking areas, such as North Africa, during the second century. The first Christian texts written in Latin date from around 200, and include writings from the apologist Tertullian and the *Martyrdom of SS Perpetua and Felicitas*, a text which also exists in a Greek version, although the Latin is generally thought to be the original (Heffernan 2012). These

---

[15] See, for example, I Corinthians 14, where Paul recommends speaking to be understood in Church: 'Yet in the church I had rather speak five words with my understanding, that by my voice I might teach others also, than ten thousand words in an unknown tongue' (verse 19, King James Version). Women, however, are told to keep silent in church, and ask their husbands to explain what is said to them at home (I Corinthians 14:34–5).

texts are not, however, as far removed from literary registers of Latin as some of the Greek books of the New Testament were from the standard of the day. The early Latin translations of the Bible from Greek were probably also made in the third century. We know from the comments of Augustine and Jerome that these were of varying quality, and some contained straightforward mistakes and mistranslations. For example, Augustine discusses Latin versions which render the Greek 'their feet are swift to shed blood' as 'their feet are sharp to spread blood', or 'false plants do not put down deep roots' as 'false calves do not put down deep roots' (*De doctrina Christiana* 2.12.18). Even so, a recent study of the language of the first Latin translations (the *Vetus Latina*) has shown them to be closer to the educated standard of the day than they have generally been given credit for (Burton 2000). Later Latin Christian writers, however, show signs of embarrassment (a linguistic cringe, as it were) about the language of the first Latin Bible translations. Thus the apologist Lactantius, writing in the second half of the third century, thinks that the Christian message has not got through to scholars and princes because the apparent coarseness of its language seems to the educated 'stuff for old women, stupid and vulgar' (*Divine Institutes* 5.1.16, translated A.J. Bowen). Lactantius further acknowledges that Tertullian writes rough and uneven Latin and does not always make his meaning clear (*Divine Institutes* 5.1.23). Lactantius himself writes with Classical elegance, studding his prose with citations from Cicero.

The apparent tolerance towards non-standard features of language among early Christian writers has already been exemplified by Origen's defence of solecisms in the gospels, and by Augustine's acceptance of *h*-dropping. Augustine further expands on the subject of solecisms and barbarisms in another passage of his work on Christian doctrine (*De doctrina Christiana* 2.13.19–20), which helps to clarify his attitude to correct language. Immediately after his discussion of inferior translations of the Bible into Latin, Augustine notes that some apparent mistakes in Latin are not important, since they do not affect the meaning. Take the preposition *inter* 'between', which is followed in Classical Latin by a noun in the accusative case, as *inter homines* 'between men'. In non-standard Latin registers from the first century CE on, speakers and writers sometimes use a different case form, the ablative (hence *inter hominibus* 'between men'); this development is often seen as an important stepping stone towards the eventual loss of case distinctions in languages descended from Latin. Since there is no difference of meaning between *inter homines* and *inter hominibus*, Augustine says that the learned reader should have no problem with the variation:

> But the weaker men are, the more they are troubled by such matters. Their weakness stems from a desire to appear learned, not with a knowledge of things, by which we are edified, but with a knowledge of signs, by which it is difficult not to be puffed up in some way. (*De doctrina Christiana* 2.13.20, translation from Green 1995: 77)

Augustine argues that debates over correct language can prove distracting, and since the linguistic signs are not as important as the message they convey, it is easiest to remove the source of distraction. In this way, he comes to argue for a continuation of the Classical rules of grammar. We should note that, in this passage, as elsewhere in his writings, Augustine does not question the accepted ancient view that language is built on authority and custom, as well as reason. As Burton has pointed out (2007: 176–7), submission to authority is usually seen by Augustine as a desirable quality, particularly when the authority has been shown to be efficacious and capable of producing good results. Language is no different, and there is therefore no reason for Augustine, or other Christian writers, to try to overturn the linguistic prescriptions in which they were educated.

The steady progress towards the higher registers of both Greek and Latin among some Christian writers from the second to fifth centuries certainly reflects a broadening of their appeal to educated classes and among members of the elite of ancient society. But authors such as Lactantius and John Chrysostom did not turn their back on the lower classes, or write only for the rich. On the contrary, Lactantius criticizes pagan learning for its lack of involvement with women, slaves and barbarians (*Div. Inst.* 3.25). John Chrysostom had rock-star appeal among the common people, and lost his post as Archbishop of Constantinople through alienating the wealthy, including the emperor's wife. It is hard for a modern audience to reconcile the use of highfalutin, archaic diction with populism, and we are inclined not to take seriously the claim made by Isidore of Pelusium, in a letter to a grammarian, that John's clarity was achieved because he 'Atticized in his speech' (*Epist.* 2.42, Migne *PG* 78, 484, cited in Kelly 1995: 82). But it is important not to lose sight of the gap between written text and everyday spoken language. By the third and fourth centuries, all literary or written forms of Greek and Latin, even the more humble styles associated with martyrdoms and saint's lives, were learned varieties. The composition of any written text required a command of different vocabulary, spelling rules and even syntax and word-endings. Christians still relied on the same methods of education as earlier generations, including rote learning of sections of the classical canon as well as drills in spellings and explanations of texts, even though Christian literature was now likely to feature alongside the pagan classics. Augustine records that learning to write Latin was as difficult and painful as learning Greek (*Confessions* 1.13.20). Greek- and Latin-speaking communities had become 'diglossic', accustomed to deal in a different variety for written composition and formal occasions from the language of the street. An individual who could master the formal 'high' register with competence might therefore have been more intelligible to the masses than one who mixed forms from different registers, or who did not observe the conventions of the higher register.

The body of Christian texts written in Greek and Latin in the first five centuries after Jesus covered a wide spectrum of topics, intended for a range of different audiences. While theologians and orators such as John Chrysostom, Lactantius and Augustine were able to adopt and adapt the idioms of earlier Greek and Latin classics, other less high-flown texts continued to be written and circulated. Unfortunately, many of these low-level Christian texts (such as the apocryphal gospels, or the stories of the childhood of Jesus or Mary) do not survive in complete form, and are only known from stray scraps of papyrus or parchment surviving from the first millennium. We do, however, have copies of martyrdoms and bio-graphies, accounts of pilgrimages, and monastic rule books which were composed in language which was closer to everyday spoken Greek or Latin. However, even these texts still contain many features that by now had probably dropped out of common parlance. The much greater amount of surviving papyri from the Greek-speaking east, particularly from Egypt, allows us to set low-level literary works, such as the second-century *Martyrdom of Polycarp* (author unknown), against letters and documents written by those with minimal education. The comparison shows that the apparent simplicity and directness of the language of martyrdom narratives is actually not the result of lack of education of their authors, but reflects a conscious attempt to present straightforward prose, partly mirroring the model of the scriptures (see Horrocks 2010: 158–9 on the different levels within written Greek). In the absence of a similar wealth of surviving letters and documentary texts in the Latin language, scholars have been more liable to read texts such as the *Martyrdom of SS Perpetua and Felicitas* or the *Peregrinatio Aetheriae* (on which see below p. 163–4) as reflecting the unmitigated voice of the author or the protagonists.[16] But these texts, and others like them, build on the language of the Latin Bible versions,

---

[16] See Bremmer and Formisano (2012: 1) and Heffernan (2012: 5) for the view that Perpetua's own words are preserved in the *Martyrdom*; Palmer (1954: 153) already cautions against mistaking the *Peregrinatio* for a 'true and undistorting mirror of the spoken language.'

if not so closely on the pagan classics. Take for example the striking phrase *uideo in horomate* 'I saw in a vision' which occurs in Perpetua's narrative in the *Martyrdom of SS Perpetua and Felicitas* (10.1). A similar phrase for 'in a vision', *en horámati*, occurs several times in the Greek version of Acts (e.g. 7:31, 10:3). Jerome translates the phrase as *in uisu* in the Vulgate, but earlier translations current in North Africa during Perpetua's time may well have wanted to keep the Greek word for a Christian vision.

Modern perceptions of the language of Greek and Latin Christian texts in part reflect the history of scholarship in the last hundred years. Twentieth-century anglophone classicists in general answered the questions of Tertullian 'What has Athens got to do with Jerusalem?' (*De praescriptione* 7.9) and Jerome 'What has Horace to do with the psalter, Vergil with the gospels and Cicero with Paul?' (*Epist.* 22.29) in the way that the questioners had intended: Christian texts have nothing to do with the classical world. This has led to a growing divergence between the study of pagan and Christian authors, and growing compartmentalization between theological and classical students. The separation has had a lasting effect on views of the history of the Greek and Latin languages, which may be best seen in the compilation of two of the standard weapons in the classicist's arsenal, the Latin and Greek dictionaries. The *Oxford Latin Dictionary* (Glare 1982), fifty years in the making, was completed in 1982. The short preface to the work discloses nothing of the tempestuous early history of the project, which resulted in the mental breakdown of the second editor, who subsequently distributed a series of slanderous pamphlets abusing Oxford lexicographers, amongst others. The preface does, however, reveal the reasoning behind the chronological restrictions of the work, which covers all Latin authors until the end of the second century CE:

> The later limit of the period covered by this dictionary is necessarily imprecise. In practice it means that most of the jurists quoted in Justinian's Digest have been included, although they run over into the third century, while patristic writings from the last years of the second century have not been drawn upon. (A proposal that the Dictionary should be extended to include Christian Latin had been finally rejected in 1951.)
> (Glare 1982: vi)

The monumental ninth edition of the *Greek–English Lexicon* (*LSJ*), published in 1940, also excluded Christian Greek authors of the fourth century CE and later from consideration, even though words from them had been included in earlier editions. Indeed, a separate lexicon of 'patristic' Greek was already underway when the ninth edition was published (eventually to appear as Lampe 1961–8). The segregation of the classical and the Christian is perhaps most evident in the lexicographic world, but it did not stop there. Classical and theological studies developed distinct traditions of text publication, commentary and even language tuition. This institutional divide doubtless contributed to the certainty expressed in the preface to the *Oxford Latin Dictionary* that there is a distinct variety of 'Christian Latin', which was to be carefully filtered out of what the classical student might need. The notion of a separate 'Christian Latin' was given scholarly respectability by a number of studies by Dutch scholars associated with the Catholic University of Nijmegen, most notably Josef Schrijnen (see for example Schrijnen 1935), and Christine Mohrmann (see Mohrmann 1958–77), who pointed out stylistic and lexical features particular to Latin Christian texts.

However, in recent years, particularly with the surge of interest in late antiquity among ancient historians, the barriers between Classics and Theology departments have steadily been coming down. At the same time, confidence in the linguistic distinctiveness of Christian texts has gradually evaporated (see Coleman 1987 and Burton 2011 for discussion of Christian Latin). True, Christian writers both in Latin and in Greek have some specialized items of vocabulary to define Christian concepts, rituals or objects. But these words, if not too arcane, are also found in the works of non-Christians. There are certainly 'non-classical' features that can be found in the language of Christian writers. Some of these, particularly in Greek authors, reflect the language of the Septuagint or of the Greek New Testament, and may ultimately go back to Semitic influence. But other features are no doubt the reflection of the gradual evolution of the written literary standard, with a gradual expansion of its vocabulary, or the extension of existing patterns of syntax or word-formation. Since pagan authors disappear from the written record in the fifth and sixth centuries, many of the linguistic forms or structures which were thought to be representative of 'Patristic Greek' or 'Christian Latin' are simply the outcome of the same continuous process of change which all languages, even written literary forms, undergo.

Christianity and local languages in the Roman Empire

The *Peregrinatio Aetheriae*, a travelogue recording the trip to the Holy Land by a late fourth-century nun, variously identified by the name Aetheria, Egeria or Silvia, customarily makes an appearance in the final chapter of books on the history of the Latin language. The work, the earliest surviving substantial prose work written by a woman, is written in a low-level register of Latin which, although still with literary pretensions, is further from the classical canons which underlie the language of her contemporaries Augustine and Jerome (on the language of Aetheria, see most recently Adams 2011: 258–63). Linguists have devoted much time to the investigation of the chatterbox Aetheria's language and style, but what she says can also be of interest. At the end of her travels, she explains the language situation in Aelia Capitolina, the Roman city built next to the site of Jerusalem after its destruction following the Bar Kokhba revolt of 132–6 CE:

> And since in that province some of the people know both Syrian and Greek, but others Greek alone or Syrian alone, and since, therefore, the bishop (although he may know Syrian) always speaks Greek, and never Syrian, a priest always stands by who interprets in Syrian what the bishop says in Greek, so that all may understand the explanations. And since it is necessary that the lessons read in church shall be read in Greek, a man stands by who interprets in Syrian that the people may receive instruction. And that the Latins, who know neither Syrian nor Greek, may not be saddened, an explanation is also given to them in Latin by those brothers and sisters present who understand both Greek and Latin. (*Peregrinatio Aetheriae* 47.3, translation adapted from John H. Bernard)

Note that Aetheria, like other Latin writers, uses 'Syrian' (Latin *siriste*) to refer to the Semitic language of Judaea that we have earlier called Aramaic (Millar 2006: 387). The picture Aetheria presents, of a priest speaking or reading in Greek followed by individual adaptations and explanations in the local language, has been adopted as the model for the early church both within the Roman Empire (Metzger 1977: 286 for the early Latin church) and outside its borders (Thomson 1978: 295 on the Armenian Moses of Chorene *History* 3.36). The general silence about translation in church in other sources is in keeping with the customary reluctance to mention interpreters (although note that another pilgrim from the west, the fifth-century Antoninus of Piacenza, refers to multilingual abbots and interpreters at a monastery in the Sinai peninsula, *Itinerarium* 37). It may be significant that Aetheria comments in detail on the languages used during a mass in the Near East, since her description suggests that contemporary readers in the western Empire were not familiar with simultaneous translation during church services.

The *Peregrinatio* extract also gives important information about the status of Aramaic and Greek in the church in the Roman Near East. Aramaic, although permitted in use in church and by priests, is clearly subordinate to Greek, which is the language in which the lessons are read and the bishop addresses the congregation. Indeed, the prohibition of the bishop from speaking in Aramaic in church, although he may know the language, recalls the position of Latin (and later Greek) as the only language(s) permitted for a Roman magistrate on official business (see Chapter 2 above). Jerome also mentions 'Syrian' in restricted use in churches in Judaea (*Epist.* 108.29) where it features as one of the languages of the psalms sung over the corpse of the saintly Paula. Note also that Aetheria explicitly states that the lessons in church were read in Greek, but it is known that there were Bible translations made into the Syriac dialect of Aramaic already by the fourth century. We saw in the opening section of this chapter that Syriac and Coptic were the only two local languages to have any status in the church within the Roman Empire, and in this final section I shall examine the reasons for the rise to prominence of these two languages, and no others.

Unlike the other dialects of Aramaic in use in the Roman Near East, Syriac came to be the vehicle for a substantial corpus of written literature (mostly, but not entirely, Christian), including numerous translations from Greek works. One indication of the far-reaching interaction between Greek and Syriac is the number of Greek loanwords in the language, including the name of its distinctive looping variety of the Aramaic script, *estrangelā*, a borrowing from the Greek adjective *stroggúlē* 'rounded'.[17] Syriac was originally associated with the kingdom of Osrhoene, a quasi-independent kingdom between Rome and Parthia situated between the Tigris and Euphrates in an area which is now divided between Turkey and Syria. Osrhoene encompassed the cities of Edessa in the west, now Urfa in Turkey, and Nisibis in the east, now Nusaybın, just north of the Turkish border with Syria. After the successful military campaigns of Lucius Verus against the Parthians in the 160s, Osrhoene's independence lessened, and Edessa became a Roman *colonia* in 212/13. Osrhoene was a polyglot kingdom, with Greek widely spoken as well as Syriac, and probably varieties belonging to the Iranian sub-family of Indo-European. The borderland between Rome and Parthia seems to have provided fertile soil for multi-lingualism. Palmyra (modern Tadmur in Syria) and Dura-Europos (now located to the east of the Syrian border with Iraq), two towns to the south of Osrhoene, provide better epigraphic and documentary evidence for the language situation in the early centuries of the Christian era than their northern neighbour. In Palmyra, an oasis city-state with pretensions to

---

[17] This account largely follows Millar (1993: 437–8); for Greek loanwords in Syriac, see Brock (1996).

independence, the public epigraphy features many bilingual Palmyrene (another Aramaic dialect) and Greek inscriptions, and some with three languages, Palmyrene, Greek and Latin. In Dura, which switched between Roman and Parthian control before its destruction in the third century, excavations have revealed texts and inscriptions in a smorgasbord of Near Eastern languages: various dialects of Aramaic (including both Syriac and Palmyrene), Greek, Latin, and the Iranian languages Parthian and Middle Persian (see Kaizer 2009 and Andrade 2013: 211–41 for recent overviews). The earliest surviving Christian text from this whole region was found at Dura, a fragment of a gospel harmony (a compilation which ties together the four different gospel accounts) dating from the end of the second or beginning of the third century, written in Greek. Throughout this region, local traditions of writing in the vernacular continued in the Roman period.

So why did Syriac alone develop an extensive literature? The answer may be that there was already a literary culture in the kingdom before it came under Roman control. Although it later became associated specifically with Christianity, Syriac was already in use in Osrhoene before the arrival of Christian missionaries. Indeed, the first Bible versions in Syriac may have been parts of the Hebrew Scriptures translated in diaspora Jewish communities (Ameling 2009: 222), and Syriac was also the language of most of the teachings of Mani (216–76 CE), the founder of the Manichaean religion. Mani grew up in a Jewish/Christian village in southern Mesopotamia, outside the Roman Empire. As Mani's biography shows, Syriac had a healthy life on both sides of the border, not just among Christians, and the continued production of Syriac writings east of the Euphrates sustained the Syriac readers on the west bank. The translation of the Bible and the creation of Christian literature in Aramaic dialects thus seem to be a result of particular local circumstances, and are not well explained by the assumption that there was a resurgence of local pride among Aramaic-speaking communities, and a desire for autonomy from Rome.[18] Indeed, Greek remained widely in use in the cities of the Near East, and language does not seem to have been utilized as a political tool in the local tussles with central authority. This is seen most clearly in the career of the third-century renegade Bishop of Antioch (modern Antakya in Turkey), Paul of Samosata, who appears to have continued to use Greek rather than adopting Syriac, although in revolt against the Orthodox Church of the time (Millar 1971).

---

[18] As was proposed by MacMullen (1966); see the discussion in Chapter 3.

In Egypt too, the creation of the Coptic versions of the Bible was dependent on a pre-existing tradition of using the language for everyday documentation (Bagnall 1993: 235–50; Richter 2009). The rise of Coptic in the third century occurs around the same time as the demise of writing in the Demotic script, the last stage in the evolution of Egyptian hieroglyphs. The transition to the new script may have been in part due to experimentation among the scribal class; indeed, many Egyptian scribes were literate in both Greek and Egyptian written in Demotic script (Vierros 2012), and some had experimented using Greek letters to write the Egyptian language already in the third century BCE. Although the last Demotic texts and the earliest Coptic ones are close in time, the language of the latter is closer to the spoken idiom of the day; Demotic avoids using Greek loanwords, but Coptic is stuffed full of them. According to Hopkins (1991: 146), 'Christianity was an important stimulus to maintaining and spreading literacy in Coptic among the underprivileged ... Coptic originated as a script of protest'. But others have taken more nuanced views, which fit better into the picture given by papyrus archives (such as those from Kellis discussed in Chapter 5) that show communities happily switching between Greek and Coptic and reflect the fact that early biblical texts surviving from Egypt display a preference for bilingual versions, with the Greek and Coptic languages written side by side (Bagnall 1993: 253–4). Thus Frankfurter assigned a key role in the creation of the written form of Coptic to the power of writing in magic spells and curses (Frankfurter 1998), and other scholars have stressed the importance of Gnostic writings and early translations of Manichaean texts as well (Richter 2009: 415). Indeed, there is some evidence that Coptic versions of Manichaean texts may have been directly translated from Syriac Aramaic, without going through the medium of Greek, as shown by the survival of a Syriac-Coptic glossary of Manichaean terms at Kellis (Römer 2009: 639).

The translation of the Bible into the Aramaic dialects and Coptic in the eastern Roman Empire thus arises from special circumstances. In both cases, there were existing traditions of literacy in the vernacular. Aramaic received further support from communities outside the Empire, and Coptic from a scribal class who were proficient both in writing in Greek and a second language. Despite the claims of the church fathers given at the opening of this chapter, there were no other serious engagements with other local languages in the Roman Empire, no translation of biblical or other texts into the vernacular. Although Augustine records his search for a Punic-speaking bishop for the congregation at Fussala, we never learn whether he actually found one. Peter Brown thought that Christian evangelism delivered the knock-out blow to the minority languages of the Roman Empire. Latin was the marker of the universal church, whereas local languages had been associated with local religious use. To become a fully paid-up member of the Christian church, the believer in the west had to embrace Latin.

> Latin won its final triumph as the spoken language of most of the former territories of the Roman empire in the very last, more desperate centuries of Roman rule. Had the empire fallen when the 'Roman peace' was at its height, in the second century AD, Latin would have vanished along with the empire in much of western Europe. Celtic would have re-emerged as the dominant language in Gaul and much of Spain. France and Spain might well have become Celtic-speaking countries, as Brittany and Wales are today. It was only in the last century of the empire that the slow pressure of bureaucrats, landowners and the Christian clergy ensured that Latin replaced languages which had existed since prehistoric times. (Brown 2013: 232)

Like all alternative histories, this vision of Celtic triumphalism is thought-provoking, but difficult to assess. Linguistic evidence alone offers little help. It is true that some of the common words in Romance seem to have a particularly Christian timbre. For example, modern western Romance languages use a derivative of *parabola* to mean 'word', rather than the normal Latin term *uerbum* (French *parole*, Italian *parola*, Spanish *palabra* and Portuguese *palavra*). The term *parabola* is a borrowing from Greek, which entered the language through the translations of the gospels, as the special term to refer to the stories that Jesus tells (English *parable* has the same origin). However, the widespread adoption of a Christian term does not necessarily mean that the majority of the inhabitants of the western Empire only learnt Latin after the second century. Vocabulary can spread quickly among a wide population of speakers over a diverse area, as easily demonstrated from any number of lexical changes in English around the globe, where *stores* are replacing *shops*, and *ice-cream cornets* have largely been replaced by *ice-cream cones*.

Indeed, as we saw in Chapter 5, the demise of local languages in the Roman Empire may have taken place over many generations, and involved lengthy periods of bilingualism, where Latin was spoken in some domains, and the vernacular in others. Documentary evidence from before the rise of Christianity suggests that Latin had already penetrated deeply into local societies in the west. Bilingual archives, such as the second-century firing records from the pottery factory at La Graufesenque in southern Gaul (see Chapter 3), show Latin used alongside the local variety among the same group of speakers, many of them hardly members of the Roman aristocracy, but slaves. Greek loanwords in Coptic and Aramaic,[19] and Latin loanwords in British varieties of Celtic, in Basque and in Albanian[20] show that even among the languages which survived Roman rule, there had been periods of intense linguistic interaction between the local populations and their overlords. Furthermore, the apparently speedy demise of local languages after the introduction of Christianity may be a result of the bias of our sources. One of the few domains in which Gaulish, Punic and Phrygian had continued in written usage involves local religion and cult, so it is no surprise that the textual evidence for this diminishes after the fourth century. We cannot deduce from this that the spoken languages themselves necessarily did not continue to be spoken, particularly in out-of-the-way areas or close-knit communities. In other documented cases of history where minority languages die out in the face of a dominant major language, the moribund variety may continue in oral use for decades or even centuries after its last use in written form. In summary, there is no secure way of knowing the date of the triumph of Latin in the west, whereas it can be stated for certain that the Arab invasions from the seventh century on cut short the story of Greek in the east.

This chapter opened with the translation of the Bible into Gothic, and the story of the afterlife of Gothic can act as a fitting coda, and an example of the long-term survival of a language after it has fallen out of written use. When Bishop Wulfila did his missionary work in the third century, the Goths inhabited the Balkans and an area north of the Black Sea. But after the influx of the Huns in the fourth and fifth centuries into their homeland, the Goths themselves moved en masse into the Roman Empire; the Gothic sack of Rome under Alaric in 410 CE is one of the traditional endpoints of the ancient world. Gothic kingdoms were briefly established in Italy, France and Spain, and it is during the reign of Theodoric the Great (died 526 CE), king of the Ostrogoths in Italy, that the surviving codex of the Bible in Gothic, written with silver letters on purple parchment, was created. The Goths themselves appear to have adopted the language of the Romans over time, and after the seventh century there are no surviving written records in Gothic. The written sources suggest, therefore, that Gothic died out in the seventh century. But Gothic was still spoken in the

[19] For Greek loanwords in Coptic, see Förster (2002); in Syriac, Brock (1996).
[20] For a collection of Latin loanwords in British Celtic, see Jackson (1953) (see Adams (2007: 579–93) for a criticism of Jackson's conclusions about the nature of British Latin); for Latin loanwords in Basque, see Segura Mungula and Etxebarria Ayesta (1996); for Latin loanwords in Albanian, Orel (2000: 23–37).

Crimea until at least the sixteenth century, when the diplomat Ogier Ghiselin de Busbecq served as ambassador for the Habsburgs at the Ottoman court (Stearns 1978). Busbecq recounts in the fourth of his *Turcicae Epistolae* (*Turkish Letters*) how he met at court two delegates from the Goths of Crimea, and records some of their vocabulary and expressions. Although Busbecq's native Flemish may have led him to overstate the similarity of Gothic to Germanic languages with which he was more familiar, there is little doubt that the language is a later development of one in which the Gothic Bible was composed. Gothic was still in use nearly a thousand years after our last written record.

Conclusion
Dead languages?

Historians 'have long been aware that the texts they employ offer only partial glimpses of life as lived' (Osborne 2011: 25). Osborne's statement occurs in a plea to historians to be more aware of evidence from sources other than the written, illustrated by his consideration of what can be learnt from Classical Greek representations of the human body. He argues that categories of thought with which text-based historians might choose to operate, such as free or enslaved, Greek or barbarian, may be reframed or refocused by paying closer attention to visual media. In this book, I have shown another way in which the historian can supplement the direct evidence given by surviving ancient literature, documents and inscriptions, namely through an examination of the languages and idioms in which texts were written. Authors, scribes, stone-cutters and engravers all made choices when they committed a text to a written medium. Some decided to write in a particular language or dialect which was not the same as their native tongue, others chose to record bi- or multilingual versions of the same message. Even monolingual speakers made conscious selections of lexical items, constructions or idioms. The linguistic choices made by ancient writers are rarely without a wider significance, and I have demonstrated how language use can be revealing both of the imperial ambitions of cities and states and of local attitudes towards empires. The vocabulary of a particular individual can shed light on his or her class, gender, age and ethnicity; it may reveal religious or political sympathies and antipathies.

Inscriptions, documents and literary works do not allow a 360-degree view of ancient life as lived, and neither do they give a complete picture of language as spoken. All the languages discussed in this book are 'dead languages', an expression that neatly encapsulates the truism that languages live in the minds and mouths of their speakers. Understanding how an ancient language really worked from examination of the written remains is a task similar to figuring out how dinosaurs moved, or what they ate, from the fossil record. It is possible to draw a number of conclusions about the way ancient languages were used, or how extinct creatures lived, through comparison with current spoken languages, or existing fauna respectively, combined with the scientific understanding of what is possible furnished either by linguistics or by biology. Given the amount of surviving text for Greek and Latin, it has been possible to build up a fairly comprehensive picture of the languages, but even so our understanding of either language could be dramatically changed by a new find, just as the new discovery of a fossilized skeleton has the potential to enrich our view of the build or the habits of the plesiosaur or pterodactyl. For some of the other ancient languages discussed in this book, we have far less material to go on, and 'palaeolinguists' have had to match the ingenuity of palaeontologists in constructing a model of a minor language from extremely meagre and often ambiguous evidence. New texts in ancient languages are turning up every year, and they will continue to improve our knowledge of the different languages spoken in the ancient world.

The comparison between languages and dinosaurs is, however, misleading in one crucial respect. Fossils preserve the actual bones or cartilage or their imprint on surrounding material. Ancient languages are known only through a written medium, and script is not the same as speech. Indeed, I have argued throughout this book that it is often much more difficult to match writing to speech than is assumed in some works on ancient languages and linguistics. The acquisition of literacy was always an arduous and unpleasant task in ancient societies. Although Horace (*Sat.* 1.25–6) and Jerome (*Ep.* 128.1) mention that the bitter pill of learning the alphabet was sometimes sweetened through the gift of cakes, perhaps in the shape of letters, most ancient accounts make it clear that the rod was generally the most-favoured educational aid. Learning to write was not only painful, it was also costly and time-consuming. We have already seen at various points in this book how, by the end of the Classical period, the literary forms of Greek and Latin were far removed from the everyday spoken language. This can sometimes lead us to imagine an early stage of the languages when people wrote as they spoke. But written language is always removed from speech. Not only do we omit from the written record the manifold slips of the tongue and non-sequiturs that may be caused by tiredness, inebriation, lack of concentration or confusion, we also adapt speech to the conventions of writing. When occupied in making a permanent or semi-permanent record, speakers have time to reflect on their words in a way that seldom happens in day-to-day conversation, and they are able to iron out inconsistencies, avoid some vocabulary items at the expense of others, and adopt learned phrases or stylistic idioms. Learning letters inculcates models of how to write, how to express different messages, and what vocabulary and grammatical endings to use. There does not seem to have been any time or circumstance in the ancient world when this 'writing up' of speech into script did not take place. Most early Greek writing, for example, demonstrates the care taken in its composition by virtue of the fact that it is expressed in the medium of verse, not prose (Powell 1991). Moreover, the influence of earlier written models can even be traced on texts that appear to us to be very personal and direct, such as curses carved onto lead tablets, intended for the sight of gods and demons rather than for human eyes, or boasts of sexual performance hastily scratched on brothel walls.[1]

Although we can strive to bridge the gulf between the written and the spoken when researching the history of dead languages, it is important never to forget the limitations of our evidence. The investigation of written texts necessarily involves consideration of ancient education and literacy, topics which deserve, and have received, book-length treatments of their own.[2] As we have seen in this book, literacy can change the way speakers viewed their own language: perceptions of what counts as 'correct' language and attitudes towards linguistic variation differ between largely literate societies and predominantly oral cultures, and high levels of literacy can have an effect on the spoken language. Assumptions about ancient education, or about levels of literacy, can also affect the way we view the surviving texts from antiquity. If we think that only a minority of speakers were able to read, then we may be tempted to associate the language of classical literate texts with a small class of elite individuals, and by extension imagine that the general population spoke something different. Such an idea has been commonplace in the study of Latin, where the term 'Vulgar Latin' has been used to describe the spoken idiom of the underclass, perhaps radically different from the speech of their masters and patrons, which itself corresponded to the written Latin encountered in Classical texts.[3] Adams (2013) has shown that this 'two-tier' view of Latin cannot be upheld, since statements by elite authors, such as Cicero or Augustine, make it clear that they did not write as they spoke either. Furthermore, features of Latin that had previously been classed as 'Vulgar' sometimes

---

[1] See Kruschwitz and Halla-aho (2007) and Clackson (2011c: 37) for examples of the influence of spell-books on curse-tablets and stock phrases in graffiti.
[2] In addition to the bibliography cited at p. 97, see Thomas (1992), Morgan (1998), Cribiore (2001).
[3] See Adams (2013: 7) for references to works on Vulgar Latin taking this view.

appear in high-register literary texts. Perhaps then, we need to reposition our conceptual boundaries so that we no longer view a division between the (spoken and written) language of the educated elite and the (spoken) language of the illiterate, but instead draw the line between writing and speech.

What does the distance between the spoken and written language mean for the student of ancient languages? It could be argued that it is pointless to attempt to make sense of ancient linguistic variation through the methods of modern linguistic research, which are largely grounded in speech, not writing. Does it make sense to discuss the ancient Greek dialects with the same terminology used by twenty-first century dialectologists, given that most modern dialects do not have a written form? Or, consider the study of sociolinguistic variation: linguists such as Labov can make use of recordings, acoustic measurements, and sufficient data to allow for statistical testing, but for the ancient world we have to make do largely with texts transmitted through a manuscript tradition, which may tell us more about an author's skill at caricature than about the speech habits of individuals. The language of speakers in Aristophanes, Roman comedy or Petronius' *Cena Trimalchionis* is situated at several removes from any real spoken event. I hope, however, that the studies in this book have shown that, provided the researcher is aware that written language is not identical to speech, it is nevertheless possible to use the methods of modern linguistics to gain some insight into ancient verbal behaviour. Habits of speech sometimes leak through the filters imposed by education, or are revealed through hypercorrection errors, where writers overcompensate for what they perceive as a flaw in their own usage. Metalinguistic comments, parodies, anecdotes and statements of grammarians can all be revealing about what was really going on in the spoken language.

Furthermore, the recognition that writing is a medium at one remove from speech can help us to refocus on the fact that the inscribed, drawn or painted texts of the ancient world are themselves features of a physical object. Study of ancient epigraphy has in recent years paid increasing attention to the materiality of inscriptions, their location and their interaction with associated monuments or works of art.[4] We saw in the discussion of the bilingual texts in Chapter 3 and the account of the dedications in the temple of Artemis Orthia by victors in the boys' games (p. 61) that choice of unusual linguistic forms is often accompanied by careful selection

---

[4] See for example Carroll (2006) and Laurence and Sears (2013).

of script, letter-forms and decoration. Consideration of the language of these texts makes better sense when integrated with an understanding of the object as a whole. In our investigation of the written remains of antiquity, we must be sure that we pay as much attention to the language of our written sources as their authors did.

Bibliographic essay

SOURCES

A substantial body of literary and subliterary material written in Greek and Latin has been passed down from antiquity through copying and recopying of manuscript material. In addition, we have direct evidence for the languages from tens of thousands of surviving inscriptions and documents on wood, papyrus or other materials. Some of the other languages discussed in this book, such as Hebrew, Armenian and Old Irish, are attested both in inscriptions and in a manuscript tradition, but the majority of them are known only from epigraphic sources. Keeping track of this vast range of inscriptional material is made much easier by the bibliography edited by Bérard et al. (2010, with annual supplements available online), which gives full information on published inscriptions both in Latin and Greek and in a range of other languages from India to Ireland. Bérard et al. (2010) includes documentary material written on wooden tablets, but does not generally cover texts written on papyrus, for which see Bagnall (ed.) (2009). Papyrologists also benefit from a number of corpora and search platforms on the web, for which see www.papyri.info. Understanding epigraphy requires knowledge of the history of writing, and the different varieties of script, from hieroglyphs to abjads and alphabets. The most comprehensive account of the development of writing around the world is Daniels and Bright (1996), which includes scholarly accounts of the development of local scripts in the Near East and Mediterranean. For the local varieties of the early Greek alphabet *LSAG* is unsurpassed.

The Classical languages have been extensively studied, and are well served by grammars, dictionaries and handbooks. The standard reference grammar for Greek is Kühner, Blass and Gerth (1890–1904), with more historical and dialectal material in Schwyzer (1959–66); for Latin Kühner and Holzweissig (1912) covers phonology and morphology and Kühner, Stegmann and Thierfelder (1966) syntax; historical phonology and morphology are described in Leumann (1977) and Weiss (2009). There are also numerous grammars of individual Greek dialects, including Threatte's work on Attic inscriptions (Threatte 1980 and 1996), which sets a standard that few other grammars can hope to match. The authoritative dictionaries for Greek and Latin into English are Liddell, Scott and Jones (1940, with the revised supplement of Glare 1996) and Glare (1982). Two recent publications in the Leiden Indo-European Etymological Dictionary Series, Beekes (2010) and de Vaan (2008), provide up-to-date information in English on a bulk of Greek and Latin etymologies, with full references. Two handbooks of Greek have been published in the last ten years (Christidis ed. 2007 and Bakker ed. 2010); they are largely complementary, and together cover a large range of topics in the history of Ancient Greek and its many varieties. Horrocks (2010) is a single-author history of the language, which takes Greek from antiquity to the present day. For Latin, there is also a recent handbook (Clackson ed. 2011), and discursive history of the language (Clackson and Horrocks 2007).

For the non-classical languages of the ancient world the bibliography is enormous, and I have given indications of reliable accounts of the languages I discuss in this book other than Latin and Greek in footnotes. For a good survey of many of the non-classical languages, including indications of where to find out more, Woodard (ed.) (2004) is recommended. Languages of the Indo-European family, including some of the smaller varieties known only from isolated inscriptions or glosses, are further described in Fortson (2010). New discoveries of inscriptions from ancient Spain, Italy and Anatolia are constantly extending our knowledge of the ancient languages of these regions; the journals *Palaeohispanica* and *Studi Etruschi* publish annual surveys of epigraphic finds from Spain and Italy, and most of the new material in languages other than Latin and Greek from Anatolia and Greece finds its way into the journal *Kadmos*.

LINGUISTICS

Making sense of how ancient languages worked and how they are linked both in family relationships and by grammatical influence and vocabulary-borrowing requires some knowledge of linguistics. There are many extremely good introductions to linguistics, and to the specific branches that I have had most recourse to in this book, historical linguistics and sociolinguistics. For initial introductions to the study of language and linguistics, Trask (1999), Crystal (2010) and Yule (2010) are all recommended for the clarity of their writing and breadth of coverage. For historical linguistics and sociolinguistics there are also many readable and reliable single- or double-author introductions, and an increasing number of edited handbooks and companions. For historical linguistics, the study of how languages change over time, Trask and McColl (2007) and Crowley and Bowern (2010) are ideal for the beginning reader, while Hale (2007) and Ringe and Eska (2013) are geared towards a more advanced audience; the handbook of Joseph and Janda (eds) (2003) also contains many useful chapters. The concerns of sociolinguistics are very varied, and include the synchronic study of language variation, the association of features of language with social groups, and the use of multiple languages by individuals. Romaine (2000), Coulmas (2005) and Wardhaugh (2010) are general introductions to the field, and many topics are covered in the voluminous edited handbooks of Coulmas (ed.) (1997), Mesthrie (ed.) (2011),

Bayley, Cameron, and Lucas (eds) (2013), and Wodak, Johnstone and Kerswill (eds) (2013). Since language variation and language change are intricately linked, there are also edited volumes that straddle socio- and historical linguistics, such as Chambers, Trudgill and Schilling-Estes (eds) (2002) and Hernández Campoy and Conde Silvestre (eds) (2012).

References

Adams, J. N. (1977) *The Vulgar Latin of the Letters of Claudius Terentianus (P. Mich. VIII, 467–72)*. Manchester: Manchester University Press.
  (1982) *The Latin Sexual Vocabulary*. London: Duckworth.
  (1984) 'Female speech in Latin comedy'. *Antichthon* 18, 43–77.
  (1990) 'The latinity of C. Novius Eunus'. *Zeitschrift für Papyrologie und Epigraphik* 82, 227–47.
  (2002) 'Bilingualism at Delos'. In Adams et al. (eds) 103–27.
  (2003a) *Bilingualism and the Latin Language*. Cambridge: Cambridge University Press.
  (2003b) 'Petronius and new non-literary Latin'. In J. Herman and H. Rosén (eds) *Petroniana: Gedenkschrift für Hubert Petersmann*. Heidelberg: Winter, 11–23.
  (2005) 'Neglected evidence for female speech in Latin'. *Classical Quarterly* 55, 582–96.
  (2007) *The Regional Diversification of Latin, 200 BC–AD 600*. Cambridge: Cambridge University Press.
  (2011) 'Late Latin'. In Clackson (ed.) 257–83.
  (2013) *Social Variation and the Latin Language*. Cambridge: Cambridge University Press.
Adams, J. N., Janse, Mark and Swain, Simon (eds) (2002) *Bilingualism in Ancient Society: Language Contact and the Written Text*. Oxford: Oxford University Press.
Allan, Keith and Burridge, Kate (2006) *Forbidden Words: Taboo and the Censoring of Language*. Cambridge: Cambridge University Press.
Allen, W. S. (1987) *Vox Graeca*. (3rd edition). Cambridge: Cambridge University Press.
Amadasi Guzzo, Maria Giulia (1990) *Iscrizioni fenicie e puniche in Italia*. Rome: Libreria dello Stato, Istituto Poligrafico e Zecca dello Stato.
Ameling, Walter (2009) 'The epigraphic habit and the Jewish diasporas of Asia Minor and Syria'. In Cotton et al. (eds) 203–34.
  (2012) '*Femina Liberaliter Instituta*: some thoughts on a martyr's liberal education'. In Bremmer and Formisano (eds) 78–102.
Amphoux, C.-B., Elliott, J. Keith and Outtier, Bernard (eds) (2012) *Textual Research on the Psalms and Gospels/Recherches textuelles sur les psaumes et les évangiles*. (Supplement to *Novum Testamentum* 142). Leiden and Boston: Brill.

Anderson, Henning (ed.) (2003) *Language Contacts in Prehistory: Studies in Stratigraphy*. Amsterdam and Philadelphia: Benjamins.

Andrade, Nathanael J. (2013) *Syrian Identity in the Greco-Roman World*. Cambridge: Cambridge University Press.

Anthony, David W. (2007) *The Horse, The Wheel, and Language: How Bronze-Age Riders from the Eurasian Steppes Shaped the Modern World*. Princeton: Princeton University Press.

Antonini, Rosalba (2007) 'Contributi Pompeiani II-IV'. *Quaderni di studi pompeiani* 1 (*Miscellanea pompeiana*), 47–114.

Arnaud, P. (2001) 'Les Ligures: la construction d'un concept géographique et ses étapes de l'époque archaïque à l'Empire Romain'. In Fromentin and Gotteland (eds) 327–46.

Austin, Colin and Olson, S. Douglas (2004) *Aristophanes Thesmophoriazusae. Edited with Introduction and Commentary*. Oxford: Oxford University Press.

Ax, Wolfram (2011) *Quintilians Grammatik* (Inst. Or. 1,4–8). *Text, Übersetzung und Kommentar*. Berlin / Boston: de Gruyter.

Bagnall, Roger S. (1993) *Egypt in Late Antiquity*. Princeton: Princeton University Press.

(2011) *Everyday Writing in the Graeco-Roman East*. Los Angeles and Berkeley: University of California Press.

(ed.) (2009) *The Oxford Handbook of Papyrology*. Oxford: Oxford University Press.

Bagnall, Roger S. and Cribiore, Raffaella (2006) *Women's Letters from Ancient Egypt, 300 BC–AD 800*. Ann Arbor, Mich.: University of Michigan Press.

Bagnall, Roger S. et al. (eds) (2013) *The Encyclopedia of Ancient History*. Malden, Mass. and Oxford: Wiley-Blackwell.

Bain, David (1984) 'Female speech in Menander'. *Antichthon* 18, 24–42.

(1991) 'Six Greek verbs of sexual congress'. *Classical Quarterly* 41, 51–77.

(1999) 'The avoidance of euphemism: basic language in Greek medical texts'. In De Martino and Sommerstein (eds) 259–81.

Bakker, E. J. (ed.) (2010) *The Blackwell Companion to the Ancient Greek Language*. Malden, Mass. and Oxford: Wiley-Blackwell.

Bakker, Peter (1997) *A Language of Our Own: The Genesis of Michif, the Mixed Cree-French Language of the Canadian Métis*. Oxford: Oxford University Press.

Balz, Horst Robert et al. (eds) (2004) *Theologische Realenzyklopädie*. Berlin: de Gruyter.

Bayley, Robert, Cameron, Richard and Lucas, Ceil (eds) (2013) *The Oxford Handbook of Sociolinguistics*. Oxford: Oxford University Press.

Beard, Mary et al. (eds) (1991) *Literacy in the Roman World*. (*Journal of Roman Archaeology* Supplementary Series no. 3). Ann Arbor, MI: Journal of Roman Archaeology.

Beekes, Robert (2010) *Etymological Dictionary of Greek*. Leiden: Brill.

Benedetti, L. (2012) *Glandes perusinae. Revisione e aggiornamenti*. Rome: Quasar.

Benelli, Enrico (1994) *Le iscrizioni bilingue etrusco-latine*. Florence: Olschki.

Bennet, John and Driessen, Jan (eds) (2002) *A-na-qo-ta. Studies Presented to J. T. Killen. (Minos 33–34).* Salamanca: Universidad.

Bérard, François et al. (2010) *Guide de l'épigraphiste.* (4th edition). Paris: Rue d'Ulm.

Bers, Victor (1997) *Speech in Speech: Studies in Incorporated Oratio Recta in Attic Drama and Oratory.* Lanham, MD: Rowman & Littlefield.

Bhatia, Tej K. and Ritchie, William C. (2013) 'Introduction'. In Bhatia and Ritchie (eds) xxi-xxiii.

Bhatia, Tej K. and Ritchie, William C. (eds) (2013) *The Blackwell Handbook of Bilingualism and Multilingualism.* (2nd edition). Malden, Mass. and Oxford: Wiley-Blackwell.

Bickerman, Elias J. (1952) 'Origines gentium'. *Classical Philology* 47, 65–81.

   (1985) *Religions and Politics in the Hellenistic and Roman Periods.* Como: Edizioni New Press.

Bile, Monique, Brixhe, Claude and Hodot, René (1984) 'Les dialectes grecs, ces inconnus'. *Bulletin de la Société de Linguistique de Paris* 79, 155–203.

Bispham, Edward (2007) *From Asculum to Actium: The Municipalization of Italy from the Social War to Augustus.* Oxford: Oxford University Press.

Black, Matthew (1967) *An Aramaic Approach to the Gospels and Acts.* Oxford: Clarendon Press.

Blass, Friedrich, Debrunner, Albert and Rehkopf, Friedrich (2001) *Grammatik des neutestamentlichen Griechisch.* (18th edition). Göttingen: Vandenhoeck & Ruprecht.

Blom, A. H. (2009) 'Lingua gallica, lingua celtica: Gaulish, Gallo-Latin, or Gallo-Romance?', *Keltische Forschungen* 4, 7–54.

Bombi, R. et al. (eds) (2006) *Studi linguistici in onore di Roberto Gusmani.* Alessandria: Orso.

Bonfante, G. and Bonfante, L. (2002) *The Etruscan Language: An Introduction.* (rev. edition). Manchester: Manchester University Press.

Borst, Arno (1959) *Der Turmbau von Babel: Geschichte der Meinungen über Ursprung und Vielfalt der Sprachen und Völker.* Vol. II *Ausbau*, Teil 2. Stuttgart: Hiersemann.

Bourguet, Émile (1927) *Le dialecte laconien.* Paris: Champion.

Bowen, Anthony and Garnsey, Peter (2003) *Lactantius Divine Institutes: Translated with an Introduction and Notes.* Liverpool: Liverpool University Press.

Bowman, Alan K. (1994) *Life and Letters on the Roman Frontier.* London: British Museum Press.

Bowman, Alan K. and Woolf, G. (eds) (1994) *Literacy and Power in the Roman World.* Cambridge: Cambridge University Press.

Boyce, B. (1991) *The Language of the Freedmen in Petronius' Cena Trimalchionis.* Leiden: Brill.

Brandenstein, W. and Mayrhofer, M. (1964) *Handbuch des Altpersischen.* Wiesbaden: Reichert.

Bremmer, Jan N. and Formisano, Marco (2012) 'Perpetua's passions: a brief introduction'. In Bremmer and Formisano (eds) 1–13.

Bremmer, Jan N. and Formisano, Marco (eds) (2012) *Perpetua's Passions: Multidisciplinary Approaches to the Passio Perpetuae et Felicitatis*. Oxford: Oxford University Press.

Brennan, T. C. (1998) 'The poets Julia Balbilla and Damo at the Colossus of Memnon'. *Classical World* 91, 215–34.

Briant, Pierre, Henkelman, W. F. M. and Stolper, M. W. (eds) (2008) *L'archive des fortifications de Persépolis: état des questions et perspectives de recherches: actes du colloque organisé au Collège de France par la 'Chaire d'histoire et civilisation du monde achéménide et de l'empire d'Alexandre' et le 'Réseau international d'études et de recherches achéménides' (GDR 2538 CNRS), 3–4 novembre (2006)*. (*Persika* 12). Paris: de Boccard.

Brixhe, Claude (1987) *Essai sur le grec anatolien au début de notre ère*. Nancy: Presses Universitaires de Nancy.

(1988) 'La langue de l'étranger non grec chez Aristophane'. In Lonis (ed.) 113–38.

(2004) 'Phrygian'. In Woodard (ed.), 777–88.

Brixhe, Claude (ed.) (1993) *La Koiné grecque antique I. Une langue introuvable?* Nancy: Presses Universitaires de Nancy.

Brixhe, Claude and Michel Lejeune (1984) *Corpus des inscriptions paléophrygiennes*. Paris: Recherche sur les civilisations A.D.P.F.

Brock, S. P. (1996) 'Greek words in Syriac: some general features'. *Studia Classica Israelica* 15, 251–62.

Brown, Peter (1968) 'Christianity and local culture in Late Roman Africa'. *Journal of Roman Studies* 58, 85–95.

(2013) *The Rise of Western Christendom: Triumph and Diversity, A.D. 200–1000*. (10th anniversary revised edition). Oxford: Blackwell.

Browning, Robert (1983) *Medieval and Modern Greek*. (2nd edition). Cambridge: Cambridge University Press.

Brunt, P. A. (1976) 'The Romanization of the local ruling classes in the Roman Empire'. In Pippidi (ed.) 161–73.

Bruun, Patrick et al. (1975) *Studies in the Romanization of Etruria*. (Acta Instituti Romani Finlandiae V). Rome: Bardi.

Buck, Carl Darling (1913) 'The interstate use of the Greek dialects'. *Classical Philology* 8, 133–59.

Burrell, Barbara (2009) 'Reading, hearing and looking at Ephesos'. In Johnson and Parker (eds) 69–95.

Burton, Philip (2000) *The Old Latin Gospels: A Study of their Texts and Language*. Oxford: Oxford University Press.

(2007) *Language in the Confessions of Saint Augustine*. Oxford: Oxford University Press.

(2011) 'Christian Latin'. In Clackson (ed.) 485–501.

Campbell, Lyle and Poser, William J. (2008) *Language Classification: History and Method*. Cambridge: Cambridge University Press.

Carleton Paget, James and Schaper, Joachim (eds) (2013) *The New Cambridge History of the Bible, Volume 1. From the Beginnings to 600*. Cambridge: Cambridge University Press.

Carroll, Maureen (2006) *Spirits of the Dead: Roman Funerary Commemoration in Western Europe*. Cambridge: Cambridge University Press.

Cartledge, Paul (2007) 'Greeks and "barbarians"'. In Christidis (ed.) 307–13.

Casey, Maurice (1998) *Aramaic Sources of Mark's Gospel*. Cambridge: Cambridge University Press.

(2002) *An Aramaic Approach to Q: Sources for the Gospels of Matthew and Luke*. Cambridge: Cambridge University Press.

(2007) *The Solution to the 'Son of Man' Problem*. London and New York: T. & T. Clark.

Cassio, Albio (ed.) (1999) Κατὰ διάλεκτον: *Atti del III Colloquio Internazionale di Dialettologia Greca*. (*AION* 19, 1997). Naples: Istituto universitario orientale.

Chadwick, John (1967) *The Decipherment of Linear B*. (2nd edition). Cambridge: Cambridge University Press.

(1976) 'Who were the Dorians?', *Parola del Passato* 31, 103–17.

Chahoud, A. (2004) 'The Roman satirist speaks Greek'. *Classics Ireland* 11, 1–46.

Chambers, J. K., and Trudgill, Peter (1998) *Dialectology*. (2nd edition). Cambridge: Cambridge University Press.

Chambers, J.K., Trudgill, Peter and Schilling-Estes, Natalie (eds) (2002) *The Handbook of Language Variation and Change*. Malden, Mass. and Oxford: Blackwell.

Charles-Edwards, Thomas (2000) *Early Christian Ireland*. Cambridge: Cambridge University Press.

Christidis, A.-F. (ed.) (2007) *A History of Greek from the Beginnings to Late Antiquity*. Cambridge: Cambridge University Press.

Cirio, Amalia Margherita (2011) *Gli Epigrammi di Giulia Balbilla: ricordi di una dama di corte e altri testi al femminile sul Colosso di Memnone*. (Satura 9). Lecce: Pensa.

Clackson, James (2007) *Indo-European Linguistics*. Cambridge: Cambridge University Press.

(2010) Review of Anthony (2007) *Journal of Hellenic Studies* 130, 286–7.

(2011a) 'Classical Latin'. In Clackson (ed.) 236–56.

(2011b) 'The social dialects of Latin'. In Clackson (ed.) 505–26.

(2011c) 'Latin inscriptions and documents'. In Clackson (ed.) 29–39.

(2012a) 'Oscan in Sicily'. In Tribulato (ed.) 132–48.

(2012b) 'Language maintenance and language shift in the Mediterranean world during the Roman Empire'. In Mullen and James (eds) 36–57.

Clackson, James (ed.) (2011) *A Companion to the Latin Language*. Malden, Mass. and Oxford: Wiley-Blackwell.

Clackson, James and Horrocks, Geoffrey (2007) *The Blackwell History of the Latin Language*. Malden, Mass.and Oxford: Wiley-Blackwell.

Clackson, James and Meißner, Torsten (2000) 'The Poet of Chester'. *Proceedings of the Cambridge Philological Society* 46, 1–6.

Coleman, K. (forthcoming) *Q. Sulpicius Maximus, Poet, Eleven Years Old*. Ann Arbor: University of Michigan Press.

Coleman, Robert (1987) 'Vulgar Latin and the diversity of Christian Latin'. In Herman (ed.) 37–52.

Colson, F. H. (1921) 'The fragments of Lucilius IX on ei and i'. *Classical Quarterly* 15, 11–17.

Colvin, Stephen (1999) *Dialect in Aristophanes*. Oxford: Clarendon Press.

(2004) 'Social dialect in Attica'. In Penney (ed.) 95–108.

Conway, Robert S. (1897) *The Italic Dialects edited with a Grammar and Glossary*. Cambridge: Cambridge University Press.

Conway, Robert S., Whatmough, Joshua and Johnson, Sarah E. (1933) *The Prae-Italic Dialects of Italy*. 2 vols. Cambridge, Mass.: Harvard University Press.

Cooley, A. E. (2002) 'The survival of Oscan in Roman Pompeii'. In Cooley (ed.) 77–86.

(2012) *The Cambridge Manual of Latin Epigraphy*. Cambridge: Cambridge University Press.

Cooley, A. E. (ed.) (2002) *Becoming Roman, Writing Latin? Literacy and Epigraphy in the Roman West.* (*Journal of Roman Archaeology*, Supplementary Series 48). Portsmouth, RI: Journal of Roman Archaeology.

Cornell, T. J. (2013) *The Fragments of the Roman Historians. Vol. 1: Introduction.* Oxford: Oxford University Press.

Cotton, Hannah (2003) 'The Bar Kokhba revolt and the documents from the Judaean desert: Nabataean participation in the revolt (P. Yadin 52)'. In Schäfer (ed.) 133–52.

Cotton, H. M., Hoyland, R. G., Price, J. J. and Wasserstein, D. J. (eds) (2009) *From Hellenism to Islam: Cultural and Linguistic Change in the Roman Near East.* Cambridge: Cambridge University Press.

Cotton, Hannah M., Lupu, Eran, Heimbach, Maria, and Schneider, Naomi (2010–12) *Corpus inscriptionum Iudaeae/Palaestinae: A Multi-Lingual Corpus of the Inscriptions from Alexander to Muhammad. Vol. I. Jerusalem.* Berlin: de Gruyter.

Cotton, Hannah M. and Yardeni, Ada (1997) *Aramaic, Hebrew and Greek Documentary Texts from Naḥal Ḥever and Other Sites: With an Appendix Containing Alleged Qumran Texts. (Discoveries in the Judaean Desert 27).* Oxford: Clarendon Press.

Coulmas, Florian (2005) *Sociolinguistics: The Study of Speakers' Choices.* Cambridge: Cambridge University Press.

Coulmas, Florian (ed.) (1997) *The Handbook of Sociolinguistics*. Oxford: Blackwell.

Crawford, Michael H. (2011) 'Introduction'. In Crawford et al. 1–63.

Crawford, Michael H. et al. (2011) *Imagines Italicae*. London: Institute for Classical Studies.

Crespo, Emilio, García Ramon, José Luis and Striano, Araceli (eds) (1993) *Dialectologica Graeca: Actas del II Coloquio internacional de dialectología griega (Miraflores de la Sierra (Madrid), 19–21 de junio de 1991).* Madrid: Universidad Autónoma de Madrid.

Cribiore, Raffaella (2001) *Gymnastics of the Mind: Greek Education in Hellenistic and Roman Egypt*. Princeton: Princeton University Press.

Cristofani, Mauro (1991) *Introduzione allo studio dell' etrusca*. (2nd edition). Florence: Olschki.

Crowley, Terry and Bowern, Claire (2010) *An Introduction to Historical Linguistics*. (4th edition). Oxford: Oxford University Press.

Crystal, David (2010) *The Cambridge Encyclopedia of Language*. (3rd edition). Cambridge: Cambridge University Press.

Cunliffe, Barry and Koch, John T. (eds) (2010) *Celtic from the West: Alternative Perspectives from Archaeology, Genetics, Language and Literature*. Oxford: Oxbow.

Curtin, P. D. (1984) *Cross-Cultural Trade in World History*. Cambridge: Cambridge University Press.

Daniels, Peter T. and Bright, William (1996) *The World's Writing Systems*. Oxford: Oxford University Press.

Dankoff, Robert (2004) *An Ottoman Mentality. The World of Evliya Çelebi*. Leiden: Brill.

Dankoff, Robert and Kim, Sooyong (2010) *An Ottoman Traveller: Selections from the Book of Travels of Evliya Çelebi*. London: Eland.

Dawkins, R. M. (ed.) (1929) *The Sanctuary of Artemis Orthia at Sparta, excavated and described by Members of the British School at Athens, 1906–1910*. London: Society for the Promotion of Hellenic Studies.

Decourt, J.-C. (2004) *Inscriptions grecques de la France*. Lyons: Maison de l'Orient et de la Méditerranée-Jean Pouilloux.

de Grummond, Nancy Thompson (2006) 'Prophets and priests'. In de Grummond and Simon (eds) 27–44.

de Grummond, Nancy Thompson and Simon, E. (eds) (2006) *The Religion of the Etruscans*. Austin, Tex.: University of Texas Press.

Delamarre, Xavier (2001) *Dictionnaire de la langue Gauloise: une approche linguistique du vieux-celtique continental*. Paris: Errance

(2012) *Noms de lieux celtiques de l'Europe ancienne (-500 / +500)*. Paris: Errance.

De Martino, F. and Sommerstein, Alan H. (eds) (1995) *Lo spettacolo delle voci*. Bari: Levante.

(eds) (1999) *Studi sull'eufemismo*. Bari: Levante.

Dench, Emma (1995) *From Barbarians to New Men: Greek, Roman and Modern Perceptions of Peoples from the Central Apennines*. Oxford: Clarendon Press.

Denniston, J. D. (1934) *The Greek Particles*. Oxford: Clarendon Press.

Dickey, E. (1996) *Greek Forms of Address: From Herodotus to Lucian*. Oxford: Clarendon Press.

(2002) *Latin Forms of Address: From Plautus to Apuleius*. Oxford: Oxford University Press.

(2012) *The Colloquia of the Hermeneumata Pseudodositheana*. Vol. 1. Cambridge: Cambridge University Press.

Dickey, E. and Chahoud, A. (eds) (2010) *Colloquial and Literary Latin*. Cambridge: Cambridge University Press.

Donner, H. and Röllig, W. (1962–2002) *Kanaanäische und Aramäische Inschriften*. 3 vols. Wiesbaden: Harrassowitz.

Dover, K. J. (1976) 'Linguaggio e caratteri aristofanei'. *Rivista di Cultura Classica e Medioevale* 18, 357–71. English translation in Dover (1987) 237–48.

(1978) *Greek Homosexuality*. London: Duckworth.

(1987) *Greek and the Greeks, Collected Papers I: Language, Poetry, Drama*. Oxford: Blackwell.

(2002) 'Some evaluative terms in Aristophanes'. In Willi (ed.) 85–97.

Driessen, Jan (2008) 'Chronology of the Linear B texts'. In Duhoux and Morpurgo Davies (eds) 69–79.

Dubuisson, M. (1983) 'Les Opici: Osques, Occidentaux ou Barbares?', *Latomus* 42, 522–45.

Duhoux, Yves (2004) 'Langage de femmes et d'hommes en grec ancien'. In Penney (ed.) 131–45

(2007) 'Eteocretan'. In Christidis (ed.) 247–52.

(2009) 'The Cypro-Minoan Tablet no. 1885 (Enkomi): an analysis'. *Kadmos* 48, 5–38.

(2013) 'Non-Greek languages of ancient Cyprus and their scripts: Cypro-Minoan 1–3'. In Steele (ed.) 27–48.

Duhoux, Yves and Morpurgo Davies, Anna (eds) (2008) *A Companion to Linear B. Mycenaean Greek Texts and their World*. Vol. 1. Louvain-la-Neuve: Peeters.

(eds) (2011) *Companion to Linear B. Mycenaean Greek Texts and their World*. Vol. 2. Louvain-la-Neuve: Peeters.

Eck, Werner (2009) 'The presence, role and significance of Latin in the epigraphy and culture of the Roman Near East'. In Cotton et al. (eds) 15–42.

Eckert, P. and McConnell-Ginet, S. (2013) *Language and Gender*. (2nd edition). Cambridge: Cambridge University Press.

Ehrman, Bart D., and Pleše, Zlatko (2011) *The Apocryphal Gospels: Texts and Translations*. Oxford: Oxford University Press.

Englund, Robert (2004) 'The state of decipherment of Proto-Elamite'. In Houston (ed.) 100–49.

Eska, J. F. (1987) 'The language of the Latin inscriptions of Pompeii and the question of an Oscan substratum'. *Glotta* 65, 146–61.

Evans, Trevor (2012) 'Linguistic and stylistic variation in the Zenon Archive'. In Leiwo et al. (eds) 27–42.

Faber, Alice (1997) 'Genetic subgrouping of the Semitic languages'. In Hetzron (ed.) 3–15.

Falileyev, Alexander (2003) Review of Delamarre (2001) *Folia linguistica historica* 24: 281–94.

(2010) *Dictionary of Continental Celtic Place-Names*. Aberystwyth: CMCS.

Falileyev, A. I. (2011) 'Issues in Ligurian linguistics: Ligurica sub specie Celto-Liguricae et Indo-Germanicae'. (In Russian). *Voprosy Jazykoznanija* 3, 85–113.

Ferrara, Sylvia (2013) *Cypro-Minoan Inscriptions. Vol. 2: The Corpus*. Oxford: Oxford University Press.

Fishman, J. A. (1965) 'Who speaks what language to whom and when?', *La Linguistique* 2, 67–88.

Fögen, Thorsten (2004) 'Gender-specific communication in Greco-Roman antiquity: with a research bibliography'. *Historiographia Linguistica* 31, 199–276.

    (2010) 'Female speech'. In Bakker (ed.) 311–26.

    (2011) 'Latin as a technical and scientific language'. In Clackson (ed.) 445–63.

Förster, H. (2002) *Wörterbuch der griechischen Wörter in den koptischen dokumentarischen Texten*. Berlin: de Gruyter.

Fortson, Benjamin W. (2010) *Indo-European Language and Culture: an Introduction*. (2nd edition). Malden, MA and Oxford: Wiley-Blackwell.

Fournet, J.-L. (2009) 'The multilingual environment of Late Antique Egypt: Greek, Latin, Coptic and Persian documentation'. In Bagnall (ed.) 418–51.

Frajzyngier, Zygmunt and Shay, Erin (2012) 'Introduction'. In Frajzyngier and Shay (eds) 1–17.

    (eds) (2012) *The Afroasiatic Languages*. Cambridge: Cambridge University Press,

Frankfurter, David (1998) *Religion in Roman Egypt: Assimilation and Resistance*. Princeton: Princeton University Press.

Freeman, Philip (2001) *The Galatian Language: A Comprehensive Survey of the Language of the Ancient Celts in Greco-Roman Asia Minor*. Lewiston, NY: Edwin Mellen Press.

Friedrich, P. and Redfield, J. (1978) 'Speech as personality symbol: the case of Achilles'. *Language* 54, 263–88.

Fromentin, Valérie and Gotteland, Sophie (eds) (2001) *Origines Gentium*. (Collection Etudes 7). Bordeaux: Editions Ausonius.

Gal, S. (1978) 'Peasant men can't get wives: language change and sex roles in a bilingual community'. *Language in Society* 7, 1–16.

    (1979) *Language Shift: Social Determinants of Linguistic Change in Bilingual Austria*. San Francisco and New York: Academic Press.

Galand, L. (1996) 'Du berbère au libyque: une remontée difficile'. *LALIES. Actes des sessions de linguistique et de littérature* 16, 77–98.

Garrett, Andrew and Weiss, Michael (eds) (forthcoming) *Handbook of Indo-European Studies*. Oxford: Oxford University Press.

George, Coulter (2010) 'Jewish Greek'. In Bakker (ed.) 267–80.

Gershevitch, Ilya (1979) 'The alloglottography of Old Persian'. *Transactions of the Philological Society* 77, 114–90.

Gildersleeve, B. L. (1907) Review of M. Bréal *Pour mieux connaître Homère* (Paris: Hachette, 1906) *American Journal of Philology* 28, 208–17.

Gilleland, M. E. (1980) 'Female speech in Latin and Greek'. *American Journal of Philology* 102, 180–3.

Gippert, Jost (2012) 'Fragments of St. John's Gospel in the Language of the Caucasian Albanians'. In Amphoux et al. (eds) 237–44.

Glare, P. G. W. (1982) *Oxford Latin Dictionary*. Oxford: Clarendon Press.

    (1996) *Greek–English Lexicon: revised supplement*. Oxford: Clarendon Press.

Godart, Luis and Olivier, Jean-Pierre (1976–85) *Recueil des inscriptions en Linéaire A*. (Études Crétoises 21, vols. 1–5). Paris: Geuthner.

Goedegebuure, Peta (2013) 'Hattic language'. In Bagnall et al. (eds) 3080–1.

Gorbachov, Yaroslav (2008) 'Nine observations on the Old Phrygian inscription from Vezirhan'. *Kadmos* 47, 91–108.

Gorrochategui, Joaquin (1995) 'The Basque language and its neighbours in antiquity'. In Hualde et al. (eds) 31–63.

Grafton, Anthony (1990) 'Petronius and Neo-Latin satire: the reception of the *Cena Trimalchionis*'. *Journal of the Warburg and Courtauld Institutes* 53, 237–49.

Grant, M. and Kitzinger, R. (eds) (1988) *Civilization of the Ancient Mediterranean: Greece and Rome*. Vol. 1. New York: Scribner's.

Green, R. P. H. (1995) *Augustine De Doctrina Christiana Edited and Translated*. Oxford: Clarendon Press.

Griffith, Sidney (2012) 'The Bible in Arabic'. In Marsden and Rutter (eds) 123–42.

Gruen, Erich S. (2011) *Rethinking the Other in Antiquity*. Princeton: Princeton University Press.

Gruppe, O. F. (1838) *Die römische Elegie. Volume 1*. Leipzig: Wigand.

Gunnarsson, Britt-Louise et al. (eds) (2003) *Language Variation in Europe*. Uppsala: Universitetstryckeriet.

Haas, Otto (1966) *Die phrygischen Sprachdenkmäler*. Sofia: Académie Bulgare des sciences.

Hale, Mark (2007) *Historical Linguistics: Theory and Method*. Malden, MA and Oxford: Blackwell.

Hall, Jonathan M. (1997) *Ethnic Identity in Greek Antiquity*. Cambridge: Cambridge University Press.

Hansen, Peter Allan (1983) *Carmina Epigraphica Graeca: Saeculorum VIII–V a. Chr. n.* Berlin: de Gruyter.

  (1989) *Carmina Epigraphica Graeca: Saeculi IV a. Chr. n. (CEG 2)*. Berlin: de Gruyter.

Harris, W. V. (1989) *Ancient Literacy*. Cambridge, Mass.: Harvard University Press.

Hawkins, Shane (2012) 'A linguistic analysis of the vase inscriptions of Sophilos'. *Glotta* 88, 122–65.

Heffernan, Thomas J. (2012) *The Passion of Perpetua and Felicity*. Oxford: Oxford University Press.

Henderson, J. (1975) *The Maculate Muse: Obscene Language in Attic Comedy*. New Haven: Yale University Press.

Herman, J. (ed.) (1987) *Latin vulgaire – latin tardif. Actes du Ier Colloque international sur le latin vulgaire et tardif, Pécs, 2–5 septembre 1985*. Tübingen: Niemeyer.

Hernández Campoy, Juan Manuel and Conde Silvestre, Juan Camilo (2012) *The Handbook of Historical Sociolinguistics*. Malden, Mass. and Chichester: Blackwell.

Hetzron, Robert (ed.) (1997) *The Semitic Languages*. Abingdon and New York: Routledge.

Hinge, George (2006) *Die Sprache Alcmans: Textgeschichte und Sprachgeschichte.* Wiesbaden: Reichert.

Hoffmann, F., Minas-Nerpel, M. and Pfeiffer, S. (2009) *Die dreisprachige Stele des C. Cornelius Gallus: Übersetzung und Kommentar.* Berlin: de Gruyter.

Hopkins, Keith (1991) 'Conquest by book'. In Beard et al. (eds) 133–58.

Hopkinson, Neil (2008) *Lucian: A Selection.* Cambridge: Cambridge University Press.

Horrocks, Geoffrey C. (2010) *Greek: A History of the Language and its Speakers.* (2nd edition). Malden, Mass. and Oxford: Wiley-Blackwell.

Horsley, R. A. (2009) 'The language(s) of the kingdom: from Aramaic to Greek, Galilee to Syria, oral to oral-written'. In Z. Rodgers (ed.) *A Wandering Galilean: Essays in Honour of Seán Freyne.* Leiden: Brill, 401–26.

Housman, A. E. (1931) 'Praefanda'. *Hermes* 66, 402–12.

Houston, Stephen D. (ed.) (2004) *The First Writing: Script Invention as History and Process.* Cambridge: Cambridge University Press.

Hualde, José Ignacio, Lakarra, Joseba A. and Trask, R. L. (eds) (1995) *Towards a History of the Basque Language.* Amsterdam: Benjamins.

Hunter, Richard, and Rutherford, Ian (eds) (2009) *Wandering Poets in Ancient Greek Culture: Travel, Locality and Panhellenism.* Cambridge: Cambridge University Press.

Isaac, Benjamin, (2009) 'Latin in cities of the Roman Near East'. In Cotton, Hoyland, Price and Wasserstein (eds) 43–72.

Isaac, Ephraim (2012) 'The Bible in Ethiopia'. In Marsden and Rutter (eds) 110–22.

Jackson, Kenneth (1953) *Language and History in Early Britain: A Chronological Survey of the Brittonic Languages, First to Twelfth Century A.D.* Edinburgh: Edinburgh University Press.

Jim, Theodora S. F. (2011) Review of Missiou (2011), *Bryn Mawr Classical Review* 2011.11.02.

Jocelyn, H. D. (1980) 'A Greek indecency and its students: *LAIKAZEIN*'. *Proceedings of the Cambridge Philological Society* n.s. 30, 12–66.

Johnson, William A. and Parker, Holt A. (eds) (2009) *Ancient Literacies: The Culture of Reading in Greece and Rome.* Oxford: Oxford University Press.

Jones, Charles and Stolper, Matthew W. (2008) 'How many fortification tablets are there?' In Briant et al. (eds) 27–48.

Joseph, Brian D. and Janda, Richard D. (eds) (2003) *The Handbook of Historical Linguistics.* Malden, Mass. and Oxford: Blackwell.

Joseph, John Earl (1987) *Eloquence and Power: The Rise of Language Standards and Standard Languages.* London: Pinter.

Kaczko, Sara (2009) 'From stone to parchment: epigraphic and literary transmission of some Greek epigrams'. *Trends in Classics* 1, 90–117.

Kahle, Wilhelm (1918) *De vocabulariis graecis Plauti aetate in sermonem latinum vere receptis.* Münster: ex officina societatis typograph. Westf.

Kaimio, J. (1975) 'The ousting of Etruscan by Latin in Etruria'. In Bruun et al. 85–245.

Kaizer, T. (2009) 'Religion and language in Dura-Europos'. In Cotton et al. (eds) 235–53.

Karakasis, E. (2005) *Terence and the Language of Roman Comedy*. Cambridge: Cambridge University Press.

Karali, M. (2007) 'The use of dialects in literature'. In Christidis (ed.) 972–98.

Kaster, Robert A. (1988) *Guardians of Language: The Grammarian and Society in late Antiquity*. Berkeley: University of California Press.

Keegan, P., Sears, G. and Laurence, R. (eds) (2013) *Written Space in the Latin West 200 BC to AD 300*. London: Bloomsbury.

Kelly, Amanda (2012) 'The Cretan slinger at war – a weighty exchange'. *Annual of the British School at Athens* 107, 273–311.

Kelly, J. N. D. (1995) *Golden Mouth: The Story of John Chrysostom, Ascetic, Preacher, Bishop*. Ithaca, NY: Cornell University Press.

Kennell, Nigel M. (1995) *The Gymnasium of Virtue: Education and Culture in Ancient Sparta*. Chapel Hill: University of North Carolina Press.

Kent, Roland G. (1953) *Old Persian. Grammar, Texts, Lexicon*. (2nd edition). New Haven: American Oriental Society.

Khanoussi, M., Ruggeri, P. and Vismara, C. (eds) (1996) *L'Africa romana: atti dell'11. Convegno di studio, 15–18 dicembre 1994, Cartagine, Tunisia*. Sassari: Il Torchietto.

Kilmer, Martin F. and Develin, Robert (2001) 'Sophilos' vase inscriptions and cultural literacy in Archaic Athens'. *Phoenix* 55, 9–43.

Kirchhoff, A. (1863) *Studien zur Geschichte des griechischen Alphabets*. Berlin: Ferdinand Dümmler.

Koch, John T. (2010) 'Paradigm shift? Interpreting Tartessian as Celtic'. In Cunliffe and Koch (eds) 187–295.

Kruschwitz, Peter (2012a) 'Language, sex and (lack) of power: reassessing the linguistic discourse about female speech in Latin sources'. *Athenaeum* 100, 197–230.

    (2012b) 'How to avoid profanity in Latin: an exploratory study'. *Materiali e discussioni* 68, 9–38.

Kruschwitz, Peter and Halla-aho, H. (2007) 'The Pompeian wall-inscriptions and the Latin language: a critical reappraisal'. *Arctos* 41, 31–49.

Kühner, Raphael, Blass, Friedrich and Gerth, Bernhard (1890–1904) *Ausführliche Grammatik der griechischen Sprache*. (3rd edition). Hannover: Hahn.

Kühner, Raphael and Holzweissig, Friedrich W. (1912) *Ausführliche Grammatik der lateinischen Sprache. Bd.1. Elementar-, Formen- und Wortlehre*. Hannover: Hahn.

Kühner, Raphael, Stegmann, Carl, and Thierfelder, Andreas (1966) *Ausführliche Grammatik der lateinischen Sprache. Teil 2. Satzlehre*. (4th edition). Hannover: Hahn.

Kuhrt, Amélie (2007) *The Persian Empire: A Corpus of Sources from the Achaemenid Period*. London and New York: Routledge.

Labov, William (1966) *The Social Stratification of English in New York City*. Washington D.C.: Center for Applied Linguistics.

(1972) 'The social stratification of (r) in New York City department stores'. In William Labov *Sociolinguistic Patterns,* Philadelphia: University of Pennsylvania Press, 43–54.

(1994) *Principles of Linguistic Change. Vol. 1: Internal Factors.* Oxford: Blackwell.

(2006) *The Social Stratification of English in New York City.* (2nd edition). Cambridge: Cambridge University Press.

Lallot, Jean (1998) *La grammaire de Denys le Thrax. Traduite et annotée.* (rev. edition). Paris: CNRS.

Lambert, Pierre-Yves (2003) *La langue gauloise: description linguistique, commentaire d'inscriptions choisies.* (rev. edition). Paris: Errance.

Lampe, G. W. H. (1961-8) *A Patristic Greek Lexicon,* Oxford: Clarendon.

Lang, V. (2001) 'Interpreting archaeological cultures'. *Trames* 5, 48–58.

Langslow, David (1988) 'Languages and dialects'. In Grant and Kitzinger (eds) 183–207.

(2000) *Medical Latin in the Roman Empire.* Oxford: Oxford University Press.

(2002) 'Approaching bilingualism in corpus languages'. In Adams et al. (eds) 23–51.

(2012) 'Integration, identity, and language shifts: strengths and weaknesses of the linguistic evidence'. In Roselaar (ed.) 289–310.

Lasserre, François (1966) *Die Fragmente des Eudoxos von Knidos.* Berlin: de Gruyter.

Laurence, Ray, and Sears, Gareth (2013) 'Written space'. In Keegan, Sears and Laurence (eds) 1–9.

Lazzeroni, R. (1991) 'Contatti di lingue e di culture nell' Italia antica: un bilancio'. In Enrico Campanile (ed.) *Rapporti Linguistici e Culturali tra i popoli dell' Italia antica.* Pisa: Giardini, 177–85.

Lee, John A. L. (2013) 'The Atticist grammarians'. In Porter and Pitts (eds) 283–308.

Leiwo, M., Halla-aho, H. and Vierros, M. (eds) (2012) *Variation and Change in Greek and Latin.* (Papers and monographs of the Finnish Institute at Athens 17). Helsinki: Finnish Institute at Athens.

Leumann, M. (1977) *Lateinischen Laut- und Formenlehre.* (5th edition). Munich: Beck.

Levin-Richardson, Sarah (2011) '*Facilis hic futuit*: graffiti and masculinity in Pompeii's "purpose-built" brothel'. *Helios* 38, 59–78.

Lewis, D. M. (1994) 'The Persepolis tablets: speech, seal and script'. In Bowman and Woolf (eds) 17–32.

Lewis, Geoffrey (1999) *The Turkish Language Reform: A Catastrophic Success.* Oxford: Oxford University Press.

Lewis, M. Paul (ed.) (2009) *Ethnologue: Languages of the World.* (16th edition). Dallas, Tex.: SIL.

Lewis, Martin and Pereltsvaig, Asya (2015) *The Indo-European Controversy: Facts and Fallacies in Historical Linguistics.* Cambridge: Cambridge University Press.

Liddell, H. G., Scott, R. and Jones, H. S. (1940) *A Greek–English Lexicon.* (new 9th edition). Oxford: Clarendon Press.

Lonis, Raoul (ed.) (1988) *L'étranger dans le monde grec: Actes du colloque organisé par l'Institut d'Études Anciennes*. Nancy: Presses Universitaires de Nancy.

López Eire, Antonio (1993) 'De l'attique à la koiné'. In Brixhe (ed.) 41–57.

(1999) 'Nouvelles données à propos de l'histoire de l'attique'. In Cassio (ed.) 73–107.

López Eire, Antonio and Ramos Guerreira, Agustín (eds) (2004) *Registros lingüísticos en las lenguas clásicas*. Salamanca: Universidad de Salamanca, 173–91.

Lowe, N. J. (1988) 'Sulpicia's syntax'. *Classical Quarterly, n.s.*, 38, 193–205.

McClure, L. (1999) *Spoken like a Woman: Speech and Gender in Athenian Drama*. Princeton: Princeton University Press.

McDonald, Katherine (2012) 'The Testament of Vibius Adiranus'. *Journal of Roman Studies* 102, 40–55.

McHardy, Fiona and Marshall, Eireann (eds) (2004) *Women's Influence on Classical Civilization*. London: Routledge.

MacMullen, Ramsay (1966) 'Provincial languages in the Roman Empire'. *American Journal of Philology* 87, 1–17.

Mairs, Rachel (2011) 'Translator, traditor: the interpreter as traitor in classical tradition'. *Greece & Rome* 58, 64–81.

(2012) 'Interpreting at Vindolanda: commercial and linguistic mediation in the Roman Army'. *Britannia* 43, 17–28.

Mairs, Rachel and Muratov, Maya (forthcoming) *Interpreters of Foreign Languages in the Ancient World*.

Malcolm, Noel (2007) 'Comenius, Boyle, Oldenburg, and the translation of the Bible into Turkish'. *Church History and Religious Culture* 87: 327–62.

Manuwald, Gesine (2007) *Cicero, Philippics 3–9. Edited with Introduction, Translation and Commentary*. Berlin and New York: de Gruyter.

Marchesini, Simona (2009) *Le lingue frammentarie dell'Italia antica: manuale per lo studio delle lingue preromane*. Milan: Hoepli.

(2012) 'The Elymian Language'. In Tribulato (ed.) 95–115.

Marcotte, D. (2001) 'Samnites, Lucaniens et Brettiens: L'Italie sabellique dans l'ethnographie grecque'. In Fromentin and Gotteland (eds) 285–95.

Marsden, Richard and Rutter, E. Ann (eds) (2012) *The New Cambridge History of the Bible. Vol. 2: From 600 to 1450*. Cambridge: Cambridge University Press.

Masson, O. (2007) 'Eteocypriot'. In Christidis (ed.) 243–6.

Mastandrea, Paolo (1985) *Massimo di Madauros: (Agostino, Epistulae 16 e 17)*. Padua: Editoriale Programma.

Mather, Patrick-André (2012) 'The social stratification of /r/ in New York City: Labov's department store study revisited'. *Journal of English Linguistics* 40, 338–56.

Matras, Y. (2002) *Romani: A Linguistic Introduction*. Cambridge: Cambridge University Press.

Mees, Bernard (2003) 'A genealogy of stratigraphy theories from the Indo-European West'. In Anderson (ed.) 11–44.

(2011) 'Words from the well at Gallo-Roman Châteaubleau'. *Zeitschrift für Celtische Philologie* 58, 87–108.

Meiggs, Russell, and Lewis, David (1988) *A Selection of Greek Historical Inscriptions to the End of the Fifth Century B.C.* (rev. edition). Oxford: Clarendon Press.

Meißner, Torsten (2007) 'Notes on Mycenaean spelling'. *Cambridge Classical Journal* 53, 96–111.

(2009–10) 'Das Hieronymuszeugnis und der Tod des Gallischen'. *Zeitschrift für celtische Philologie* 57, 107–12.

Méndez Dosuna, Julián (2004) '¿Sociofonología y sociomorfología en griego antiguo?' In López Eire and Ramos Guerreira (eds) 173–91.

Mesthrie, Rajend (ed.) (2011) *Cambridge Handbook of Sociolinguistics*. Cambridge: Cambridge University Press.

Metzger, Bruce M. (1977) *The Early Versions of the New Testament*. Oxford: Clarendon Press.

Mickey, K. (1981a) *Studies in the Greek Dialects and the Language of Greek Verse Inscriptions*. Oxford: Oxford University Press.

(1981b) 'Dialect consciousness and literary language: an example from Ancient Greek'. *Transactions of the Philological Society* 79, 35–66.

Millar, Fergus (1968) 'Local cultures in the Roman Empire: Libyan, Punic and Latin in Roman Africa'. *Journal of Roman Studies* 58, 126–34.

(1971) 'Paul of Samosata, Zenobia and Aurelian: the church, local culture and political allegiance in third-century Syria'. *Journal of Roman Studies* 61, 1–17, reprinted in Millar 2006: 243–74.

(1993) *The Roman Near East (31BC– AD 337)*. Cambridge, Mass.: Harvard University Press.

(1998) 'Ethnic identity in the Roman Near East, AD 325–450: language, religion and culture'. *Mediterranean Archaeology* 11: 159–76, reprinted in Millar 2006: 378–405.

(2006) *Rome, the Greek World, and the East. Vol. 3: The Greek World, the Jews, and the East.* (Edited by Hannah M. Cotton and Guy M. Rogers). Chapel Hill, NC: University of North Carolina Press.

Missiou, Anna (2011) *Literacy and Democracy in Fifth-Century Athens*. Cambridge and New York: Cambridge University Press.

Mohrmann, C. (1958–77) *Études sur le latin des chrétiens*. 4 vols. Rome: Edizioni di storia e letteratura.

Morgan, Theresa (1998) *Literate Education in the Hellenistic and Roman Worlds*. Cambridge: Cambridge University Press.

Morley, Neville (2007) *Trade in Classical Antiquity*. Cambridge: Cambridge University Press.

Morpurgo Davies, Anna (1987) 'The Greek notion of dialect'. *Verbum* 10, 7–28.

(1992) 'Mycenaean, Arcadian, Cyprian and some questions of methodology in dialectology'. In Olivier (ed.) 415–32.

(1993) 'Geography, history and dialect: the case of Oropos'. In Crespo, García Ramon and Striano (eds) 261–79.

Mossman, J. (2001) 'Women's speech in Greek tragedy: the case of Electra and Clytemnestra in Euripides' "Electra"'. *Classical Quarterly* 51, 374–84.

Mullen, Alex (2012) 'Introduction: multiple languages, multiple identities'. In Mullen and James (eds) 1–35.

  (2013) *Southern Gaul and the Mediterranean: Multilingualism and Multiple Identities in the Iron Age and Roman Periods.* Cambridge: Cambridge University Press.

Mullen, Alex and James, Patrick (eds) (2012) *Multilingualism in the Graeco-Roman Worlds.* Cambridge: Cambridge University Press.

Müller, R. (2001) *Sprachbewußtsein und Sprachvariation im lateinischen Schrifttum der Antike.* Munich: Beck.

Munkhammar, Lars (2011) *The Silver Bible: Origins and History of the Codex Argenteus.* Uppsala: Selenas.

Nettle, Daniel (1999) *Linguistic Diversity.* Oxford: Oxford University Press.

Neumann, Günter (1977) 'Die Normierung des Lateinischen'. *Gymnasium* 84, 199–212.

  (1988) *Phrygisch und Griechisch.* (Sitzungsberichte der Österreichischen Akademie der Wissenschaften. Philosophisch-Historische Klasse 499). Vienna: Österreichische Akademie der Wissenschaften.

Nichols, Johanna (1992) *Linguistic Diversity in Space and Time.* Chicago: University of Chicago Press.

Noy, David (1993–5) *Jewish Inscriptions of Western Europe.* Cambridge: Cambridge University Press.

Olivier, Jean-Pierre (2007) *Édition holistique des textes chypro-minoens.* Rome: Fabrizio Serra.

Olivier, Jean-Pierre (ed.) (1992) *Mykenaika.* Paris: École française d'Athènes.

Olivier, Jean-Pierre and Godart, Louis (1996) *Corpus Hieroglyphicarum Inscriptionum Cretae.* (*Études Crétoises* 31). Paris: de Boccard.

Olsen, Magnus (1906) 'Ligur. *Porcobera* (flussname)'. *Zeitschrift für vergleichende Sprachforschung* 39, 607–9.

Oosterhuis, D. (2013) 'In love with Greek (or one particular Greek?): *Catalepton* 7 and Virgilian reception'. Unpublished paper delivered at the American Philological Association Annual Meeting, Seattle, 5 January 2013.

Orel, Vladimir E. (2000) *A Concise Historical Grammar of the Albanian Language: Reconstruction of Proto-Albanian.* Leiden, Boston and Cologne: Brill.

Osborne, Robin (2004) *The Old Oligarch: Pseudo-Xenophon's 'Constitution of the Athenians'.* (2nd edition). Cambridge: Cambridge University Press.

  (2011) *The History Written on the Classical Greek Body.* Cambridge: Cambridge University Press.

Page, Denys (1951) *Alcman: The Partheneion.* Oxford: Clarendon Press.

Palaima, T. G. (2002) 'Special vs. Normal Mycenaean. Hand 24 and writing in service of the king?' In Bennet and Driessen (eds) 205–21 and 371–5.

  (2011) 'Scribes, scribal hands and palaeography'. In Duhoux and Morpurgo Davies (eds) 137–68.

Palmer, Leonard R. (1954) *The Latin Language.* London: Faber.

Palmer, L. R. and Chadwick, J. (eds) (1966) *Proceedings of the Cambridge Colloquium on Mycenaean Studies.* Cambridge: Cambridge University Press.

Parsons, Peter (2007) *The City of the Sharp-nosed Fish: Greek Lives in Roman Egypt.* London: Weidenfeld and Nicolson.

Peek, Werner (1955–7) *Griechische Vers-Inschriften.* Bd.1, *Grab-Epigramme.* Berlin: Akademie Verlag.

Penney, J. H. W. (ed.) (2004) *Indo-European Perspectives: Studies in Honour of Anna Morpurgo Davies.* Oxford: Oxford University Press.

Pippidi, D. M. (ed.) (1976) *Assimilation et résistance à la culture gréco-romaine dans le monde ancien.* Bucharest: Editura Academiei.

Plant, I. M. (2004) *Women Writers of Ancient Greece and Rome: An Anthology.* London: Equinox/University of Oklahoma Press.

Poccetti, P. (2012) 'Reflexes of variations in Latin and Greek through neither Latin nor Greek documentation: names of Greek religion and mythology in the languages of ancient Italy'. In Leiwo et al. (eds) 71–96.

Pollock, Sheldon (2006) 'Response for third session: power and culture beyond ideology and identity'. In Sanders (ed.) 283–92.

Porter, S. E. and Pitts, A. W. (eds) (2013) *The Language of the New Testament: Context, History and Development.* Leiden: Brill.

Powell, Barry B. (1991) *Homer and the Origin of the Greek Alphabet.* Cambridge: Cambridge University Press.

Powell, J. G. F. (2010) 'Hyperbaton and register in Cicero'. In Dickey and Chahoud (eds) 163–85.

Prauscello, Lucia (2009) 'Wandering poetry, "travelling" music: Timotheus' muse and some case-studies of shifting cultural identities'. In Hunter and Rutherford (eds) 168–94.

Preisigke, Friedrich, et al. (1915-) *Sammelbuch griechischer Urkunden aus Ägypten.* Strassburg: Trübner.

Renfrew, Colin (1987) *Archaeology and Language: The Puzzle of Indo-European Origins.* Cambridge: Cambridge University Press.

Renfrew, Colin and Bellwood, Peter (2002) *Examining the Farming/Language Dispersal Hypothesis.* Cambridge: McDonald Institute for Archaeological Research.

Richter, Tonio Sebastian (2009) 'Greek, Coptic and the "language of the Hijra": the rise and decline of the Coptic language in late antique and medieval Egypt'. In: Cotton et al. (eds) 401–46.

Ringe, Don and Eska, Joseph F. (2013) *Historical Linguistics: Toward a Twenty-First Century Reintegration.* Cambridge: Cambridge University Press.

Risch, E. (1966) 'Les différences dialectales dans le mycénien'. In Palmer and Chadwick (eds) 150–7.

(1979) 'Die griechisch Dialekte im 2. vorchristlichen Jahrtausend'. *Studi Micenei ed Egeo-Anatolici* 20, 91–111.

Rix, Helmut, et al. (1991) *Etruskische Texte: editio minor.* 2 vols. Tübingen: Narr (= ET).

(2002) *Sabellische Texte: Die Texte des Oskischen, Umbrischen und Südpikenischen.* Heidelberg: Winter.

Robb, John (1993) 'A social prehistory of European languages'. *Antiquity* 67, no. 257, 747–60.

Rochette, Bruno (2011) 'Language policies in the Roman Republic and Empire'. In Clackson (ed.) 549–63.

Römer, Cornelia (2009) 'Manichaeism and Gnosticism in the papyri'. In Bagnall (ed.) 623–43.

Romaine, Suzanne (2000) *Language in Society: an Introduction to Sociolinguistics.* (2nd edition). Oxford: Oxford University Press.

Roselaar, Saskia T. (ed.) (2012) *Processes of Integration and Identity Formation in the Roman Republic.* (*Mnemosyne* supplements. History and archaeology of classical antiquity, 342). Leiden and Boston: Brill.

Rowlandson, Jane (2004) 'Gender and cultural identity in Roman Egypt'. In McHardy and Marshall (eds) 151–66.

Rubin, Aaron D. (2008) 'The subgrouping of the Semitic languages'. *Languages and Linguistics Compass* 2.1, 61–84.

Rubin, Z. (2002) 'Res Gestae Divi Saporis: Greek and Middle Iranian in a document of Sasanian anti-Roman propaganda'. In Adams et al. (eds) 267–97.

Rubio, G. (2006) 'Writing in another tongue: alloglottography in the Ancient Near East'. In Sanders (ed.) 33–70.

Russo, Joseph, Fernández-Galiano, Manuel and Heubeck, Alfred (1992) *A Commentary on Homer's Odyssey.* Volume 3. *Books xvii–xxiv.* Oxford: Clarendon Press.

Rutter, Keith (2001) *Historia Numorum. Italy.* London: British Museum.

Sacconi, A., Del Freo, M., Godart, L. and Negri, M. (eds) (2008) *Colloquium Romanum: Atti del XII colloquio internazionale di micenologia (Roma, 20–25 febbraio 2006).* Pisa and Rome: Fabrizio Serra.

Salmeri, Giovanni (2000) 'Dio, Rome and the civic life of Asia Minor'. In Swain (ed.) 53–92.

Sanders, Seth L. (ed.) (2006) *Margins of Writing, Origins of Cultures.* Chicago: Chicago Oriental Institute.

Sandøy, H. (2003) 'Types of society and language change in the Nordic countries'. In Gunnarsson et al. (eds) 53–76.

Schäfer, P. (ed.) (2003) *The Bar Kokhba War Reconsidered: New Perspectives on the Second Jewish Revolt against Rome.* Tübingen: Mohr.

Schäferdiek, Knut (2004) 'Wulfila'. In Balz et al. (eds), vol. 36, 374–8.

Schironi, Francesca (2009) *From Alexandria to Babylon: Near Eastern Languages and Hellenistic Erudition in the Oxyrhynchus Glossary (P.Oxy 1802 + 4812).* Berlin: de Gruyter.

(2010) 'Technical languages: science and medicine'. In Bakker (ed.) 338–53.

Schmitt, Rüdiger (2004) 'Old Persian'. In Woodard (ed.) 717–41.

Schniedewind, William (2006) 'Aramaic, the death of written Hebrew, and language shift in the Persian period'. In Sanders (ed.), 135–52.

Schrader, Otto (1883) *Sprachvergleichung und Urgeschichte: linguistisch-historische Beiträge zur Erforschung des indogermanischen Altertums*. Jena: Costenoble.

Schrijnen, Josef (1935) 'Le latin chrétien devenu langue commune'. *Revue des Études Latines* 12, 96–116.

Schumacher, Stefan (2004) *Die rätischen Inschriften: Geschichte und heutiger Stand der Forschung*. Innsbruck: Innsbrucker Beiträge zur Sprachwissenschaft.

Schwyzer, Eduard (1959–66) *Griechische Grammatik*. Munich: Beck.

Sechidou, I. (2005) 'Finikas Romika: a Greek Para-Romani variety'. *Romani Studies* 15, 51–80.

Segura Mungula, Santiago and Etxebarria Ayesta, Juan Manuel (1996) *Del latín al euskara*. Bilbao: Universidad de Deusto.

Shipley, Graham (2011) *Pseudo-Skylax's Periplous: The Circumnavigation of the Inhabited World*. Exeter: Bristol Phoenix Press.

Shipp, G. P. (1954) 'Plautine terms for Greek and Roman things'. *Glotta* 34, 139–52.

(1972) *Studies in the Language of Homer*. (2nd edition). Cambridge: Cambridge University Press.

(1977) 'Linguistic notes'. *Antichthon* 11, 1–9.

Simkin, Oliver (2012) 'Language contact in the pre-Roman and Roman Iberian peninsula: direct and indirect evidence'. In Mullen and James (eds) 77–105.

Simone, Carlo de (2011) 'La nuova iscrizione 'tirsenica' di Lemnos (Efestia, teatro): considerazioni generali'. *Rasenna* 3.1, 1–34.

Sims-Williams, Patrick (2006) *Ancient Celtic Place-Names in Europe and Asia Minor*. Oxford: Blackwell.

Soares, P. et al. (2010) 'The archaeogenetics of Europe'. *Current Biology* 20.4, R174–R183.

Solin, H. (1996) *Die stadtrömischen Sklavennamen. Ein Namenbuch*. Vols 1–2. (Forschungen zur antiken Sklaverei, Beiheft 2). Stuttgart: Franz Steiner.

Sommerstein, Alan H. (1995) 'The language of Athenian women'. In De Martino and Sommerstein (eds) II 60–85.

Stanford, W. B. (1947–8) *The Odyssey of Homer*. London: Macmillan.

Stearns, MacDonald (1978) *Crimean Gothic: Analysis and Etymology of the Corpus*. Saratoga: Anma Libri.

Steele, Philippa M. (2013) *A Linguistic History of Ancient Cyprus: The Non-Greek Languages and their Relations with Greek, c. 1600–300 BC*. Cambridge: Cambridge University Press.

Steele, Philippa M. (ed.) (2013) *Syllabic Writing on Cyprus and its Context*. Cambridge: Cambridge University Press.

Stern, Sacha (2012) *Calendars in Antiquity: Empires, States and Societies*. Oxford: Oxford University Press.

Stolper, Matthew W. and Tavernier, Jan (2007) 'From the Persepolis Fortification Archive Project, 1: An Old Persian administrative tablet from the Persepolis Fortification'. *ARTA: Achaemenid Research on Texts and Archaeology* 2007.001, 1–28.

Strassi, Silvia (2008) *L'archivio di Claudius Tiberianus da Karanis*. Berlin and New York: de Gruyter.

Stüber, Karin (1996) *Zur dialektischen Einheit des Ostionischen*. Innsbruck: Institut für Sprachwissenschaft der Universität Innsbruck.

Swain, Simon (2002) 'Bilingualism in Cicero? The evidence of code-switching'. In Adams et al. (eds) 128–67.

Swain, Simon (ed.) (2000) *Dio Chrysostom: Politics, Letters and Philosophy*. Oxford: Oxford University Press.

Tallerman, Maggie and Gibson, Kathleen R. (2012) 'Introduction: The evolution of language'. In Tallerman and Gibson (eds) 1–35.

Tallerman, Maggie and Gibson, Kathleen R. (eds) (2012) *The Oxford Handbook of Language Evolution*. Oxford: Oxford University Press.

Taylor, D. G. K. (2002) 'Bilingualism and diglossia in late antique Syria and Mesopotamia'. In Adams et al. (eds) 289–321.

Thomas, Rosalind (1992) *Literacy and Orality in Ancient Greece*. Cambridge: Cambridge University Press.

Thompson, R. J. E. (1999) 'Dialects in Mycenaean and Mycenaean among the dialects'. *Minos* 31–2, 313–33.

(2002) 'Special vs. Normal Mycenaean Revisited'. In Bennet and Driessen (eds) 337–70.

(2008a) 'Mycenaean scribes and dialect: interpreting linguistic variation in the Linear B documents'. Paper presented to the Aegean Round Table on Writing and Non-Writing in the Bronze Age Aegean, Sheffield 16–18 January 2008.

(2008b) 'Mycenaean non-assibilation and its significance for the prehistory of the Greek dialects'. In Sacconi et al. (eds) 753–65.

Thomson, Robert W. (1978) *Moses Khorenats'i History of the Armenians. Translation and Commentary*. Cambridge, Mass. and London: Harvard University Press.

Threatte, Leslie (1980) *The Grammar of Attic Inscriptions. Vol. 1. Phonology*. Berlin: de Gruyter.

(1996) *The Grammar of Attic Inscriptions. Vol. 2. Morphology*. Berlin: de Gruyter.

Trapp, M. (2003) *Greek and Latin Letters: An Anthology with Translation*. Cambridge: Cambridge University Press.

Trask, R. L. (1999) *Language: The Basics*. London and New York: Routledge.

Trask, R. L. and McColl Millar, Robert (2007) *Trask's Historical Linguistics*. (2nd edition). London: Hodder.

Tribulato, Olga (2010) 'Literary dialects'. In Bakker (ed.) 388–400.

(2011) 'The stone-cutter's bilingual inscription from Palermo (*IG* XIV 297 = *CIL* X 7296): a new interpretation'. *Zeitschrift für Papyrologie und Epigraphik* 177, 131–40.

(2012) '*Siculi bilingues*? Latin in the inscriptions of early Roman Sicily'. In Tribulato (ed.) 291–325.

Tribulato, Olga (ed.) (2012) *Language and Linguistic Contact in Ancient Sicily*. Cambridge: Cambridge University Press.

Trigger, Bruce G. (2004) 'Writing systems: a case study in cultural evolution'. In Houston (ed.) 39–68.

Trudgill, Peter (1974) *The Social Differentiation of English in Norwich*. Cambridge: Cambridge University Press.

(2010) *Investigations in Sociohistorical Linguistics*. Cambridge: Cambridge University Press.

Trümpy, C. (1986) *Vergleich des Mykenischen mit der Sprache der Chorlyrik*. Berne: Peter Lang.

Turfa, Jean MacIntosh (2006) 'The Etruscan Brontoscopic Calendar'. In de Grummond and Simon (eds) 173–90.

Turner, Nigel (1976) *A Grammar of New Testament Greek by James Hope Moulton*. Vol. 4. *Style*. Edinbugh: T. & T. Clark.

Untermann, Jürgen (1977) 'Korreferat zu Günter Neumann: die Normierung des Lateinischen'. *Gymnasium* 84, 279–83.

(1980) *Monumenta Linguarum Hispanicarum*. Bd. 2. *Die Inschriften in iberischer Schrift aus Südfrankreich*. Wiesbaden: Reichert.

(1990) *Monumenta Linguarum Hispanicarum*. Bd. 3. *Die iberischen Inschriften aus Spanien*. Wiesbaden: Reichert.

(1997) *Monumenta Linguarum Hispanicarum*. Bd. 2. *Die tartessischen, keltiberischen und lusitanischen Inschriften*. Wiesbaden: Reichert.

(2006) 'Ligurisches'. In Bombi et al. (eds) 1759–69.

Vaan, Michiel de (2008) *Etymological Dictionary of Latin*. Leiden: Brill.

van Alfen, P. G. (2008) 'The Linear B inscribed vases'. In Duhoux and Morpurgo Davies (eds) 35–42.

van der Meer, L. B. (1987) *The Bronze Liver of Piacenza: Analysis of a Polytheistic Structure*. Amsterdam: Gieben.

van Heems, Gilles (2011a) 'De la variation et des langues anciennes'. In van Heems (ed.) 9–14.

(2011b) 'Essai de dialectologie étrusque: problèmes théoriques et applications pratiques'. In van Heems (ed.) 69–90.

van Heems, Gilles (ed.) (2011) *La variation linguistique dans les langues de l'Italie préromaine*. (CMO 45). Lyons: Maison de l'Orient et de la Méditerranée.

Vierros, Marja (2012) *Bilingual Notaries in Hellenistic Egypt: A Study of Greek as a Second Language*. Brussels: Koninklijke Vlaamse Academie van België voor Wetenschappen en Kunsten.

Wachter, Rudolf (1991) 'Abbreviated writing'. *Kadmos* 30, 49–80.

Wallace, Rex. E. (2007) *The Sabellic Languages of Ancient Italy*. Munich: Lincom.

(2008) *Zikh Rasna: A Manual of the Etruscan Language and Inscriptions*. Ann Arbor and New York: Beech Stave.

Wardhaugh, Ronald (2010) *An Introduction to Sociolinguistics*. (6th edition). Malden, Mass. and Oxford: Wiley-Blackwell.

Wasserstein, Abraham and Wasserstein, David J. (2006) *The Legend of the Septuagint: From Classical Antiquity to Today*. Cambridge: Cambridge University Press.

Watson, Alan (1998) *Digest of Justinian translated, edited. Vol. 3*. Philadelphia: University of Pennsylvania Press.

Watts, Victor (2004) *The Cambridge Dictionary of English Place-names.* Cambridge: Cambridge University Press.

Weinreich, Max (1945) 'Der YIVO un di problemen fun undzer tsayt'. *YIVO Bleter* 25.1, 3–18.

Weiss, Michael (2009) *Outline of the Historical and Comparative Grammar of Latin.* Ann Arbor and New York: Beech Stave.

West, M. L. (1977) 'Erinna'. *Zeitschrift für Papyrologie und Epigraphik* 25, 95–119.

Whitmarsh, T. (2004) *Ancient Greek Literature.* Cambridge: Polity.

Willi, Andreas (2002a) 'The language of Greek comedy: introduction and biographical sketch'. In Willi (ed.) 1–32.

(2002b) 'Languages on stage: Aristophanic language, cultural history and Athenian identity'. In Willi (ed.) 111–50.

(2003) *The Languages of Aristophanes: Aspects of Linguistic Variation in Classical Attic Greek.* Oxford: Oxford University Press.

(2008) *Sikelismos: Sprache, Literatur und Gesellschaft im griechischen Sizilien (8.-5. Jh. v. Chr.).* (Biblioteca Helvetica Romana 29). Basle: Schwabe Verlag.

(2009) 'Opfer des Lateinischen: zum Sprachtod in Altitalien'. *Gymnasium* 116, 573–98.

(2010) 'Register variation'. In Bakker (ed.) 297–310.

(2012) '"We speak Peloponnesian": Tradition and linguistic identity in post-classical Sicilian literature'. In Tribulato (ed.) 265–87.

Willi, Andreas (ed.) (2002) *The Language of Greek Comedy.* Oxford: Oxford University Press.

Williams, Peter (2013) 'The Syriac versions of the Bible'. In Carleton Paget and Schaper (eds) 527–35.

Wilson, Andrew (2012) 'Neo-Punic and Latin inscriptions in Roman North Africa: function and display'. In Mullen and James (eds) 265–316.

Winkler, Gabriele (1994) *Koriwns Biographie des Mesrop Maštoc': Übersetzung und Kommentar.* (Orientalia Christiana Analecta 245). Rome: Pontificio Istituto Orientale.

Wodak, Ruth, Johnstone, Barbara and Kerswill, Paul (eds) (2013) *The Sage Handbook of Sociolinguistics.* London: Sage.

Woodard, Roger (1986) 'Dialect differences at Knossos'. *Kadmos* 25, 49–74.

Woodard, Roger (ed.) (2004) *The Cambridge Encyclopedia of the World's Ancient Languages.* Cambridge: Cambridge University Press.

Woods, C. (2007) 'Bilingualism, language learning, and the death of Sumerian'. In Sanders (ed.) 95–124.

Woodward, A. M. (1929) 'Inscriptions'. In Dawkins (ed.) 285–377.

Woolf, G. (1998) *Becoming Roman: The Origins of Provincial Civilization in Gaul.* Cambridge: Cambridge University Press.

Younger, John G. (1999) 'The Cretan hieroglyphic script: a review article'. *Minos* 31–2, 379–400.

Yule, George (2010) *Introducing Language.* Cambridge: Cambridge University Press.

Zucca, R. (1996) 'Inscriptiones latinae liberae rei publicae Africae, Sardiniae et Corsicae'. In Khanoussi et al. (eds) 1425–89.

Index

Index